COMETH THE ¥UAN

Mark Newham

Published by MoriartiMedia.com

First edition 2014 published by MoriartiMedia.com
Copyright © 2013 Mark Newham
Cover illustration by Kim Murphy

All rights reserved. Without limiting the rights under copyright reserved above, no part of this publication may be reproduced, stored in or introduced into a retrieval system, or transmitted, in any form, or by any means (electronic, mechanical, photocopying, recording, or otherwise) without the prior written permission of the copyright owner of this book.

ISBN 978-0-9926625-5-4

About the Author

During a thirty-year career as a print and broadcast journalist **Mark Newham**'s coverage of international affairs has appeared in almost every quality British newspaper, in international news magazines and on the BBC.

Newham has also acted as a media consultant to the United Nations, the World Bank, the European Union and China's state-run Xinhua news agency.

He accepted the Xinhua posting for one reason only – to gain firsthand, inside knowledge of the rules governing China's media mind games... and to see how much both could be bent.

Cometh the Yuan is the second in a trilogy charting China's growing influence on the world. The first – **Limp Pigs** – was published in 2011 and ranked Number One in Amazon's censorship category for several weeks. The BBC called it 'Unique... Inspiring....'

Mark Newham can (sometimes) be contacted through mail@moriartimedia.com

To Tom Welsh
mentor extraordinaire

chapter one

Clawing his way along the traffic-clogged artery en route to the gathering of MCC high priests that never was, Sir Victor Turnball afforded himself a small, sly smile.

While his mistake in choosing the M25 freeway section on a Friday night would doubtless be met with tuts of disapproval for not making his own meeting on time, if what he had to tell his fellow inner sanctum members didn't have them proclaiming him a living god he'd break the habit of a lifetime and buy that old windbag Bleauforth lunch.

As Turnball inched his way glacially westwards cursing the man who'd made the meeting necessary in the first place, the source of his derision flashed past him, gliding imperiously down the motorway's eastbound traffic-free toll lane feeling equally pleased with himself.

Apart from being one of a privileged few still able to afford such luxuries in a country that remained economically egg-bound a full ten years on from the 2008 financial crash, Harry Wong knew he was within an ace of ticking off a prime item on his lifetime ambitions list.

Unless he was very much mistaken – and he very rarely was – nothing could now stop him being acclaimed China's reincarnation of Kerry Packer, the man who forty years earlier had singlehandedly changed the face of world cricket.

* * *

Had Turnball spotted Wong heading away from the meeting, he wouldn't have been in the least surprised. Wong was one of a pair of fellow Marylebone Cricket Club committee members specifically left off Turnball's star chamber invite list. If either Wong or the redoubtable and unspeakable Baroness Daphne DeWitt got wind of his scheme for nipping China's pernicious little insurgency plan in the bud, there'd be precious little anyone could do to prevent the MCC and western civilisation itself succumbing to the infidel invader from the East.

Being omitted from Turnball's list was one of two things – and two things only – that Wong and DeWitt had in common.

The other was a connection to Dinsdale Stewart-Krabbs and, by association, to his debt collector-dodging neighbour Simon Middlethorpe. It was a connection the MCC pair would have rued ever having made had they so much as sniffed how central the Stewart-Krabbs/Middlethorpe partnership would become to Turnball's strategy for spiking the guns of an unholy – and wholly unlikely – alliance.

Thanks to the pair, Turnball now had a battle plan for countering the devastating impending barrage the collective arsenal of the Wong/DeWitt/People's Republic of China troika stood poised to unleash on one of the central, load-bearing pillars of the civilised world.

Failure to prevent it meant only one thing. If the MCC bastion of decency and social order was lost to the barbarian hordes sweeping down on it from the Orient then nothing was safe from the inexorable spread of the dragon's dreadful, looming shadow.

chapter two

Middlethorpe hadn't intended to be untruthful or deceitful. He'd just thought it best not to overburden a heavyweight potential investor like Wong with the finer points of how the government's idiotic attempts to balance the country's burning economic books had sent him and his company cartwheeling towards a financial precipice.

'For all the good the government's economic balancing act has done,' Middlethorpe had raged at one of the newly-formed Free Radical Party's anti-Tory rant therapy sessions, 'they might as well have tried to balance Boris Johnson's mind.'

As pleased as he was with the parallel, Middlethorpe thought now might not be the time to work it into his conversation with Wong.

Apart from not knowing if the London mayor's reputation for eccentric behaviour had registered on the Hong Konger's radar, Middlethorpe thought it best not to get distracted from his primary mission – convincing Wong that the Middlethorpe enterprise had come through the last eight years of global economic meltdown unscathed.

If Wong was going to be persuaded to invest, he needed reassurance of the company's financial viability and he needed it, Middlethorpe was quite sure, in a language that wouldn't have Wong thinking he was in the presence of one of nature's business world throwbacks. So…

'Well, I wouldn't say the crash helped,' Middlethorpe had said in answer to Wong's query, picking his words carefully in an attempt to replicate the language he'd heard coming out of the mouths of big money world spin doctors, 'but we're still very much in the game and the underlying metrics are sound. There's still health in the market for products like mine and the industry's diagnostics remain extremely buoyant going forward.

'Everyone's seen order book condensation and ongoing workforce revision but the current economic climate has given us all a heads-up regarding production efficiency leverage. I'm confident we're well-positioned to recover lost ground and begin competing again in a world that's leaner and fitter and ready to take advantage of the opportunities presented by global restructuring.'

As Middlethorpe continued in this vein, Wong listened impassively hoping his face wasn't betraying his inner thoughts. The only effect this sort of American business school corporate jargobabble had on Wong was to make him wince.

Whenever it made an entrance into the conversation Wong knew two things. The babbler not only had something to hide but felt he could get away with treating his audience like a dim-witted client a jobbing builder thought could be fobbed off with a clearly substandard job.

In Wong's estimation, resorting to such prattle was, as Samuel Johnson might have put it, the last refuge of the scoundrel and under normal circumstances, whenever he heard the scoundrel taking refuge in it, the Hong Konger's immediate reaction was to suddenly discover he had an urgent appointment to get to.

Unfortunately for Wong, the circumstances he found himself in with Middlethorpe were anything but normal and on this occasion Wong had been forced to suffer the scoundrel's blather in its entirety.

Trapped in a Stewart-Krabbs/Middlethorpe pincer movement

at the cricket tournament Wong himself had organised, it was only through a mumbled accession to Middlethorpe's plea to meet later to talk business formally that he'd managed to extract himself and escape to the sanctuary of his private box.

Safe from the outside world, Wong collapsed into his automatically body-contouring viewing chair relieved to be rid of the Middlethorpe annoyance. He hadn't come all this way to be pestered by business associate wannabes. He was here to relax and watch the cricket and that was what he was determined to do.

It was not to be. The more Wong tried to concentrate on the game, the more he felt an unwelcome sensation gnawing at his bones – one he thought had long since been excised from his psyche. Conscience was back, that human failing the father he worshipped had commanded he eradicate forthwith if he wanted to get anywhere in the business world.

For years he hadn't had an attack. But now, thanks to the blatant business meeting lie he'd fobbed Middlethorpe off with, he was experiencing his second in as many months and Wong was worried.

Coming so soon after the fleeting tremor of remorse he'd felt after inadvertently running over a neighbour's cat and clandestinely depositing the remains on the driveway of another, Wong fretted that he might be losing his touch. Allow this to continue, he told himself, and conscience might even stop him palming fake medicines off onto unsuspecting HIV sufferers the length and breadth of Africa.

His father was right. Guilt really was bad for business. But how to stop it intervening? Wong thought he'd had it licked. He'd obviously been wrong. He'd obviously not learned his lesson well enough and now there was no father to turn to for advice. Unless…

As the cricket edged towards its climax, Wong was elsewhere, communing with his long-dead father through a secret meditational technique Wong had relieved a Shaolin master of during a trip to the furthest reaches of Tibet.

It had been time well spent. In a voice that was loud, clear and unequivocal, Wong's father boomed his advice in his son's head.

'The only sure way of seeing a problem like this off is to buy it off,' he told Wong Jnr emphatically. 'Your lie has clearly displeased the Middlethorpe ancestors and now they need appeasing. Pump a bit of petty cash into the man's business. You never know, it might even reap dividends. Even patently obvious disaster zones like Middlethorpe can be rehabilitated given a bit of judicious realignment – starting, I would suggest, by getting the prat to stop behaving like a bloody politician.'

It was like preaching to the converted. As Wong was only too aware, just like the country's political elite, people like Middlethorpe had started believing their own propaganda. Despite record unemployment rates telling them the exact opposite a full eight years on from the 2008 crash, the government still insisted that recovery was on track and somehow the lie had contaminated the business community.

Despite the inescapable fact that companies were continuing to go under faster than graves could be dug for them, the country's business leaders refused to be dissuaded from their belief that the current situation was but a blip. One that would go away once the world came to its senses, realised that nothing could compete with British products for quality, and overseas buyers began returning cap in hand to their former suppliers.

Wong could only find such sentiments touching. And hopelessly naïve. As one who'd spent his life criss-crossing the planet in search of profit, the one thing of which Wong was sure was that UK plc was deluding itself through its teeth. What Middlethorpe and countless millions like him needed, Wong had decided, was a dose of heavy reality. Something that would put an end, once and for all, to a condition he termed 3D syndrome – denial, delusion and, well, der.

* * *

Propped unsteadily against the bar of the train carrying him home that night, Middlethorpe calculated that that had all gone pretty well. Not only had he managed to prise Wong's phone number out of him but the Hong Konger hadn't baulked at Middlethorpe's suggestion that they continue the discussion at a more appropriate time. The third innings was about to start and Wong was clearly itching to get back to his hospitality box.

As it got underway, Middlethorpe found himself whooping with joy. Not only was his side giving the opposition a good run for their money but he was sure he'd found someone who could be persuaded to rescue him from the workhouse. The only thing tempering his jubilation was Stewart-Krabbs' frown. Surely his fellow Sussex County Cricket Club devotee should be equally euphoric. Whatever helped Middlethorpe would help Stewart-Krabbs, the man who'd backed Middlethorpe when no others could be found.

But Stewart-Krabbs would have none of it. 'I haven't come all the way to Lord's to bother myself with business,' was all he'd had to say on the subject. With the fourth innings now underway and Sussex closing in on the Yorkshire total, their side needed all the encouragement they could get if they were to lift the 2016 Double Tops cricket trophy.

Only in the train after they'd clinked glasses to celebrate a glorious Sussex victory was Stewart-Krabbs willing to help put Middlethorpe's mind at rest.

'Relax, man,' he'd commanded as Middlethorpe fretted that

Stewart-Krabbs had spotted something that might make Wong think twice about investing.

'Really can't think why you're worrying. Wong being the sort of bloke he is, I'm sure he saw us as just a couple of over-worked businessmen escaping their busy offices for a relaxing day at the cricket,' Steward-Krabbs had managed between stifled snorts of barely concealed sniggering. If Wong hadn't spotted the scuffed, charity shop-bought jeans, the three-day growth of stubble and the Special Brew stains decorating Middlethorpe's five year-old Sussex CCC supporters shirt, his friend was home and dry.

'Deep down, Wong's not that much different to you and me,' added a lip-biting Stewart-Krabbs by way of trying to comfort the beer-can clutching personification of lost opportunity swaying before him. 'He knows as well as anyone that cricketers use the game primarily to get away from their day-to-day troubles. Well, that and to make new business contacts of course.'

That, as Stewart-Krabbs was confident Wong would be fully aware, was part and parcel of the cricket world – the business leads you got out of it and the contacts you made.

He'd know as well as anyone that few people played the game just to get their heads dented by surprise, express delivery bouncers from the West Indian ringer playing for the opposition. Becoming part of the cricket fraternity was, after all, as much to do with getting on as getting in and in that respect joining a cricket club wasn't that much different to joining the Freemasons or the Rotary Club. Wearing fancy dress to meetings and indulging in even fancier rituals was but a minor part of being a Freemason/Rotarian/cricketer.

So when Stewart-Krabbs had bumped into his former Oxford college-mate during the Double Tops final and had introduced Wong to Middlethorpe, Middlethorpe hadn't needed reminding of the cricket contact protocol – begin by talking cricket, steer the conversation round to business and never give any impression that yours was anything less than booming.

Which was how Middlethorpe had managed to get through the complete fifteen-minute conversation with Wong without making any reference to the halving of government subsidies to Britain's solar energy sector, just one of a raft of savage public spending cuts which had left the Middlethorpe business holed below the waterline and his world a pale reflection of its former, gloriously materialistic, self.

* * *

In the four years since the subsidy had been hacked to death, Middlethorpe had seen famine rapidly overtake feast.

Along with orders for solar panels had gone the gleaming Middlethorpe five-litre babe magnet, the plans for the swimming pool, the three holidays a year, the house in the Algarve where he took his daughters when there was no other female company available and any hope the former Mrs Middlethorpe might be harbouring of screwing him for a crippling divorce settlement. His empty order book had done that already.

In place of the Middlethorpe dream was a dented seven year-old pick-up parked next to the abandoned half-dug hole where the pool should have been, a debt mountain to test the pick of Nepalese Sherpas, a stack of solicitors letters threatening legal action unless he fulfilled the terms of the warranties given on thousands of now-dysfunctional solar panels and two heartless daughters giving him grief over the state of the world and his role in allowing things to get this bad through turning a blind eye to the bleedin' obvious for so many years.

No longer a regular on charter flights to the sun belt, Middlethorpe had seen his universe shrivel to the point at which its outer limits were now marked by the Ousedon village cricket club, the nearby Ousedon Arms and the house of a neighbour which served as the Free Radical Party's local HQ.

Of the three, only the last was witnessing a regular intake of new recruits, the party's membership growing exponentially as the brigade of feather-spitting, former Tory loyalist small businessmen kneecapped by the effects of the public spending cuts grew ever larger.

Even in this truest and bluest of Tory strongholds where vocalised anti-Tory sentiment was treated as a hanging offence, the political tide seemed to be turning. Of all the political parties, the only one in the ascendancy was the one with no real agenda other than getting its own back on the Cameron cronies, a government that had singularly failed to protect its most loyal support base from the ravaging effects of the post-2008 austerity measures.

'I don't care what anyone says,' griped Middlethorpe to his fellow FRP confederates, 'whatever economic recovery we've seen is bugger all to do with government policy. It's down to overseas carpetbaggers knowing a soft target when they see one. They're the ones behind most of the so-called growth, investing because there's easy money to be made out of a British workforce made destitute by this bloody government.

'I don't mind admitting that I'd be taking advantage of it too if I had the cash. But I don't. This fuckwit government has seen to that.'

To say that Middlethorpe was bitter would be like describing Al Qaeda as a protest movement. As Britain's worst economic slump since the 1930s inched it way out of the abyss leaving the likes of Simon Middlethorpe behind, a burning fury had consumed him. Whatever he tried, the government seemed to have another trick up its sleeve to unseat him and as the

Middlethorpe company's prospects sank ever lower he'd finally found himself facing a stark and inescapable reality.

Of all the things that had ever had any real meaning for him, just three now remained – his daughters, his newly-adopted party's plan for wreaking vengeance on those who'd failed to stop the world going into financial meltdown, and cricket.

With the future looking as bleak as a damp day at Headingley, Middlethorpe might well have lost the will to live had it not been for the great game. At least he still had that to look forward to and there was nothing any idiot politician could do to take it away from him. Cricket was his sanctuary, his one weekly moment of oblivion when all other concerns were relegated to subordinates of the match leaving his mind liberated, free of all cares save for the application of willow on leather.

There was nothing Middlethorpe knew of to beat it. Not gliding through a sun-bleached Alpine pass in an open-topped Mercedes. Not the taste of lobster bisque cooked to perfection by a scantily-clad temptress on an Algarve beach as he sipped nectar from a fluted crystal glass. Not even being there when his precious England team took the wicket that sent the bloody Aussies home without the Ashes. He'd give all that up for just one more effortless creamed drive through the covers to the boundary.

In fact he had. It wasn't as if he'd had much choice in the matter. By early 2016, the world of Simon Middlethorpe had shrunk to the size it'd been when his parents grounded him for getting caught on camera dogging in the car park of the Poundstretcher store in nearby Uckfield.

Had it been Waitrose, they'd told him, they'd have understood. But as it wasn't, for a complete month the then spotty, penniless, hormone-ravaged adolescent had been forbidden from travelling further than the boundaries of Ousedon village and the banks of the river running through it.

Now, through no fault of his own, the bitter memory of those days had returned and it was only when he discovered he could get into the newly-introduced Double Tops matches for just a few quid that his post solar subsidy-cut world had expanded to include the Sussex County Cricket Club ground in Hove and now Lord's, the Mecca of world cricket.

With more than enough time on their hands, he and the equally cash-strapped Dinsdale Stewart-Krabbs had taken full advantage of a competition heavily-subsidised by China's Ke-Ching mega-corporation, the People's Republic's answer to eBay.

With tickets costing little more than the price of the bus fare to the ground, the pair had indulged themselves in every local Double Tops game, whooping with delight as Sussex made it through to play Yorkshire at Lord's in the competition's inaugural final.

By tightening the belt one more notch, the pair had managed to amass just enough for a couple of day-return, off-peak, economy class train tickets to get them to the game, it being still a few months before third class was due to be re-introduced.

Thanks to the chance meeting with Wong, Middlethorpe had declared it to have been money well-spent. Stewart-Krabbs' old college mate was the one man Middlethorpe had met in recent times who seemed to share his vision of solar still having the potential to be the next big thing.

'All the industry needs,' Wong had said with a knowing look in Middlethorpe's direction, 'is a serious injection of cash to bring the economies of scale into play and a collection of companies capable of handling the sort of money I'm talking about.'

'Bugger me,' Middlethorpe had thought. 'Is he referring to MY company?' and suddenly both the Middlethorpe mind and mouth were racing.

* * *

Almost as soon as he'd said it, Wong regretted it. It had set Middlethorpe off on one of the voyages of delusion he'd heard so often from British business, voyages which did nothing to convince Wong that the country had moved on from those dark days when the banks failed and the whole of the western financial world imploded.

The man's artless attempt to convince his audience there was nothing intrinsically wrong with his business that a bit of repositioning couldn't fix was an almost a word-for-word regurgitation of the delusory fabrications issued by US and European banks prior to the 2008 crash. Just switch the names Middlethorpe and Lehman Brothers, thought Wong, and you'd be back in the days when western industry and governments alike found themselves sucked into a banking crisis that looked likely to bring down the Eurozone itself.

As memory of those hugely profitable days for Wong returned, the Hong Konger found an inner smile replacing the grimace the Middlethorpe memory had generated. It wasn't every day you found yourself at the forefront of a major world currency bail-out programme.

To the man-in-the-street, the euro had been saved by Germany, the European Central Bank and the International Monetary Fund partnering up to prevent the worst-affected Eurozone economies going tits-up.

Wong knew better. There were other forces at work and Wong knew who they were. People like himself.

With a collapse of the euro being to China's distinct disadvantage, Beijing's reaction was to call on the likes of Wong to channel vast sums of Chinese money into the economies of Eurozone countries on the brink of collapse. For reasons of its own, China wanted to keep its involvement in saving the euro to itself.

Although never officially informed as to the reasons, Wong had a pretty good idea what they were. If news of China's intervention in the financial markets leaked there was every possibility of its follow-up phase leaking also, a follow-up phase, so Wong's sources informed him, that was so pernicious it made the Hong Konger shudder with envy.

Even by China's own duplicitous standards, phase two of its plan to recover the world domination status Europe and then the US stole from it in the nineteenth and twentieth centuries was devilment incarnate.

chapter three

As Harry Wong was being caressed into oblivion by the soothing hands of the birdlike masseuse who came with every SinAir emperor class ticket to Beijing, the executive of the Marylebone Cricket Club was locked in grim-faced deliberation in a chilly Lord's committee room.

'Gentlemen,' said MCC committee chairman Sir Oliver Gainsborough, 'it seems we live in interesting times.'

The use of this backhanded Chinese curse as the overture to the committee's discussion on the finance director's end-of-2017 season report had struck Gainsborough as especially appropriate in light of who was now undoubtedly pulling the strings of the world economy.

'The simple truth of the matter is that without the support of Ke-Ching and its representative-on-Earth, Hu Nei, Lord's would be... how can I put this... facing a bigger follow-on deficit than it already does. The one thing that cannot be fudged is that we have the Chinese to thank for helping keep the deficit to manageable proportions and for putting food on the Lord's table.'

'Entrée the dragon, eh?' mumbled Lord Bleauforth to no one in particular.

'And there'll always be Hu Nei for tea,' added Sir Victor Turnball taking up the theme.

'Quite,' said Gainsborough with a look over his half-moon spectacles the pair might have recognised from their schooldays.

Gainsborough had always had reservations over the club's

decision to co-opt the two former cricket correspondents onto its executive after their talents had been deemed surplus to their respective failing newspapers' requirements. Word play double-acts like the one he'd just scotched might have their place in TV and radio commentary boxes. Here in the committee room, they just got in the way of getting through the business in hand and Gainsborough, also the chairman of one of the most prestigious investment banks in the country, was not best known for his love of unnecessarily drawn-out committee meetings.

'However,' Gainsborough continued, allowing the look to rest on the pair as he spoke, 'such support, as we all know, is tenuous. The vicissitudes of the economy can mean the minds of one's backers can change with the direction of the economic wind and long-term support is not something that can always be relied upon.'

The committee's twenty-two other members nodded sagely at the observation. Apart from Bleauforth, Turnball and a couple of others, every one of them was a leading light in the business world and knew full well that support like Ke-Ching's could be withdrawn at any moment. They also knew how vital it was in helping tide the club over until its bank completed its investigations into how the MCC account had been mysteriously drained of its reserves.

With all the signs pointing to a computer hack, the board had been assured that should this prove to be the case, such a security breach would be the sole responsibility of the bank and that reimbursement of the funds to the club was just a matter of time.

But that assurance had been received months ago and still there was no word on the investigation's outcome. Had it not been for Ke-Ching, the MCC would have been left begging for a substantial bank bridging loan, the interest on which would have left the club facing the likelihood of defaulting on its regular overdraft repayments.

Ke-Ching had almost romped to the club's rescue once news of the apparent hack reached its ears. After all, it said, the MCC's ground was used to stage the company's Double Tops final. It could hardly stand by and see the spiritual home of cricket boarded-up while the bank's investigations were underway. Such investigations, it knew, generally took far longer than anyone was prepared to admit.

The Chinese company had only one condition for coming to the MCC's rescue – that the club hold an extraordinary general meeting to re-elect the board. Rumours abounded that the hack had only been made possible thanks to 'someone' not logging off properly after checking the MCC's bank balance and Ke-Ching was keen to give the club's rank and file the chance of demonstrating their level of confidence in the committee.

It was not the unanimous show of support for which the committee had been hoping. Angered by what they perceived as the executive's gross negligence over allowing such a thing to happen, the ordinary members had staged what was, in MCC terms, a palace revolution. Fully half the board found themselves back in the ranks to be replaced by members who at least knew how to turn a computer off.

Taking the place of the coterie of retired colonels and minor aristocracy who seemed to have been in residence on the board since Thomas Lord founded the MCC in 1787, was a new coterie, a regular wardrobe of 'suits'.

True, the new intake were to a man from the sort of stock which put their offspring's names down at birth for MCC membership and Britain's foremost public schools in that order, and that the newly-appointed committee members' rise in the business world wasn't wholly unconnected with their membership of both, but it was a change from the way things had been done until the club's lower orders staged their flannel revolution.

Taking their seats, the new members' prime responsibility was not lost on them. It was to get the club back on the financial rails, an issue their chairman was now addressing.

* * *

'So, gentlemen,' Gainsborough said with a look round the table he hoped inspired memories of his boyhood hero Winston Churchill, 'while the bank's investigations into the fund disappearance issue remain ongoing, I'm sure there's no reason to have to remind you that it's this body's responsibility to ensure that the future of the great institution of which we are the custodians remains assured.

'It is for this reason that I present to you today a proposal received by my office which could, if approved by your good selves, provide us with a solid foundation for achieving that end.'

While he was speaking, Gainsborough's personal assistant had begun placing slim folders on the conference table in front of each board member, timing the distribution to end at precisely the moment the chairman's soliloquy reached its climax.

'Before you open your folders, gentlemen,' said Gainsborough, 'I urge a moment's reflection on the MCC's current financial predicament in order that the proposal's contents might be viewed in that context. They will not, I am sure, be to everyone's taste.

'But the follow-on looms,' he intoned, adopting his Churchillian gravitas once more, 'and we are the last pair at the wicket. Saving the test is all that matters and in such circumstances each batsman must ask himself a question. Do I have the gumption to take the onslaught on the chin for the good of the team? Indeed, for the good of the very country itself…'

* * *

Swooping in to Beijing's sparkling pink Norman Foster-designed international airport built to coincide with the opening of the 2008 Olympics, Harry Wong smiled happily to himself. The trip could hardly have gone better.

Apart from gathering a few more business souls to add to his already voluminous collection, he was virtually certain that the name of his client Ke-Ching would soon be appearing on the Lord's letterhead as the MCC's sole operations partner and Wong would be one step closer to achieving a lifetime ambition.

How could they resist? The proposal Ke-Ching had, for reasons of its own, asked him to present to Gainsborough contained nothing, surely, to which any of the board members could object. In return for the stunningly generous long-term support the Chinese company was offering should the club's bank find itself innocent of any blame regarding the computer hack, all it wanted was the MCC's endorsement of its product, a few minor alterations to the Double Tops competition playing regulations and a seat on the board. Surely that wasn't too much to ask. Any prospective partner would expect like representation… especially one that had already demonstrated its commitment to supporting English cricket.

Although only two seasons old, the Wong-inspired Ke-Ching Double Tops tournament had already proved a staggering success, bringing people who hadn't been to a cricket match for years back to the game.

By simply combining two forms of the game into one and keeping ticket prices to affordable levels, Wong's inspiration had singlehandedly revitalised English cricket, packing out the grounds of clubs who'd almost forgotten that the term 'sell-out' had any connotation beyond that associated with the words 'soul', 'devil' and 'down the river'.

Called in by Ke-Ching in 2014 to advise on how the company

might promote its internet shopping services in the UK, it hadn't taken the cricket-mad Wong long to work his obsession into a promotional campaign for an organisation which, in terms of relevance to its operations, rated cricket right up there with the search for the Higgs boson particle.

To begin with, Wong felt he'd have had more success trying to sell the Higgs boson concept to Ke-Ching's finger-drumming promotions director Hu Nei, but slowly and gradually he won her round.

'The thing about cricket,' he enthused, 'is that it's a sport which, if such a thing is possible, is as much a source of conversation to the British as the weather. Become associated with cricket and you instantly become a household name,' Wong exaggerated to a now more attentive Hu.

'It's a known fact that those who've sponsored English cricket find themselves ranked alongside the likes of Coca-Cola for brand awareness. Competition for cricket sponsorship in Britain is as fierce as that for a seat on a train out of Beijing Central at Chinese New Year and a lot less gentlemanly. The British have even been known to miss tea for a chance of getting in on the cricket sponsorship act.'

Hu Nei frowned. 'Surely that'd mean having to oust an existing sponsor to gain a foothold.'

'It would if we wanted to sponsor an existing competition,' countered Wong, 'but that's not the plan. My research shows the British are desperate for something new, something different now that the novelty of the two shortened versions of the game has worn off. What I'm proposing is that we capitalise on that and introduce a wholly new cricket format, one that takes the best aspects of the twenty-over and fifty-over formats and combines them into one.'

After patiently explaining what an over was to Hu who'd

interrupted again to ask if there was also something called an under, Wong went on to outline the core features of his masterplan.

To be called 'Double Tops' after the term used by darts players for a double twenty, the new competition would consist of two twenty-over innings per side using every technological aid known to man to maintain pace and excitement.

Once established, the plan was to raise the Double Tops profile until it eventually took over as the single standard short form of the game in the UK. That, he was certain, was the way to win Ke-Ching a place in the hearts and minds of the great British public, a public that never failed to be bowled over – ho ho – by two-for-the-price-of-one sales offers.

'And while we're on the subject of money,' Wong went on, 'it's crucial that tickets to the games are pitched at a level to suit the average cricket follower's pocket. The one sure way of killing support for the competition is to put the games beyond the budget of the regular joe.

'Cricket in England has become a rich man's game and it's alienating millions of people. Although TV coverage of the major games gives the impression that cricket is well-supported, what the pictures don't show is that the game has come to exemplify the UK's growing rich/poor divide. The only people you'll find attending the bigger matches are those with pockets deep enough to afford the sky-high ticket prices. Those whose aren't – millions upon millions of them – are left out in the cold.

'While the issue has become a problem for English cricket, to my mind it represents a major opportunity for Ke-Ching. Think of the goodwill the company will attract by introducing a tournament geared to the pocket of the ordinary consumer – the very people who're most likely to be attracted to using an economy-shopper website like Ke-Ching.'

Wong knew from Hu Nei's eyes that he'd hit a nerve. Although, on the surface, Ke-Ching was the very personification of unreconstructed capitalism, the blood of revolutionary socialist zeal still coursed strongly through Chinese veins and Wong knew that any proposal likely to further China's mission to help promote the class war and hammer a few more nails into the coffin of western imperialism was guaranteed to find an appreciative audience.

'So what I'm proposing is that Ke-Ching should subsidise the Double Tops competition tickets heavily. By keeping the entrance cost to an easily affordable level, full houses – and consequently live TV coverage – at every game can be virtually guaranteed, not to mention the undying gratitude of the British cricket-loving public.'

As Wong neared the end of his presentation, Hu's eyes began to shine. The more she thought about it, the more it appealed to her. If sponsoring English cricket achieved what Wong said it would, her job was not only done on several different levels but done well within the parameters of Ke-Ching's UK promotions budget.

As much as she'd have liked to have rubber-stamped the proposal there and then, Wong's idea first needed to be floated to the Ke-Ching board, leaving Wong waiting several weeks for an answer.

When it came, it was worth waiting for. Not only did they like the idea but since he was the only one who knew the first thing about the game, perhaps he should be the one to overlord the plan's implementation, working with Hu to see it to fruition.

Expecting nothing less, Wong had used the waiting time to lay the groundwork for setting the Double Tops wheels in motion and within days of agreeing to act on Ke-Ching's behalf he and Hu were heading for London for a meeting with the England Cricket Board.

It'd been a done deal the moment Wong opened his mouth. Drooling over the prospect of a new sponsor with deep pockets wanting to support the game, the ECB had sanctioned the idea in record time, asking only whether a 2016 launch date would be too early for Wong.

As Wong had confidently predicted it would be, the Double Tops competition had been received with greedy hands by Britain's cash-strapped public, tickets for the first Lord's final selling out within hours prompting TV companies to enter a bidding war in their desperation to cover it.

It was the same for the 2017 final and, as the match reached its climax, Wong had even noticed the odd flicker of a smile replacing the customary scowls etched across the brows of the MCC's most traditionalist members.

Having held their noses while accepting the support of the Chinese of all people to bail them out of their financial fix, their mood seemed to be softening. Maybe, Wong could hear them thinking, the hearts of these wily Orientals might be in the right place after all.

Not only had they come to the rescue of their beloved Lord's Cricket Ground but, by setting ticket prices for the Ke-Ching competition at levels last seen in the 1990s, they were responsible for almost single-handedly putting new life into the game the length and breadth of the country.

* * *

New life was also what the competition's success had put into its creator.

In the Double Tops' early days Wong had lost sleep worrying that the new format might be received with suspicion in a land where the waters of tradition ran deep.

Those worries now looked to be behind him and Wong had at last breathed out.

His Double Tops success wouldn't just help sway the MCC committee when it came to their vote on the MCC/Ke-Ching partnership proposal. It would prove invaluable when it came to the launch of Wong's campaign to fulfil a long-held dream – the bagging of the biggest prize in world cricket.

chapter four

From his soundings-out of individual board members over the previous few weeks, Wong had received nothing but positive reactions to his MCC/Ke-Ching partnership proposal... albeit accompanied by that most English of knowing half-smiles. The one Wong had long ago learned was the Englishman's way of signalling a mix of pity on the recipient for not having had the good fortune to have been born English coupled with grudging, supercilious, condescending interest without actual commitment.

They were canny these English, Wong thought, but it wasn't anything he hadn't learned how to handle during his years at Oxford.

Arriving to read politics, philosophy and economics in the mid-1980s, his fellow Oxonians had afforded him similar 'respect' which, in his then-naïve Oriental way, he'd taken to mean unreserved acceptance into the fold.

Only later, on trying to gain membership of the notorious Bullingdon club, did he discover the true meaning behind that little smile.

It was a smile that told him, without the words having to be spoken, that maybe THIS club wasn't really for him. That the Bullingdon set weren't *really* his sort of people. That maybe he might feel more at home with, well, people of his own... calibre.

'Not on your intellectual level you see, old chap. You might find them a little... boisterous. But apply for membership by all means, old man, although, quite frankly, not really sure it'd be worth your while. Got to have a sponsor, you see, and they're a bit of a scarce commodity at this present moment in time. Had a lot of chaps wanting to join recently so sponsorship is looking a bit thin on the ground…'

Wong had treated the Bullingdon club rejection as a learning experience. Despite his best efforts to fit in with English ways, it clearly hadn't been enough and he'd subsequently vowed to use his days at Oxford to overcome his Oriental roots and become, for the time being anyway, as English as the English. Only then would he stand a chance of being accepted into English society's inner circles – the core reason for his coming to Oxford in the first place.

It'd been his father's idea, Harry Wong Snr being determined that his son should penetrate deeper into the English fortress than he'd managed himself. Without the right background, Wong Snr had found his progress halted at the stage of being reluctantly accepted into the business fold as one who could deliver on time and on budget with few questions asked.

It was a humiliation Wong Snr was anxious to redress through his son. To recover family 'face' lost by this shaming rebuttal he'd decided Wong Jnr should be schooled in the dark arts of becoming an English gentleman. Hence the private tuition in Hong Kong and the place at Oxford University won more by the bursary Wong Snr had offered Christ Church College than by his son's academic prowess.

Christ Church had been chosen for one very specific reason. Wong Snr's research revealed that of the twenty-six Oxford-educated British prime ministers who'd held office since the mid-eighteenth century, fully half were Christ Church alumni.

To Wong Snr, this was a no-brainer. For his son to 'get on', he needed to rub shoulders with Britain's future leaders and so it was to Christ Church he would go. No other college would do.

Harry Wong Jnr had readily complied. Anything less would

have been to show disrespect not only for a father who'd risen from the gutter to become one of Hong Kong's richest men but for his father's quest to recover, through his son, the family honour.

With neither the breeding nor the learning to slot neatly in with his fellow Oxonians, Wong arrived at Oxford ill-equipped for the job. Even so, eager to satisfy his father's wishes, he'd instantly set about ingratiating himself with those seen as the country's rising political stars, many of whom were to be found amongst the ranks of the Bullingdon club.

Being rebuffed from a club whose membership qualification revolved more around what you had in your wallet than what you had in your head would have killed the resolve of lesser mortals. But Wong was made of sterner stuff.

From the Taoist teachings of his father, Wong knew that from every bad experience a flower grows. And so it was that, with this in mind, Wong had reassessed his own limitations, isolated his deficiencies and formulated a plan he hoped would restore him to good grace in his father's eyes. The Oxford newcomer resolved to become as English as apple pie which just went to show how far he was from achieving his desired end.

* * *

While Wong might have been a bit shaky on the distance that separated English English from its American equivalent, of one thing he was certain. No foreigner would ever get beyond the outer fringes of English society unless he knew the basics of the game of cricket.

Being as central to the English psyche as food was to the Chinese, Wong knew that unless he gained some understanding of this most English of games and could drop curiously-phrased cricketing terms into conversations that had nothing to do with cricket, he'd never be seen as anything more than an interloping outsider.

In Wong's experience, the English seemed incapable of communicating without making reference to the game and, whether they knew it or not, in the process had set the ultimate Englishness test.

Unless you knew that 'coming off a long run' related both to the length of a bowler's run-up AND to the degree of power injected into an argument, you were never likely to qualify. And if you really wanted to feel the full weight of an Englishman's withering pity for having been born a foreigner, all you needed do was assume the phrase had been injected to signal a conversation change to the time needed to recover from a marathon – something he'd heard one unfortunate American do to his eternal social cost.

Harry Wong Jnr had arrived at Oxford a cricket innocent knowing nothing more about the game than the indisputable fact that those who played or followed it stood a far better chance of getting on in English society than those who didn't.

The English who'd taken up residence in his native Hong Kong joined the colony's cricket clubs as much to mix with people of influence as to play the game. As such, Wong wasn't slow to realise, the relationship between cricket and English society wasn't that much different to that existing between mah-jong and the Chinese Triads and, taken in that context, here was a game he had no option but to master.

Looked at superficially it seemed simple enough. Bowler bowls ball, batsman hits ball to score runs and the team with the highest number of runs wins. What was complicated about that?

But, he reminded himself, that was also how mah-jong looked to the outsider. Dig deeper and it was as complex as Chinese society itself. And so it proved with cricket.

Wong's quest to unravel the mysteries of the game began with him watching – from a safe distance – any match that was in progress within the confines of the Oxford college playing fields. That, he was sure, was where the real game was to be found.

Gradually it began to make some sense and, to fill in the gaps, Wong began pulling cricket books from the library. Which was when he'd had his first cricket epiphany.

This wasn't a game. This was a publishing sensation. A whole cottage industry existed of people who filled the long English winter nights poring over the previous season's statistics and converting them into heavyweight tomes while struggling to hear scratchy radio commentaries on the England team's progress on the Indian sub-continent.

The library shelves buckled under the weight of lavishly-illustrated hardcover volumes documenting cricket tours, cricket series, cricket biographies, cricket trivia, cricket collector's items, cricket anthologies, the art of preparing a cricket wicket, the psychology of cricket, great cricket teas, great cricket tea *preparers*, the list went on and on.

To Wong's amazement there was even a book about a man called Puss Achong, a West Indian of Chinese extraction who played test match cricket in the 1930s and was credited with the invention of a new bowling delivery which came to be known as 'the Chinaman'.

And then Wong's most astounding discovery of all – an intriguing tome entitled 'The Laws of Cricket'.

'Laws?' thought Wong. 'They have special courts to rule on cricket disputes? This thing is bigger than I thought.'

He wasn't far wrong. Further investigations were to reveal that one club and one club alone in the whole of the cricketing firmament was responsible for drafting, updating and overseeing what Wong had once erroneously referred to as the rules of the game before being roundly chastised for this schoolboy howler and rapidly correcting himself.

Somehow, the Marylebone Cricket Club had become the game's unopposed custodian, presiding with magisterial pomp over the laws that governed the sport from its palatial Lord's Cricket Ground sanctuary in St John's Wood in central London, the accepted spiritual home of the game.

The finding came as something of a surprise to Wong. He'd never suspected there to be a political dimension to the game. Since the MCC's original eighteenth century membership was restricted to members of the British aristocracy, it stood to reason in the young, under-informed, Hong Konger's mind that that's how Lord's must have got its name – from the House of Lords.

Were he to have known then that jumping to such an erroneous conclusion would rebound on him in the way it was to do some three decades later, he might have lingered longer over his readings of MCC history.

But since he didn't until years later, Wong the undergraduate went through the whole of his college career unaware that the name of the ground pertained to that of its creator, one Thomas Lord, a misconception that was not only allowed to take root but to propagate.

On trips back home, people too polite to excuse themselves when Wong was in full cricket flow found themselves 'educated' into the young man's misreading of the MCC's heritage, a misreading that some of his listeners found so intriguing it sparked a ripple effect of onward misreporting that was to return to engulf him years later.

* * *

Of everything Wong was to learn about the game of cricket, it was the laws that enthralled him most.

The book that contained them fascinated him, not least because its contents revealed that here was a game to rival war itself for complexity.

No cricket game could proceed, the book told him, unless it accorded with the sort of gentlemanly conduct and rules of engagement as might have been employed at Waterloo. There was, Wong discovered, as much not allowed as was with every miniscule detail documented in paralegal language in sub-sections to sub-sections contained in pages of basic laws covering every aspect of the game.

This, it was clear to Wong, wasn't just a game, it was a civilisation unto itself, one whose mystery and cipher could rival anything North Korea or the Vatican had to offer.

As Wong voyaged deeper into the cricket jungle he felt himself beginning to understand why the English had trouble hiding the superiority they so clearly felt over the mere mortals who made up the rest of the world.

Not only had they created a game of staggering sophistication but they'd somehow got their former colonies addicted to it whilst remaining in complete control of their creation. Even the Chinese, Wong finally ended up admitting to himself, would have trouble competing with this degree of control and complexity and they had some five thousand years of dynastic civilisation to draw upon.

It was the finer detail contained in the darker recesses of the book that captivated him most. It was here that he was to discover that yes, you can be stumped off a wide ball. No, you can't put more than two fielders backward of square leg. And, confusingly, that the word 'wicket' has at least three separate and distinct meanings, something he thought competed strongly for confusion with the four tones of Mandarin applied to give different meanings to the same basic words.

He'd always thought English an easy language. Now, it was clear it was a dragon in lizard's clothing and the degree of respect he held for the English rose sharply. If they'd had different-shaped eyes they could pass for Chinese, he thought, the highest compliment of all in Wong's secret estimation.

* * *

At the end of his first season as a cricket follower, Wong felt just sufficiently confident in his understanding of the game to join his fellow students in the seated areas around the Oxford colleges' verdant playing fields. It was here that he'd listened more than he spoke, soaking up the language of the game and honing his appreciation of the finer points. For reference purposes, to every game he took a condensed version of the laws and, for experimentation, a scorebook.

Here again, he'd had an epiphany. The amount of detail needing to be entered in the book was breathtaking and meant that the scorer couldn't relax for a second.

At the end of every ball at least two different entries were needed even if the ball had flown harmlessly past the batsman to the wicketkeeper with no run scored. And when runs or wickets *were* being scored or taken anything up to ten separate entries were required and Wong started to understand why aloofness and cold detachment was a distinct trait of all cricket scorers and statisticians. The outcome of the match could depend on one false stroke of the scorer's pencil.

Or pencil*s* in Wong's case. Once he'd got used to the basic techniques of scoring and felt confident he was getting things right, he'd added an extra dimension of his own creation. By using a different coloured pencil for each bowler he could tell at a glance who'd been bowling at which batsman and how their bowling was being treated. Come the season's end, it would assist enormously in compiling the statistics.

So besotted with this newfound passion was Wong that he never missed a Christ Church home game, no matter whether it be the first XI or one of the lesser teams and no matter what tricks the weather was playing that day.

Along with him went his scorebook, his pencils, his binoculars, a thermos flask of green tea, a cushion for his backside, a blanket for his knees and a host of other items he'd found indispensible to the dedicated cricket follower, all packed with military precision into his voluminous backpack.

By and large, others at the games eyed him with amused curiosity, rarely addressing him directly. Oxford was full of quirky oddballs and this quiet Oriental was regarded by his fellow cricket watchers as someone more to have a conversation about than with.

Wong wasn't put out by their reaction. From his training in the philosophy of Taoism received at his father's knee he knew that eventually their curiosity would crack and that someone would approach him with questions as to his presence at *their* game. All he had to do was wait.

In late May of 1986 his patience was rewarded. Sitting alone in the terraced seats close to the pavilion during the break between innings on a cold and blustery midweek afternoon, Wong was busying himself checking back on the Christ Church second XI's miserable runs tally when he felt a presence at his shoulder.

'My God, you're scoring the match! I thought you were doing some sketching,' exclaimed the presence. 'Looks like you know what you're doing too. Love the colours. Your own invention?'

Wong looked up at the bear-like shape looming over him and nodded. 'I find it helps when tracking back,' he said.

'Very pretty,' said the shape.

'And functional,' retorted Wong dryly.

'Absolutely,' said the bulky blonde figure sinking into the seat next to Wong to scrutinise the book.

'Stewart-Krabbs,' said the figure holding out his hand.

'Wong,' said Wong taking it.

'No it isn't,' said Stewart-Krabbs.

'What isn't,' said Wong.

'My name,' said Stewart-Krabbs. 'It isn't wrong. It's hyphenated… with a hyphen… between Stewart and Krabbs. First name Dinsdale. Sorry. Bit of a mouthful. People call me Dusky. After the initials.'

Wong looked at Stewart-Krabbs blankly. He looked anything but dusky but that was British humour for you.

'Part Scottish, part German, you see,' Stewart-Krabbs went on. 'Two very serious families who married into each other back when God was a boy and my great great great something grand mama wasn't prepared to give up her name so they hyphenated both to avoid a war. Been stuck with it ever since. God knows what would happen if I married a double-barrelled filly who refused to give up her family name. Wouldn't half give the registrar a headache, eh? And pity the poor little blighters who issued from that conjoining. So what's your name?'

'Wong,' said Wong.

Stewart-Krabbs looked blank for a second before enlightenment dawned.

'Ohhhh… I see… Sorry, old chap. Bit of an audio blip there. No offence meant.'

'None taken,' said Wong.

'Grand,' said Stewart-Krabbs. 'So you're a bit of a cricket nut then?'

'I love the complexity,' replied Wong thoughtfully. 'Cricket reminds me of chess. Many different permutations and moves to contemplate. And when you're scoring, you discover the real meaning of the game. Like life itself, the game can change in a moment – and at any moment – so it's necessary to remain vigilant at all times.'

'Blimey,' said Stewart-Krabbs. 'Never thought of it like that. I got roped in cos I played at school and, well, you just do, don't you. Part of the fabric etcetera. It sort of comes with the territory when you're one of the lesser species in the intellectual food chain here.'

Stewart-Krabbs looked set to expand on his thesis but was interrupted by the bell sounding to announce the start of the second innings with Christ Church fielding.

'Shouldn't you be out there?' asked Wong when his newfound friend showed no sign of stirring.

'Nah,' said Stewart-Krabbs. 'Touch of the old hamstring, old boy. I'm just the drinks carrier today.'

While Wong was trying to decipher this, Stewart-Krabbs had launched back into his family history monologue which Wong had trouble following. He'd found his mind torn between his companion's *tour de force* and his task of recording in the scorebook the outcome of the opening over which had resulted in fifteen runs, most of them the product of wild deliveries slung hopelessly wide of leg stump, whistling past the startled wicketkeeper to the boundary.

This was a first for Wong. He'd never had to listen and score at the same time. It was a virtual impossibility and Wong began to fully comprehend why proper scorers seemed congenitally bad tempered. In his early days at the cricket, he'd inadvertently stood in front of one while the game was in progress only to be angrily shooed away, his ears ringing with the sort of expletive the BBC would have felt obliged to bleep out of recorded highlights had they been covering the match.

Eventually the bowler delivered a ball the batsman could get a bat on and it was clouted to the midwicket boundary where it lodged under the heavy tarpaulin covers. That's covers as in covering the wicket to protect it from bad weather, Wong reminded himself, not as in the fielding position of the same name on the off side of the field nor the two other fielding positions in the vague vicinity of cover called extra cover and cover point.

When Wong had first heard the terms used together in a BBC radio commentary – 'that was a fine shot through the covers but it'll take a while to dig the ball out from its resting place under the covers' – the confusion had sent him scurrying to the books for illumination, especially since he thought the term offside related to football. It had taken him a week to sort the muddle out and now he could converse with the best of them on confusions caused by poorly thought-through cricket terminologies.

With the ball proving difficult to retrieve, a lengthy break in proceedings ensued allowing Wong to tune back in to Stewart-Krabbs' monologue which had reached the part about him inheriting his father's peerage 'once the old boy turns his toes up.'

'That's when I get his Lords seat and finally get to have a say in government policy,' Stewart-Krabbs was saying.

The information came as something of a revelation to Wong. Until now, he'd had no idea that a member's son wasn't permitted to occupy his father's seat until his father died, nor that government policy was regularly debated at Lord's. He longed to inquire further but decided that discussing the imminent demise of Stewart-Krabbs' father might not be accepted etiquette and opted instead to ask which side his father sat.

'Oh, on the cross benches, old boy. Always on the cross benches. Family has done since the flood.'

The response left Wong none the wiser. From what he'd seen of Lord's on the TV, there were nothing but cross benches flanking the steps up to the pavilion in the members' area and he'd never heard of the ground flooding.

'It's not really common knowledge,' Stewart-Krabbs went on, 'but the cross benches are frequently where government policy lives or dies. Those who occupy them have far more power in the land than people realise.'

With the ball now recovered – as in retrieved, not as in putting a new cover on it, Wong found himself thinking – and play underway once more, Wong turned his attention back to the cricket but found it hard to concentrate.

His mind was churning with Stewart-Krabbs' confirmation of his suspicions concerning the Lord's/British politics connection. It was the very thing he needed to justify his interest in cricket to contemptuous anti-western colonialism acquaintances back home in Hong Kong – acquaintances who would, without Wong knowing it, be instrumental in causing something of a misunderstanding some thirty years later when Ke-Ching's sponsorship of English cricket came up for debate by one of the more shadowy committees of the Chinese Communist Party's central executive.

chapter five

Dozing in his fully-reclined, fully-equipped, fully body self-shaping SinAir seat as the plane carrying him to his meeting with the England Cricket Board banked into its approach to Heathrow airport, Wong couldn't help reflecting on his first, somewhat less cosseted, trip to the UK some thirty years earlier.

Keen that his son should experience some of the rigours of his own pioneering venture westwards, Harry Wong Snr had seen fit to book Wong Jnr on an Air China flight whose Red Guard stewardess had demonstrated her contempt for anyone of Chinese extraction not confining their in-flight reading to the works of Chairman Mao by ensuring Wong ended up wearing more of his dinner than he'd eaten.

That fourteen-hour ordeal had then been followed by two more at the hands of Wong's welcoming committee, Britain's immigration authorities. With nothing he could do or say convincing them he wasn't in the country to deprive one of their three million unemployed countrymen of a job, his welcome to the UK consisted of being delayed just long enough to ensure his onward passage to Oxford coincided precisely with the start of a wildcat bus and train strike.

Equally welcoming was the Christ Church College hall porter. Arriving frozen, soaked-through and on the verge of starvation two days late for the start of term, Wong had dragged his desiccated mortal remains across the college portals only to be informed that since it'd been assumed he wasn't coming, his room had been let to someone else.

There had then followed a full week of incarceration in the unheated box room of a local landlady before a convocation of shamefaced dons arrived to lead Wong back to the room originally assigned to him.

Wong, it seemed, wasn't the only one who'd had cause to regret the incident. Realising rather late in the day that they'd somehow managed to exclude the son of the man who'd pledged to fund long overdue repairs to the college's antiquated sixteenth century sewage system, the dons had finally caved-in to the bursar's pleas to go mortar board-in-hand to their most recently-acquired overseas scholar and make amends for their gross, unacceptable oversight.

Settling in to one of the college's most sought-after rooms at last, if Wong thought his troubles were over he was about to discover the definition of disappointment. Britain's initiation rites committee hadn't finished with him yet. Along with his reinstatement had come a lesson in vindictiveness English public schoolboy-style.

Hell, Wong had heard it said, hath no fury like a woman scorned. Wong begged to differ. William Congreve, the seventeenth century British playwright who'd coined the phrase, had obviously never been on the wrong end of a former Winchester schoolboy's scorn on finding himself evicted from one of the college's best rooms to make way for the son of a rich Chinaman at a time when racial tensions were boiling over into full-blown race riots.

As every immigrant to the UK knew at the time, the sensible thing for any foreigner to do was to keep to his head down. It was a piece of advice the dons' room reinstatement action effectively deprived Wong from following. With his own as much as mounted on a spike, Wong found himself pilloried from day one, the ousted student's social group's retribution ranging from basic cold shouldering to full-on public humiliation. Not just once had Wong been suckered into believing he'd been rehabilitated, racing expectantly over to a smiling, beckoning colleague only to be told loudly and very publicly to his face to fuck off.

So deep were the scars of this treatment to a man more used to the more subtle Chinese arts of ritual backstabbing that even eighteen months later, on being beckoned by Stewart-Krabbs from the cricket pavilion balcony, Wong's immediate reaction was to ignore him.

Had Stewart-Krabbs been privy to the term-long Get Wong campaign, he might have acted differently. But since he wasn't, Stewart-Krabbs just assumed Wong to be a bit deaf and simply shouted louder.

'I say! Wong old bean! WONG! Yes you. Any chance of a gander at your scorebook? Something we need to check.'

At the words 'scorebook', 'check' and 'gander' all suspicion left the young Hong Konger.

Surely cricket etiquette forbade the employment of the game's terminologies to humiliate a fellow cricket lover.

Surely Stewart-Krabbs wouldn't risk testing the boundaries of acceptable cricket behaviour just to embarrass a foreigner.

Surely, as a cricketer he'd know such a ploy could backfire badly on him.

And anyway, Wong had to know. What was this cricketing obsession with poultry? Like the assortment of ducks cricketers were constantly referring to, did 'gander' have some cricketing significance he'd missed? There was only one way to find out and as Wong made his way towards the insistent Stewart-Krabbs he heard his own voice chiming in his head.

'My God,' he allowed himself to think. 'This is it.' After what had seemed like an eternity of feeling like the last kid on the block to get picked for a street football match, Wong was certain his presence had at last been recognised in the right way and an unaccustomed glow of warmth began to course through his body, the glow of full acceptance.

* * *

When Stewart-Krabbs had been called back to the pavilion in the third over of the opposition's innings, Wong had assumed that, curiosity satisfied, that was all he'd be seeing of his new 'friend' for the time being.

Just like the Chinese, Wong had found the English a businesslike race when it came to forging new relationships. Once they'd got what they were after, both races were in the habit of shelving familiarity until they wanted something more, leaving under-informed outsiders in a permanent state of wondering if it was something they'd said.

As one of the less under-informed outsiders in the light of his first term's experience at Christ's, Wong hadn't been surprised at being left alone for the remainder of the match and, in truth, hadn't been overly despondent. The game had turned out to be a gripper, ending in a nail-biting tie which demanded all of the young Hong Konger's attention just to keep up.

As the teams left the field shaking hands and congratulating one another on having produced a thoroughly enjoyable contest, Wong was able to relax and begin work on his last, most absorbing, job of the day – double checking the figures. Never satisfied with anything less than scorebook precision, Wong knew sleep would elude him unless every last dot ball and defensive prod had been accounted for.

Over in the pavilion it was precision that was proving elusive, the lack of it leading to an icy tension replacing good-natured bonhomie. On checking their books, both opposing scorers were taking issue with the scoreboard's tied-match conclusion, both claiming their own team had actually won by one run and a heated argument had broken out.

Despite rigorous examination of the books by both captains, no obvious errors presented themselves and the impasse was threatening to unseat the polite gentlemanly decorum normally associated with university cricket.

With neither side backing down, voices began to rise, fingers began to point and all looked set to descend into a post-match confrontation in which cricket bats might find themselves employed for a purpose other than that for which they'd been designed.

Anxious to avoid the name of Christ Church College becoming known as the place where cricket's reputation for personifying the very essence of gentlemanly conduct and fair play was finally exposed as the self-perpetuating myth for which it actually was, it was Stewart-Krabbs who finally stepped in to restore order.

'Gentlemen, gentlemen,' he boomed over the mêlée. 'It's clear this is getting us nowhere. Fortunately, there's a way of settling this if we're all in agreement. There's a third scorer in the ground who I know has kept an immaculate book throughout and frankly it's a damn sight prettier than our own tawdry efforts,' he said in a failed attempt to lighten the proceedings.

'If we're all in agreement,' he continued once the bickering had died down, 'can we take whatever outcome is recorded in his book as the final arbiter?'

After some muttering between opposing captains, the Stewart-Krabbs third party mediation proposal had been grudgingly agreed leaving the astounded Wong barely able to contain himself as he edged towards the pavilion praying he'd neither misunderstood Stewart-Krabbs' beckoning nor got the score wrong.

As he approached, the players watched through narrowed eyes, unsure what to make of the nervously grinning Oriental swamped by a cricket sunhat two sizes too big for him tentatively ascending the pavilion steps as if climbing the Forbidden City's imperial stairway for an audience with the emperor.

Their expressions changed from suspicion to astonishment the moment they saw the end-product of his dedicated labours.

Compared to their own efforts, Wong's scorebook was a veritable work of art, every bowler highlighted in a different colour, every ball recorded and the occasional note added when a delivery produced something of particular interest. It was clearly a lovingly-crafted document of record which would stand the test of any post-match audit.

It was also a document that showed beyond doubt that the result of this match was a tie.

In the frantic bedlam of the final couple of overs, both teams' scorers had managed to mis-record the runs scored, one adding a run that hadn't been taken, one missing one that had.

After a moment of solemn reflection and earnest discussion it was grudgingly agreed that Wong was right and they were wrong. So hands were shaken, backs slapped, smiles returned and Wong had stood in the middle of it all beaming as he soaked up the welcome return of respectful gentlemanly cricketing conduct.

And then, to cap it all, the opposing captains had led him to the bar and bought him a drink.

But that wasn't the end of it. The following week he'd received a surprise visit from the college first XI captain. Word had reached him of Wong's scoring and arbitration skills and, 'if you're not too busy, old chap, would you consider sitting in at the next game to assist our current scorer? He never stops griping that two eyes aren't enough for the job.'

And so began Wong's career as assistant scorer and unofficial cricket law interpreter for the Christ Church College Cricket Club first XI, known fondly to all who knew them as 5c.

It was also the moment that sparked a train of events that led to Wong's discovery that he wasn't the only Oriental at Christ's with an interest in 5c and cricket in general. Seen close-to, the features of the man who rolled the wicket were an unmistakeable blend of East and West.

* * *

Until he took up his new, official, scoring role Wong had never arrived at a match earlier than ten minutes before the start.

Now he was expected to be in residence in the scorer's box a full half hour prior to the toss-up in order to collect the team sheets, enter the names and match details in the book, make sure the scoreboard registered zero on all counts, sharpen all the pencils and just be there in case anything unexpected cropped up. And while he was doing that, the ground staff were busy preparing the wicket.

Wong had never suspected how much this involved. Until he saw the wicket preparers at work, he'd just assumed the players simply turned up, stuck two sets of stumps in the ground twenty-two yards apart and got on with it. Now he became aware that the playing area preparation process was every bit as involved as the match itself and as ritualised as the most elaborate of Oriental tea ceremonies.

First the outfield had to be trimmed to a lush green carpet. Then the grass on the wicket mowed to a mere memory, the pitch rolled with an almighty machine that roared with pain every time it was started up, batting creases whitewashed geometrically in place and the boundary rope unfurled and laid with equal precision around the outfield's perimeter.

Only when all that had been accomplished were the stumps erected to await the final sacred act, the placing of the bails on the stumps by the white-coated umpires with such reverence it made Wong wonder if religious mantras accompanied the act.

With the umpires in place, only then did the players emerge to take up their positions, the wicket preparation specialists retiring from the scene until the conclusion of the match when they re-materialised to 'put the wicket to bed'.

So time-honoured and unchanging was the whole procedure it reminded Wong of Chinese imperial ritual and he found himself being drawn to it like a moth to a flame.

There was clearly much more to this thing called cricket than he'd ever imagined and it was calling to him, demanding to be observed, studied, dissected and cogitated upon until it was fully and completely understood.

Ignoring the call, he knew, was not an option. The cricket bug had burrowed under his skin and wasn't going to let him rest until he had this infuriatingly otherworldly thing firmly nailed down.

And so it was that Wong began arriving at the ground a good couple of hours before the match and staying on afterwards to observe the full ritual from beginning to end. And how it was that he and Toby Tode became friends for life.

chapter six

Tode rode the heavy roller. That's what he did. It wasn't that he did nothing else but when it came to coaxing the infernal brute into life, no one else had Tode's touch. For him it seemed to purr with contentment. With everyone else it was as reluctant to perform as a mule with a hangover.

Some said it was his Japanese ancestry helping him 'talk' the beast into cooperating. Others said it was the Australian beast in him not taking no for an answer. Either way, no one else went near it and it was left to Tode to administer the wicket's last rites before play commenced, trundling the protesting machine up and down until all surface inconsistencies had been beasted into submission and Tode was satisfied it was 'as flat as the crap beer in this country'.

At the cricket ground, Tode's Aussie roots rose to the surface like a Bondi beach bodyboard, his Japanese ancestry kept securely submerged for the duration. No one wanted to play on a Japanese garden lawn and Tode knew it. So all instincts urging him to create water features on the wicket to balance its yin-yang elements were firmly suppressed and he concentrated instead on making the playing surface as barren and featureless as the Nullarbor Plain of the great Australian outback.

Suppressing his Japanese side at the cricket ground wasn't as difficult as in his day-to-day life. Away from the ground, his two sides were occasionally so conflicted he felt like an amphibian unsure as to whether its natural home was land or water. While one side of him yearned to light incense and practice aikido in the shadow of a Shinto shrine, the other was craving voluminous quantities of the amber nectar guzzled down while roasting roos on a billabong barbie.

With time, Tode hoped one side or the other would assume dominance and release him from this schizophrenic existence but that time looked some way off and having an English home counties accent wasn't helping.

The Aussie in him, from his mother's side, yearned to blame his Japanese father for his predicament but his Japanese side wouldn't allow it. This is your father, it kept reminding him. Respect is paramount, surpassing all other feelings towards him. Bonsai, said the Japanese. Bollocks, said the Australian.

* * *

Tode's parents had chosen to migrate to England in the 1960s on the grounds that it seemed the only place in the world where a Japanese and his Australian wife might find sanctuary. Ultra-conservative Japanese society would make their multi-racial life there hell, Aussie memories of Japanese World War II prisoner of war camps in South East Asia put paid to settling in his wife's home country and no sane Japanese was ever going near the US while Pearl Harbour was still fresh in the memory.

So it was to England they came, hoping to find anonymity in the hallucinogenic, transcendental cultural revolution sweeping the country at the time.

Tode Snr, a horticulturalist by trade, found employment with a Surrey plant nursery keen to capitalise on booming Britain's newfound obsession with eastern exotics courtesy of the Beatles and the hippie movement. While the Japanese was hard at work adding an Oriental dimension to the nursery's stock, his wife passed her days contentedly pickling vegetables and tending to their newborn son while humming along to the songs of Procol Harum and Jools Driscoll in the gardener's cottage which overlooked the village cricket pitch.

It was a lifestyle that printed itself indelibly on Tode the younger, a lifestyle which led inevitably to a career in cricket ground maintenance. To Toby Tode it was the line of least resistance, combining bits of horticultural knowledge learned at his father's knee with his toddler fascination for the noisy antics of the big boys scampering around on the village cricket field.

So a cricket field groundsman he became, beginning as a schoolboy helper to the mad local farmer who treated the cricket field as his own personal fiefdom and swore vile oaths at the players for trampling his lovingly-prepared wicket to dust.

Tode himself was no natural cricketer with either bat or ball, especially on a wicket he'd helped prepare. This, he knew, was his Japanese side emerging. Like the farmer – maybe because of him – he began to develop a spiritual attachment to the turf he'd spent hours coaxing into a smooth playing surface and found himself looking more at the wicket than at the ball on the rare occasions he was asked to make up the village team's numbers.

In the end, he gave in to the inevitable and stopped offering his playing services altogether. It was best for all concerned, he decided.

It wasn't that he didn't like the game, quite the reverse. Cricket continued to hold a profound fascination for him. But even though he raked it, spiked it, cut it and rolled it he just couldn't bring himself to mindlessly trample the wicket underfoot like all the other players. To Tode, it would be like joining in the humiliation of a sensitive best friend by a pack of village thugs for the sole purpose of being seen to be one of the boys.

So all requests to play were politely declined with Tode

confining himself to absorbing the farmer's undeniably sound knowledge of cricket wicket maintenance until the time came for him to leave school and seek employment in the wider world.

Which was when he discovered that cricket wasn't just a game played to pass the time. It was more, much more, than that.

* * *

Of all the village players, the one with whom Tode had most affinity was the local vicar. The Reverend Roger was the only one who seemed to understand Tode's reasons for not wanting to play.

In Tode, the vicar saw something of his younger self, a young man who'd fought the voice calling him before finally giving in and allowing it to guide him to his ultimate spiritual home. So the cleric had taken it upon himself to nurture the boy, encouraging his groundskeeping interest in the certain knowledge that this was Tode's true path to his own personal nirvana.

Which was how Tode found himself engaged as a trainee groundsman at Christ Church College. Knowing his protégé was in need of a guiding hand in choosing an employment direction, the Reverend Roger had engineered a meeting between Tode and the head groundsman at the cleric's former college and doors suddenly opened for a young man who, without the reverend's help, would likely never have even suspected their existence.

Four years later Tode was still there, riding out the worst of Margaret Thatcher's joblessness creation programme on the heavy roller safe in the knowledge that his empathy with the beast made him an indispensable member of the college ground staff.

While the world rocked on its axis and unemployment levels soared, Tode rode serenely on, his only concern being the appearance on the ground of a bloody Chinese with a cricket scorebook – a man whose arrival could seriously undermine his position as the college playing field's token Oriental.

At first he'd viewed Wong with the sort of wariness every Japanese feels for anyone of Chinese extraction. The year was 1986, a full fifty years on from Japan's occupation of the north China province of Manchuria and the massacre of some three hundred thousand people in Nanjing, but Chinese memories, as Tode was only too well aware, were long.

Tode's initial reaction to seeing Wong treading the sacred Christ Church cricket turf was to steer clear of chance meetings. But knowing that was just delaying the inevitable, he revised his strategy and was glad he did.

To his amazement, Tode discovered that Wong's thoughts echoed his own. The past, Wong confided in him, was the past and cricket was cricket. They were now batting for the same side in their own ways and a localised civil war wouldn't help anyone.

So an armistice had been declared, memories of Manchuria and Nanjing shelved and the pair had fallen into an unlikely alliance, one which emerged out of their mutual desire to wage war on the real enemy of the day – moles and moss.

When it came to these insidious, remorseless invaders of cricket pitches, all men were of the same colour, creed, nationality and ethnic origin. They were all just cricketers hell-bent on carrying out a genocide no court would ever convict them of. Well, not in England anyway. In Brussels they'd likely receive a crippling fine for contravening some European directive or other. But amongst the leafy lanes and perfect lawns of the home of cricket, anyone with an answer to the problem of mole infestation was held up as national hero.

Would that such classlessness extended to the game itself, was Tode's contribution to a Wong-initiated discussion on how cricket seemed to level the social playing field. The impression of all cricketers being brothers in arms, equals in pursuit of a common goal, Tode explained to a rapt Wong, was a deceitful illusion promulgated by the nobility-dominated system that governed the game.

'What you have to understand,' Tode explained, 'is that cricket is, and always has been, a bastion of the British class system. There are still those who bemoan the comparatively recent removal of the gentleman/player distinction from the game when it was quite normal for the amateur "gentlemen" and the badly-paid, lower class professional "players" to change in different dressing rooms and walk onto the cricket field through different gates. That distinction was in place until just a few years ago and it didn't just apply to English county games. Ever heard of the Bodyline Series?'

Wong hadn't but said it sounded like something from the fashion industry.

'Well, you're right and wrong at the same time,' said Tode who'd just been reading about it. 'It was a famous... or rather, infamous... series of test matches between England and Australia when England toured there in the winter of 1932-33.

'In order to intimidate the Australian batsmen, England captain Douglas Jardine ordered his main pace bowler Harold Larwood to bowl vicious short-pitched deliveries directly at the batsmen's bodies. Jardine's strategy was to pack the short leg side with fielders who took a bagful of catches as the Aussie batsmen fended the ball off. It was a pretty successful but highly controversial tactic which a lot of folk thought contravened the spirit of the game even though there was nothing in the laws to prevent it.'

'But,' intervened Wong, remembering one of the laws he'd found especially unfathomable, 'the laws say the fielding side can only have two fielders in the ninety degree quadrant between the square leg umpire and an imaginary line drawn between the stumps and the boundary behind the wicketkeeper.'

'Ah,' Tode responded, 'that's the law now, brought in specifically to stop Jardine's tactic becoming fashionable. It didn't exist back then but the real thing is this. Harold Larwood was a "player", a professional who normally worked as a coal miner when not playing cricket and as such was pretty much expected to doff his cap to his "gentleman" cricketer public school toff captain Jardine.

'If Larwood had refused to obey Jardine's order, it's likely he'd have been on the next boat home thereby losing the wage that went with the job. So he HAD to continue bowling that line and hurt a lot of batsmen to boot if he wanted to stay on the tour.

'The whole thing left such a bad taste in the mouths of the Aussies that it led to a diplomatic row between the two countries that took years to simmer down. If some Australian hadn't already burned some bails and put the ashes in a little wooden urn to represent the death of English cricket back in 1882 after Australia beat England on English soil for the first time, I reckon the Ashes Series would undoubtedly have been invented after England's 1932-33 tour.'

Tode's cricket history lecture had Wong spellbound. He'd heard the term 'The Ashes' bandied around by 5c but had no real idea what it meant nor that the law about restricting the number of short leg fielders had its antecedents in one single series of matches.

But the part that really intrigued him was the class issue. Never before had he fully realised how class-ridden cricket was and it occurred to him that that might explain why modern day China had no interest in the game.

In Mao Zedong's day, anyone showing an interest in such a sport would probably have been labelled a running dog imperialist reactionary enemy of the state and sent to a re-education camp for an unlimited term. Who knows, like the underground religious sects he knew existed in China, maybe there were also secret cricket matches being played with look-outs posted in case Mao's Red Guards turned up.

Somehow Wong doubted it. Any self-respecting/self-preserving Chinese cricketer would have fled to the British colony of Hong Kong at the onset of Mao's Cultural Revolution in 1966.

But what, he wondered, would they do when Britain's leasehold on Hong Kong ran out in 1997? Would there be an almighty exodus of Hong Kongers weighed down with bats, balls, pads and stumps when the colony reverted to Chinese ownership? Or would cricket emerge from the shadows as Deng Xiaoping's Opening-Up policy gained ground. Having taken over on Mao's death in 1976, Deng seemed keen to connect again with the West so why shouldn't cricket replace Mao's ping-pong diplomacy as a means of kick-starting the process?

Hmmm, thought Wong. Might be a business opportunity there. But would he be able to sell the idea to the people that mattered in Beijing? His father might be able to help but it would still be an uphill battle convincing the powers-that-be to back the concept. He was pretty sure he'd meet strong resistance from those who regarded anything English as a reminder of colonial rule.

On the other hand, Wong thought, he might be able to sell the idea as the means of beating the English at their own game. That might work and there was already a precedent for it. Australia's Kerry Packer had seen the money-making potential of televised cricket and had set up his own World Cricket Series in 1977, thumbing his nose at the largely English-dominated cricket establishment as he did so.

From his limited reading of cricket history Wong knew that Packer not only introduced the concept of floodlit cricket but paid serious money to attract some of the world's best players to his tournament leaving their regular national sides shorn of their best talent.

Although the World Series had only lasted a couple of years it had revolutionised the game and it was clear to Wong that this was just the start. Cricket was on the verge of moving into whole new territory and there seemed no reason why the choice of direction should be the preserve of the old guard. The field was wide open to anyone, even a Hong Kong Chinese whose knowledge of the game was at best rudimentary.

As this torrent of thoughts cascaded through his mind, Wong wasn't slow to realise that there was a lot more learning to be done before he could formulate a concrete plan of action. The problem was, how was he to get up to speed with cricket AND get a degree. He'd never win his father over to the idea if he left Oxford without that precious certificate.

Tode, he thought, might have the answer. How did *he* manage it? Sure, Tode had had a head start on Wong by having been born and gone to school in England but surely all that research into the history of the game came at the expense of proper academic study. Maybe he should consider switching to whatever course Tode was on. So...

'What is it you're reading Tode?'

'Well,' replied Tode wondering what that had to do with what they'd been talking about, 'if you must know, apart from the history of the Bodyline Series, I'm working my way through the Saint and Paul Temple books at the moment.'

Ah-HA, thought Wong. Theology. So that's how he does it. He chooses a course that doesn't involve much more than reading a few religious treatise and thinking a lot, thereby leaving plenty of time for indulging in all things cricketty.

Tode could, of course, have put his Chinese friend right in his misconception that he was conversing with a fellow scholar but therein lay a problem. Tode's Japanese side told him that correcting Wong on such a matter might cause him such embarrassment that it would be taken as undermining his friend's 'face', not the done thing at all in the East.

So no, far better to leave it to Wong's truly scholarly friends. If they didn't take a dim view of him consorting with the hired help and take him aside for a friendly word, Wong would just have to work it out for himself. That was definitely the best course of action to take.

'T'aint moi station to go 'bout correctin' the young maaasters,' Tode intoned to himself in the manner of the muddy-booted fellows he'd come across labouring for slave wages in the potting sheds of their 'betters' who'd denied them a decent education in the first place.

'No,' he'd muttered with an imaginary tug of his forelock, 'such impudence wouldn't go down at all well 'yer in Merrie Olde England.'

chapter seven

'Gentlemen, GENTLEMEN!' pleaded MCC chairman Sir Oliver Gainsborough over the hubbub engulfing the Lord's committee room.

'Please. We have little choice. It's accept these terms or say goodbye to Ke-Ching's magnanimous gesture. For my part, I shall, with great reluctance, vote in favour. A quarter of a millennium of MCC history could hang on our agreeing to make this one tiny alteration to the laws of the game. It's all that stands between a massive injection of new sponsorship money and, if the bank finds it's us who've been negligent with the club's funds, oblivion.'

'A *tiny* alteration!' exploded Lord Bleauforth, the club's reformed bad boy and now its foremost champion of cricket's grand traditions. 'Scrapping the umpires is about as *tiny* as Turnball's appetite for cake.'

Sir Victor looked up wide-eyed from his plate of chocolate mini-rolls and grinned.

'Not to mention your appetite for the exotic,' he retorted.

The rest of the executive's members smirked. Not one was ever known to miss a chance of reminding old Windy of the spliff scandal back in the eighties. It had led to a temporary MCC representation ban on their esteemed colleague and any reminder of the incident was guaranteed to raise Bleauforth's blood pressure to thrombosis levels. To this day he still insisted that the so-called 'spliff' was nothing more than a bad cigar and that the committee of the day – the one on which he now served – had got it all hopelessly wrong.

But now was not the time to be tempted down that particular path. If the committee couldn't be persuaded of the threat posed by these modern day Mongol hordes poised to sweep down on Lord's from their base camp in Woking – chosen, Bleauforth had heard it said, because of the name's familiarity to Chinese ears – then the game was doomed.

Once the umpires were gone, what next? The whites-only dress code for test matches? Grass wickets? TEA? No, he couldn't allow that. It was time to dig in, in the manner of that heroic last stand by Botham and Dilley at Headingley in 1981 when England came from a hopeless follow-on position to beat the bloody Aussies. Now THAT was cricket at its finest and no bloody Chinese was ever going to come in here with his bulging moneybags and dictate to HIM how the game should be played. NEVER!

'But it's not as if we'll never see umpires on the field ever again,' protested Gainsborough. 'This is just for the Double Tops competition. All Ke-Ching is proposing is that the competition is used as a testing ground for its latest technological widgetry. Ye gods man, it's not as if we've never allowed technology through the Grace Gates. If we hadn't, we'd still be playing on uncovered wickets cut with horse-drawn mowers.'

'Thin end of wedge,' was Bleauforth's grumbled riposte. 'Let 'em get away with this and it won't be long before umpire-less test matches are the order of the day. I tell you it's not on. Cricket just isn't cricket without the umpires. They make the game.'

'Or ruin it,' interjected Turnball. 'If we'd had the decision review system back in my day I'd have ended up with twice the number of LBWs I did get.'

'About two then,' chortled Baroness DeWitt into the collar of frills that were gallantly losing a war for recognition in the foothills of her geomorphological neck.

No one responded. Contributions from the committee's token

female member were regarded by the rest of the executive as the rough equivalent of crowd noise – a damned nuisance when you were trying to have a sensible conversation.

For two hundred and twelve years the MCC had been shamelessly gentlemen only, the policy only being rescinded in 1999 after heavy political pressure had been brought to bear on England's last bastion of male exclusivity. Ever since, women members had been admitted to the club's holy of holies, the Lord's pavilion, but only under duress. No attempt had ever been made by the male contingent to camouflage the fact that they viewed the club's females in much the way cricketers view a persistent light drizzle – never bad enough to stop play and nothing to be done about it… but always bloody there.

So whenever DeWitt tried to intervene in committee meetings, the other twenty-two members reacted by feigning acute deafness and carrying on as if twenty-two was the executive's total membership. To the male contingent it was neater that way anyway. Two full cricket teams and someone to make the tea.

It was no mean feat ignoring the baroness. Being in possession of both the stature and temperament of a mature hippo made her 'a presence felt', as Lord Bleauforth had once elegantly put it. But, as the noble lord had then gone on to say, 'we've spent the better part of two and a half centuries ignoring the elephant in the room and I see no reason to change our ways now.'

As if being a woman wasn't bad enough, DeWitt's case was hardly helped by the undisguised contempt she exhibited for the game. A woman of romance at heart, she'd been forced into playing it for her school and county by her cricket-mad, MCC card-carrying father who'd brought her up in the fashion of the male heir he'd been unable to produce. Deprived of a feminine youth, the experience had left deep, indelible scars which the baroness had vowed to inflict back on the game following her father's drowning in mysterious circumstances.

Now in possession of the family title and her own MCC membership card, the baroness had set about the task with gusto. After browbeating the other female members into helping get her elected to the committee, she'd taken her seat with one sole and singular purpose in mind – the wrecking of both it and the antediluvian traditions the other members saw as their God-given duty to defend.

To date her presence had had about as much impact as a rhubarb cricket bat. But she'd bided her time certain the day of reckoning would eventually come, a day which, thanks to Harry Wong, might have finally arrived. Wong might not know it but there was every chance of the least appreciated member of the committee finding herself the most influential when it came to voting on the Ke-Ching proposal.

* * *

Not for the first time in her gluttonous life, Baroness DeWitt was wrong. Having had every member of the MCC committee thoroughly checked out before going in to bat against them, Harry Wong did know it. Not a man to leave things to chance and knowing full well that the proposals he was putting forward on Ke-Ching's behalf would have the traditionalists gagging on their Gentleman's Relish, he'd spent a great deal of time getting to know the enemy's fielding strengths before launching his offensive.

By and large, their positions were pretty predictable. There were the valiant defenders of the faith to whom any change was anathema. There were the 'suits' who looked at virtually nothing except the financial scorecard's bottom line. And there were a couple who were so ineffectual they'd vote as their mothers told them.

But then there was Baroness Daphne DeWitt, the only true wildcard in the pack and a conundrum who didn't seem to fit any pattern or stereotype.

On the surface she was pure regulation English blue blood, riding to hounds (if a strong enough mount could be found), secretly supporting the British Nationalist Party (but only because the National Front no longer existed), eyeing all modern art as satanic imagery (but buying it anyway as hedge against inflation) and employing illegal Albanian immigrants to run her estate on which she played God at weekends.

She also kept a dual set of accounts, her money in an offshore tax haven and a well-equipped toyboy in her London flat. All pretty standard stuff for the English upper crust.

Except in the case of cricket. Here, Wong's investigations revealed, she was Che Guevara, Joan D'Arc and Moby Dick all rolled into one. Vengeance on the game, she'd decided, was hers and she'd taken a solemn oath to dispatch the whole disgusting, despicable lot to the fires of hell or go into a nunnery trying.

So when it came to voting on the Ke-Ching proposal she was the one unknown quantity on Wong's list, the one that was capable of swinging either way. If she thought its contents were likely to help save Lord's she'd most certainly vote against. On the other hand, if she viewed them as undermining the foundations of the game she so loathed, her support was guaranteed.

With the vote looking likely to go to the wire, Wong knew the baroness's vote was crucial and that he needed a strategy to win her over to the dark side. But what?

It was while watching a film on the art of spin bowling that the answer came to him. He needed to employ the strategic equivalent of the game's googly delivery wrapped up in the old three-card trick ploy. First he needed to gain DeWitt's confidence with a few easy long hops before hitting her with the devil ball – the one that looked innocuous enough but was, in fact, a bomb in cricket ball clothing.

Everything hinged on Wong appearing to be a novice bowler knowing little of his opponent's batting strengths. If she gained any inkling that he'd been poking around in her closet and come across her loathing for all things cricket, he was sunk. Success centred on convincing her he thought he was in discussion with someone who was at one with the rest of the committee in seeking ways to save Lord's and English cricket in general.

His strategy so-decided, all Wong needed now was a venue for the 'chance' encounter he'd decided to engineer with the baroness.

The field of combat chosen was the car park of the plush country restaurant the baroness favoured at weekends. Replete with *pâté de foie gras*, quail pie and vintage burgundy, DeWitt would offer an easy target for the persona Wong had selected for the occasion.

Dressed in anorak and trainers and dripping with cameras, global positioning systems and hand-held computers, Wong sat in the open side door of his jet black, antennae-swathed, custom-built transporter van apparently engrossed in conversation on his video phone and seemingly oblivious to the emergence of the baroness from the restaurant.

'I say there! Wong isn't it?' she bellowed in his direction.

Looking up from behind thick, tortoise shell-framed glasses, Wong managed a fake blank look of surprise for a second before converting it to one of recognition.

'Baroness! What a pleasure to see you. Have you been dining here?'

'Naturally. Where else would any sane person spend a chilly November Sunday afternoon? Best damned truffles this side of Normandy and the finest port ever to be smuggled out of Lisbon.

'Fraid you're a bit late for lunch though if that's your intention,' she said, scanning him disdainfully up and down for dress code compliance.

'Ah, no. I'm just packing up to head back to base. Been testing a new piece of locator divining kit in the woods over there. Can't say too much about it as it hasn't been officially released by the powers-that-be in Beijing but I can tell you it's a truly sensational example of image-enhancing nanotechnology which will revolutionise videological cadence capture when it comes out. It'll make everything else look like something from the stone age and Ke-Ching is first in line to apply it to predictive cricket diagnostics. The competition might as well pack up and go home when they see what we've got,' Wong beamed.

'Which woods?' snarled the baroness. 'THOSE woods?'

Wong nodded.

'Those, Mr Wong, are MY woods,' DeWitt hissed. 'Breed the shoot's partridges in there. And I don't recall giving anyone permission to go trampling around in them. Especially when we're bringing on the young for the Boxing Day blast!'

'Ah,' said Wong. 'Wasn't aware they were private. Didn't see any signs.'

'Don't do SIGNS,' sniffed DeWitt. 'Everyone round here KNOWS those woods are strictly off limits... and that anyone caught within its boundaries is liable to get his BALLS blown off!'

Gotcha, Wong thought. Madam DeWitt is now convinced I'm nothing but a blundering Chinese dunderhead whose boyish exuberance for techno widgetry has a habit of landing him in the mire. It was the perfect disguise for his current mission but first he needed to pacify her. She was no good to him while the inner, burgundy-fuelled orc was at the controls.

'Dreadfully sorry,' Wong fawned. 'I'd never have set foot on your property if I'd known. But you might be interested in seeing what I found in there. This little device measures heat differentials to a decimal point and can detect any living thing to a square millimetre. While I was testing it I found there's definitely a lot of game birds in there – I can even tell you how many – but that's not all. See that?'

Wong thrust the screen in front of the baroness's pulsating nose so she could see a large infrared shape edging ever closer to a cluster of smaller, less red shapes.

'Unless I'm very much mistaken that's a sizeable predator. A polecat I'd say, stalking your birds and getting pretty close. Wouldn't be surprised if it hasn't already reduced the numbers by a considerable percentage.'

'BASTARD!' shrieked DeWitt.

'Well, not sure I…'

'Not YOU Wong. THAT! I thought the numbers were down this year but I'd put it down to the gamekeeper's bottle-affected arithmetic. Now I can see I owe him an apology. And you. That bloody bastard is taking me to the cleaners. Won't be a bird left by Christmas if he isn't dealt with *tout* damned *suite*. If you've got a mo, would you mind coming up to the house to show that gadget of yours to the gamekeeper if he's sober? Need to know where to set the traps.'

'Well, I should be getting back to town… but if it's as much of a threat as you say, I'd be glad to.'

'Good man. Splendid. You might just have saved the day. Christmas just isn't the same without a bit of the old Boxing Day butchery, what!'

Wong climbed into the van's driving seat, a small smile playing on his lips. Hers weren't the only traps being set that day. The prey he was after had been irresistibly tempted by the bait and now all that remained was to get her to close the door on herself, lock herself inside and slide the key back under the door to him on the outside. By the time he was halfway back to Woking, an empty polecat box in the back of his van, she'd be purring like a contented cat inside a cage she'd yet to discover was escape-proof.

chapter eight

As they waited in the baroness's drawing room for gamekeeper Twist to arrive, DeWitt requested another look at Wong's infrared heat-seeking device, asking if operating it needed specialist skills. This could be the very thing she needed to get rid of the man she was about to order out into the night to set the traps and save on a salary that mostly seemed to find its way into the till of the scoundrel who'd refused point blank to accept her derisory offer for his goldmine pub.

'Not really,' said Wong, closing in for the kill. 'Anyone could use it given a bit of training. It's more the way it's used that's important. A bit like the new technology we want to use for the Double Tops competition, if you'll excuse the excursion into shop talk for a moment.'

Without waiting for the semi-inebriate baroness's approval, Wong moved swiftly into phase two of his vote-catching strategy.

'In my proposal to the committee I thought it best not to overburden the members with technical guff so didn't really explain the full potential of this little beauty. What you're seeing here is the hand-held version of its big brother, a device I believe will revolutionise cricket. Its actuality error-reduction potential is enormous and the best thing is that you don't need someone with a postgraduate degree in electronics to operate it. You could almost get someone in off the street and have them running the whole show in a couple of days.'

With the baroness remaining mute, Wong felt safe to press home his advantage and begin the process of reeling her in.

'If the MCC committee will back the Ke-Ching proposal, I'm sure the England Cricket Board will follow suit and allow our proposed innovations a trial run at least. And when they see it all working – and how it will attract the crowds back to the game – I'm pretty confident they'll become a permanent fixture.

'I mean, who wouldn't want to be at a game in which instant video replay makes all that tiresome appealing unnecessary? By building sensors into all the main equipment the crowd will know what's happened as soon as it's happened without having to wait for the umpire to make up his mind. The outcome will be up on the big 3D screen before anyone can even think of appealing.

'That's the beauty of the nanosensor, you see. You can implant it in bat, ball, pads, gloves, boots, stumps, creases, boundary markers, the lot, all microwave-linked back to the central umpire computer.

'I probably shouldn't really be telling you this but Ke-Ching has just agreed to use the name I thought up for the system. It's going to be known as "The Cumputire",' announced Wong, beaming with what he hoped looked like chest-bursting pride at having produced such a memorable brand name but which was really self-congratulation on the sheer, ear-grating dreadfulness of the word.

The invention of something so etymologically vile accomplished three things in one. It not only reinforced his credentials with DeWitt as a blundering technodork cricket ignoramus but one who couldn't see that such a word would have the game's dyed-in-the-wool traditionalists reaching for the defibrillator thereby guaranteeing the baroness's lifelong gratitude – and her vote.

As his host's face showed that the full implication of the cat that Wong had, in his enthusiasm, 'mistakenly' let out of the bag was dawning on her, the Hong Konger murmured an inaudible 'howzat' under his breath. Unless he was very much mistaken, he'd done her with the wrong 'un and trapped her plumb in front of the wicket.

While Wong was struggling to keep a straight face, the baroness was experiencing a similar conflict of emotions. Despite the better part of two bottles of the restaurant's best claret, DeWitt's senses weren't dulled to the likely outcome of the introduction of the technological 'improvements' Wong and Ke-Ching were proposing. They would make the game so robotic and chance-proof it would drive the traditionalists to distraction.

If there was one thing she knew about cricket, it was that its prime appeal to those who played and followed it lay in its inherent uncertainties. Despite the reams of rules and regulations, in the end the game all came down to the decision of one man whose judgement – and eyesight – wasn't always perfect. Take that out of the game and you might as well be playing it on a computer.

In fact, it had just occurred to her, that's exactly what this stupid man and his stupid company *were* proposing – making cricket a living form of computer game. They were, after all, an information technology company – and a Chinese one at that – which would presumably see nothing wrong in applying that sort of thinking to the game of cricket. Allow them free rein to manipulate it with their technological gadgetry and, for certain, the game was doomed. She almost wept with joy.

But shows of such emotion, the baroness was not unaware, would have to be suppressed for the time being. So far as she knew, Wong knew nothing of the degree to which she despised the game of cricket and all those associated with it and best to keep it that way she counselled herself.

Letting on that the MCC committee was not of one mind on the subject of the need to preserve English cricket's grand traditions might serve to put the club's prospective suitor off and now that she knew more of Ke-Ching's intentions that was the last thing she wanted. Wong seemed clearly unaware that what he'd be doing to cricket was what she'd yearned to do ever since being forced to don cricket whites as a child and face her father's pace attack without snivelling.

Her current yearning was to grab Wong by the lapels and plant a huge slobbering kiss on his forehead. But since that might give the game away she managed to restrain herself, gluing her not inconsiderable backside to the chair and forcing herself not to swoon in the manner he was now doing over the range of other technological marvels Ke-Ching had up its sleeve to bring cricket fully into the twenty-first century.

***

The primary aim, Wong explained to the now rapt baroness, was to standardise playing conditions and make the 'level playing field' adage mean exactly that.

For far too long, he enthused, the outcome of cricket matches had been dominated by the vicissitudes of the weather which in turn affected the wickets and how they played. Under such conditions it was impossible to assess the true strengths of the various teams competing against one another. Even the best players couldn't perform to their full potential if conditions were less than perfect. So Ke-Ching's intention was to capitalise on Chinese research into climate manipulation in order to take the weather variation factor out of the equation.

For years, Wong went on, the Chinese had seeded clouds to control rainfall but until recently the outcome had been somewhat hit and miss.

New techniques recently perfected made it possible to manipulate the weather with a degree of certainty and local accuracy that could previously only have been dreamt of.

In fact, Wong told the baroness in a tone that suggested it was for her ears only, the techniques had been tested as long ago as 2008 during the Beijing Olympics and then again a year later during celebrations to mark the sixtieth anniversary of Mao Zedong's declaration of the founding of the People's Republic.

Heavy rain at either event would have left egg on the face of a country obsessed with presenting itself as the best of all possible worlds so could not be allowed under any circumstances. So billions of Chinese yuan had been diverted from social welfare funds to ensure the Party leaders' hair didn't get wet while reviewing the Olympic teams and the Chinese military millions parading across Beijing's Tiananmen Square.

The results had proved so successful, continued Wong in a voice lowered to a conspiratorial whisper, that funding for micro-local weather control research had been more than trebled and the work accorded a level of classification generally applied only to top secret weapons research.

'Very few people know this but I have it on good authority that the technology has been refined to such an extent that it's made the water cannon redundant,' said Wong. 'At the first sign of social unrest in China, the public order authorities have the power to unleash the sort of weather you wouldn't send your dog out in… or even your servant,' he added to the baroness's immense amusement.

'As you can guess, that's effectively put paid to public displays of discontent across the country and was the primary reason why the Arab Spring revolts of 2011 weren't mirrored in the People's Republic. At the first sign of disquiet, the weathermen were ordered to go into action to make such protests a literal washout. It's not pleasant trying to demonstrate while you're being bombarded with hailstones the size of quail's eggs.

'By the same token, it's not pleasant trying to stage publicly-sanctioned outdoor events in inclement weather so the technology is now being employed in China to ensure perfect blue sky conditions for the entirety of any such event… cricket matches included.

'In China, the phrase "rain stopped play" is now reserved for protest rallies alone,' said Wong with a smile, 'and there seems no reason why the phrase shouldn't also be consigned to the bonfires of history in this country. Just think how much outdoor event organisers would save in weather insurance premiums alone.'

'Could do with such a machine for the hunt,' interjected the baroness. 'Have you any idea how many poor horses break their legs charging across the quagmires the bloody foxes lead them into?'

'Foxes?' said Wong before he could stop himself.

DeWitt responded with a look that would have shattered plate glass and halted a charging buffalo.

'Ah,' murmured Wong, remembering that research on the baroness had revealed she was also a Justice of the Peace and therefore not without influence in 'guiding' local magistrates in their interpretation of the law forbidding hunting with dogs.

'Well…' he croaked, scrambling for a way out of his faux pas, 'not sure the weather manipulation technology will ever become available to the private consumer… but I'm certain China's development of genetically-engineered grass will. Maybe you could plant the quagmires with it. It's staggering the range of different varieties being developed,' Wong stumbled gamely on.

'For cricket pitches, for example, there's one whose molecular structure continually regenerates so that a uniform covering is maintained regardless of wear and tear making the pitch as good at the end of the game as it was at the beginning. The idea is to eliminate any advantage being gained by the winning of the toss. In fact, the toss-up might go altogether, the two captains just agreeing who should bat first. So much more egalitarian, don't you think?'

All the baroness did was blink leaving Wong fretting that his fox blunder still reverberated, undoing all his previous good work. His only option now was to race to his next revelation, hoping it would serve to chase the issue from his hostess' mind.

'Of course the Ke-Ching innovations don't stop with grass,' he announced in a voice that seemed to have developed a mousey squeak to it.

'Pretty soon… a-HEM… Pretty soon they'll also have the technology to project full-size holographic replays of the crucial moments of a game right onto the field.' Phew. He'd got his normal sales pitch delivery back and the baroness seemed not to have noticed he'd almost lost his poise there.

'The plan,' he continued swiftly on so as to capitalise on his hostess' blank stare, 'is to replay important incidents on a neighbouring playing strip so the players don't have to move. They'll be able to watch themselves being stumped, bowled or whatever as if they were taking part in another game right on the next pitch. Neat, eh?'

'Remarkable,' replied the baroness, a faraway look clouding her eyes. While Wong had been talking she'd been imagining her toyboy's reaction to finding she'd installed just such a system in her London flat.

'And that's not all. If the demand is there, we could use the technology to project a complete game going on somewhere else in the world right on to a cricket pitch near you... or even into your living room. It's just a matter of scaling down to fit the space available.'

'Isn't that what they call "virtual reality"?'

'Much better. It takes holographic technology to a whole new level so Ke-Ching has had to invent a whole new name for it. Its proprietary name is "Holostomy" but that, if you don't mind, has to remain between you and me for the time being. Best not to let it out of the bag just yet. I'd like to keep it as a surprise for the committee when the time is right.'

'I don't think you need worry about the surprise factor,' said DeWitt almost failing to suppress the snort of pleasure that welled up at the thought of her colleagues' faces on being confronted with the word. 'I'm sure the news will have the committee struggling to contain themselves.'

'Very reassuring,' said Wong, lowering his eyes to the floor and pretending not to get it. The time had come in his pre-prepared script for his *coup de grâce* and it was important he didn't get distracted from its delivery. As one who'd banished regret from his persona, it wasn't easy pretending it was making an entrance now.

While the baroness was still smiling at her own joke, Wong took a long, slow sip of the tea his host had had brought in and made a show of frowning.

'Something wrong with the tea, Mr Wong?'

'What? No. Sorry. No, the tea's fine. It's just that while I've been babbling on... well, I've been babbling on. Not that what I've told you has any great degree of secrecy attached to it, you understand. It's just that I'm a bit worried that in my enthusiasm I might have over-stepped the mark. Not sure the powers-that-be would appreciate it given the delicate nature of the issues at hand. As a member of the committee you'll know that the MCC hasn't always been fully supportive of the introduction of new technologies in the past and there's one in particular that might set the boat rocking more than most. So, if you don't mind, perhaps I'd better stop there.'

The baroness did mind. She minded very much. Always on the look-out for new ammunition to fire in the committee's direction, she'd rather started counting on her guest to keep the rounds coming. And just as he was about to deliver the big one, he'd stopped.

To the baroness, it was like being teased towards orgasm only to find her bedding victim had gone off the boil. As unconfined as her infuriation always was in such circumstances, even the baroness knew that a reversal on these occasions could never be demanded. The only way to achieve satisfaction was to coax new life into the offending item.

And so it was with Wong. Knowing a heavy-handed approach would only make matters worse, from the weapons at her disposal the baroness chose persuasion and Wong was about to discover just how persuasive the baroness could be.

***

'Oh, Mr Wong… Harry… might I call you Harry?' she cooed in what she hoped was her most disarming manner. 'There's no reason to be concerned. You're amongst friends here. After how you've helped with the predator problem, surely you couldn't think I might be capable of betraying a confidence.'

'No. No, baroness, of course not,' Wong stuttered in what he hoped was his most shamefaced manner. 'Naturally I could never doubt your discretion. It's just that I have to be careful in such situations. Ke-Ching would certainly not thank me for revealing the material issue before it's had time to prepare its case properly. As a member of the committee, baroness, I'm sure you'll appreciate my position.'

The baroness had stopped listening after the words 'material issue'. What materials? And why were they so sensitive?

Bloody hell! Was he talking about what she thought he was talking about? If he was this was dynamite and Wong wasn't going anywhere until she'd wormed it out of him. Or, in this case, blackmailed it out.

'Why Harry! You old tease! You wouldn't lead a girl up the garden path then leave her standing at the altar would you? Tickling someone's fancy with such an intriguing titbit then leaving that someone in the lurch might be perceived as a preparedness to go back on one's word. And I'm sure you wouldn't want to find yourself landed with that sort of reputation… would you? Not something that would go down at all well with the committee. Not well at all, if you take my meaning…'

Wong did. It was difficult not to. He was being threatened with just the sort of threat he thought his mock reticence would provoke. If he didn't spill the beans – all of them and now – it wouldn't be just the baroness's vote he might not be able to count on. DeWitt would make amply sure of that.

Long before the baroness had finished delivering the threat, Wong had decided what his response should be. It was to stare even more intently at the floor ringing his hands to give the impression of one considering his position carefully.

'Hmmm. Yes. I see. Yes. You've got a point there. Such a reputation is certainly not something I'd wish to acquire. But that doesn't alter the fact that it still leaves me in a difficult position…'

'Oh come on, Harry. You can tell me. I promise it won't go beyond these four walls until you're ready to go public… Girl Guide's honour!'

Wong had no need of the 'honour' bit. He already knew that what he was about to impart would be kept firmly under wraps until the baroness saw a way of using it to further her own despicable ends.

'Well, since you put it like that,' he responded after a moment's pause purely to add fuel to the baroness's fire, 'if I have your word that what I'm about to tell you remains strictly between us, how can I resist? After all, if you'll excuse the assumption, it does seem that, like me, you're something of a technology enthusiast…?'

The baroness nodded so vigorously her teeth nearly fell out.

'As I thought. In which case I think you might appreciate this particular aspect of the Ke-Ching technology development programme, one which has stretched the company's foremost research teams to the limit. Few people know this but Ke-Ching prides itself on being something of a dog with a bone when it comes to tricky technology problems. That's what's made it one of the premier technology research organisations in China…'

'OH, COME ON, MAN!' shouted the baroness to herself trying not to let the thought register on her face. 'Enough of this foreplay. GIVE IT TO ME NOW!'

'… so when it came to tackling this particular problem it wasn't going to rest until it had the answer. It knew that if it didn't come up with something pronto, cricket would be left facing a very uncertain future.

'You see, from its research Ke-Ching has become firmly convinced that two of the game's most traditional materials are in danger of extinction and that unless moves are initiated to replace them with synthetic substitutes, cricket itself could become likewise endangered…'

'DEAR GOD!,' thought the baroness, 'I was right,' and as the thought struck her, her sides began to ache with an unconfined glee that would have to be suppressed until Wong was gone. The thought of Bleauforth's face on hearing that leather and willow were destined to go the same way as the umpires and the toss-up was just too delicious to bear.

'Substitutes, Mr Wong?' she managed through jaws so clenched her molars began biting into one another.

'Er, yes. You see, the thing is, the way Ke-Ching sees it, a degree of uncertainty hangs over the future of materials conventionally used in the manufacture of cricket balls and bats and the company is convinced action needs to be taken now to prepare for the day when leather and willow are no longer available...'

Wong's confirmation of the baroness's suspicions had her struggling to contain herself. At the mention of 'leather and willow' out of Wong's own mouth, she felt the fingers of both hands bite deep into the arms of her chair to prevent herself leaping out of it and dancing round the room in paroxysms of unconfined joy.

Wong's news exceeded by several mathematical powers anything she could possibly have hoped for and she could hardly wait for the day when the Ke-Ching proposal was placed in front of the committee. That one moment alone would be enough to compensate for all the hostility and disdain received at the hands of her fellow members ever since she'd first walked through the committee room door to find no vacant chair at the conference table.

But first things first, she forced herself to think. The priority right now was paying special attention to what Wong was saying to make certain there'd been no misunderstanding.

'... so you see, after what's happened to elm and ash over the years,' she heard him continuing, 'the company believes willow could well be next and wants to be prepared for that eventuality.

'Likewise, it's the company's opinion that the continued use of the leather ball could make cricket a target for animal rights campaigners…'

Wong never finished the sentence. There was no need. His words had already caused the baroness's eyes to start bulging in their sockets and her face to go an unhealthy shade of purple. Whether it was from the leather and willow revelation or from the mention of animal rights Wong wasn't sure, but he suspected the former.

What Ke-Ching was proposing – or what he'd told the baroness they were proposing – would, at a stroke, achieve everything the baroness had striven to achieve her whole life. Finally, the lid of cricket's coffin would have been nailed firmly shut. Take leather and willow out of the game and cricket would be cricket no longer.

Although the sight of his quarry's face was enough to convince Wong that the word 'Gotcha' might now be applied to his vote-catching mission, the Hong Konger still felt the need to add one final failsafe lock to the trap he'd sprung. The baroness needed be convinced he was as mortified as she was pretending to be over the imminent demise of one of cricket's most treasured traditions.

'I know, I know,' he murmured, ringing his hands with just enough urgency to convey his own 'horror' to his host. 'That's exactly the reaction I told them they'd get.

'But they're determined. Ke-Ching firmly believes these are very real threats that have to be addressed and wants to give synthetics a run-out during the Double Tops competition – as a softener, so-to-speak, for the time when it'll be necessary to introduce them throughout the whole game.'

With the baroness's jaw opening and closing like the fish he now knew he'd both hooked and landed, Wong knew that adding anything further would be largely superfluous and under normal circumstances he'd have stopped there.

But these weren't normal circumstances. He'd started

enjoying himself so much that, purely for his own entertainment, he'd decided to add one final flourish to his revelation. One he was certain would leave the woman in such a state of suppressed bliss it could well end with the doctor having to be called.

'When Ke-Ching told me of their plans,' Wong went on, 'my advice to them was to tread very softly over such sensitive turf but they're of a mind to move swiftly on this one.

'So swiftly in fact that they're already ready with the materials and I don't mind telling you that to my mind they've done a mighty fine job. It's virtually impossible to tell the difference between the real thing and their synthetic substitutes. And what's more, bats and balls made from the stuff are not only virtually indestructible but with 3D printing technology they can be knocked out in a matter of minutes…'

As full comprehension of the ramifications of this information gelled in the baroness's mind, her bulging eyes widened to twin full moons. It would put the cricket bat and ball-making industry out of business at a stroke, the bastard who was growing willow on her land amongst them.

Wong grinned inwardly at his own malice. As the Hong Konger knew full well from his research, although the woods in which he'd been trespassing belonged to the baroness, under an ancient statute stretching back to the time of King Alfred one section of them had been granted in perpetuity to a family of woodsmen and their descendants.

Today's incumbent was the great great grandson of a man who'd seen the potential for planting the area with willow and, to the baroness's utter horror, had expanded into the cricket bat-making business.

It had taken the baroness all of a microsecond to realise that once synthetics replaced their natural equivalents, the damned man's business would be killed off at a stroke and he might even be persuaded to hand the area back to its rightful, in the baroness's mind, owner.

Wong was right. From the baroness's eye-popping reaction to his final item of pure fabrication, it could only be a matter of moments before she forgot herself, clutched him to her monstrous bosom and attempted to swallow him whole.

So it was just as well that Twist arrived when he did. Had he left it another minute the baroness would've had some explaining to do to the red-faced blob who'd entered the room without knocking and stood hovering just inside the door wringing his cap in both hands.

'Yer wanted ter zee me, m'lady?'

'Ah… er… Twist… er… I wanted to see you? Oh yes. That's right. I did. Not dragging you away from some urgent task on the estate I trust?'

'No ma'am. Oi were juzt in me office.'

'Otherwise known as the Ousedon Arms,' stated the baroness with some measure of confidence.

Gamekeeper Twist wisely indulged in a silent staring contest with the carpet while keeping his breath out of range of his psychic employer.

'Well Twist, I've got some news for you. My good friend Wong here has been able to confirm your suspicions about the birds. He's got a bit of kit that shows they're on the menu of some damned predator… a polecat, Mr Wong?'

Wong nodded.

'So, although it irks me to say so Twist, it seems I owe you an apology… or something. It seems you were right and I was… unusually… not. The numbers are definitely down and we've got to stop the bugger before it scoffs the lot. Got to get the traps out pronto. No delays and no excuses. Wong here will show you exactly where to put 'em.'

Thirty minutes later, gamekeeper Twist was on his way to the woods while Wong was happily heading back to Woking confident of having DeWitt's vote in the bag and of being within hours of claiming the generous bounty Ke-Ching was offering in return for the MCC scalp and a place on the board of one of Britain's most influential institutions.

Three months later, he was still trying to work out which part of the word 'urgent' the MCC committee didn't fully understand.

chapter nine

Bishop Roger was not amused. He hadn't come all this way to have his after-lunch nap interrupted. It was his one little monthly respite from diocesan duties and, by and large, his fellow Lords Spiritual respected his moment of somnambulant bliss. In fact, most were likewise engaged during the postprandial 'meditation' half-hour that preceded the session's resumption, the House of Lords' tea room humming with contented clerical snoring.

But there were always one or two who seemed immune to the effects of the monthly indulgence, generally the ones whose idea of a feast was adding a smear of butter to the translucent slice of organic wholemeal gluten-free bread which accompanied their lightly-poached sliver of environmentally-sensitive line-caught sea bass.

To such sallow-complexioned, rake-thin ascetics, this was the time for intense, concerned discourse on the finer points of ecclesiastical dogma, the time to indulge in exhibitions of their understanding of the little-known works of even lesser-known theological scholars.

Known affectionately to their fellow bishops as the Great Souls, their conversations were generally kept to murmured undertones in deference to their slumbering colleagues.

Today though, one pair forgot themselves, a lapse which prompted Bishop Roger to consider inserting a capital 'R' between the words 'Great' and 'Souls' for prematurely rousing him from the arms of Morpheus.

'Oh Lord, say it isn't true!' exclaimed Bishop Vivyan to his right reverend conversation partner, Bishop Nimrod.

'By my clerical collar, that's what I heard. As you know, I'm not one for tittle tattle but on this occasion I just had to share it. After all, it wasn't as if it was something I heard in the confessional. The man was almost bellowing into his phone as he relieved himself at the urinal, oblivious to the fact that someone might be in one of the cubicles. It was all SO embarrassing that I just sat there trying not to… thingy… until he'd gone.'

'But are you SURE that's what he said? That it's the end for the umpires!'

'Completely. Eyesight's a bit wobbly these days but no need for aural assistance just yet.'

'And are you SURE it was Lord Bleauforth? No mistake?'

'Oh, absolutely. As one who's listened to the cricket on the wireless since Noah came off for bad light I'd know his voice anywhere.'

'Well that's that then. If anyone would know, it's Bleauforth. You know he's on the committee now?'

Bishop Roger was suddenly wide awake. Bleauforth might be a godless gasbag but he was generally a reliable one and, as a member of the committee of the club to which Roger had belonged for some twenty years, the bishop's noble 'friend' was privy to certain private goings-on in the world of cricket that the game's custodians preferred to keep that way.

But scrapping the umpires? Surely not. How? Why? When? This demanded immediate investigation.

* * *

'Hello? Vernon? This is Roger.'

'Roger? Ohhh… Roger the Bishop! Well, bless my unsalvageable soul,' Bleauforth blurted. 'Long time no holy see, old fruit. How the devil are you?'

'Fine, but if you don't mind and I prefer the epithet Bishop Roger in mixed company. I assume there are other people in your office…?'

'You'd assume wrong old bean. Totally alone at the moment,' Bleauforth corrected him down the phone line with a wink at his pair of research assistants seated opposite.

'Well, since you ARE alone, I was wondering if you've got a minute. Something I'd like your advice on.'

'Really? Good God. Miracles will never cease. Better take up your bed and toddle over then, old man. Tell you what… you bring the loaves and I'll rustle up some fishes. We could make a session of it… chuck another sinner on the fire and put the kettle and some soul music on.'

'Thanks. I'll be there in five minutes.'

Although frostiness wasn't in Bishop Roger's general nature, in Bleauforth's case he was willing to make an exception.

Despite his best efforts, the memory of his now fellow peer's persecution of him at their joint prep school in the sixties refused to die and appeals to a higher power for deliverance from his boyhood tormentor were clearly still in the Almighty's pending tray. Bleauforth seemed determined never to let the cleric forget how his class-topping place in religious education had led, with some perspicacity it now turned out, to the Roger the Bishop schoolboy nickname.

As Roger negotiated the Palace of Westminster's warren of oak-panelled corridors en route to Bleauforth's office, the memory of those prep school days made him shudder. But stiffening his resolve to match his clerical collar, he'd forced himself on, wracking his brains as he went for a way of approaching the umpire-scrapping issue without putting Bleauforth on his guard.

It was a vain exercise. Subterfuge came as naturally to the bishop as frostiness and, because Bleauforth had always been able to read him like the good book, by the time he reached the MCC committee man's door, Bishop Roger had pretty much decided to stick with the candour his Archbishop found unsettling but did nothing to discourage. That, at least, carried the advantage of brevity and would mean he wouldn't have to remain in Bleauforth's company any longer than was absolutely necessary.

* * *

'YOU need confirmation from ME!' Bleauforth guffawed, collapsing into the nearest chair helpless with mirth. 'God's holy incontinence pants, Bish! That's an absolute cracker. Must write it down. Anything else I can help you with? Absolution perhaps? Exorcism?'

Thank you Lord, Roger thought to himself, surreptitiously lifting his eyes to the ceiling and smiling a small smile. If proof were needed that divine intervention came in many forms, this was indisputable evidence that his God did indeed move in mysterious ways. Without realising what it was he was saying, he'd managed to put Bleauforth at ease and get him onside with one chance remark.

'Er… not quite the confirmation I was thinking of, actually. The one I had in mind was more of the cricketing variety.'

'Come again.'

'To do with the laws of the game.'

'Ah… not really my strong point old man. You'd be better off talking to a qualified umpire.'

Bishop Roger could hardly believe his luck. Bleauforth had gone straight to the nub of the issue before it had even been mentioned and the bishop once again metaphorically raised his eyes to the heavens.

'Well, as it happens, that's sort of what I wanted to ask you about.'

'Beg pardon.'

'The umpires.'

'What about them?'

'Well… what the laws say about them being there.'

'Where?'

'On the field of play.'

Bleauforth just sat there, jaw flapping with nothing coming out and in that moment Roger knew he had his man. Never before had anything he'd said left his boyhood nemesis struck dumb. Bleauforth had always had a comeback of some sort, mostly of the mocking variety. This time, it was as if he'd been stranded halfway down the wicket with the ball in the fielder's hands, the stumps at his mercy.

'Errrrr… not quite sure…'

'It's just that I want to settle a debate going on in the tea room about the laws stating that the umpires must be present on the field of play for the match to commence. What I need to know is if there are any circumstances in which the game can continue without the umpires? I thought that since you're on the MCC committee you'd know off the top of your head.'

'I see. Well… yes… I mean no… by and large. So far as I understand the laws, no game can proceed unless it's being umpired.'

'By and large?'

'More or less.'

'Hmmm.'

Vacillation, as Roger well knew, wasn't a feature of Bleauforth's general make-up. Under normal circumstances the man would simply state his case and have done with it. By wavering on such a basic issue, all he'd accomplished was the cementing in the bishop's mind of the truth behind the umpire-scrapping rumours and the certainty that the game he treasured would never be the same again.

But why? What could possibly prompt the MCC to take such a drastic step? There was a lot more to this than met the eye, he was sure. But how to get Bleauforth to come clean? A bit of informed speculation might work.

'And that requirement is set in stone? It's unlikely ever to be rescinded?'

'Look… what is it you're driving at exactly?' demanded Bleauforth, his undisguised irritation over this line of questioning serving only to encourage Bishop Roger to continue teasing at what was clearly a highly sensitive exposed nerve.

'Well… I was wondering if, in your view, you could envisage any circumstance in which the requirement might be… overlooked.'

'Overlooked?'

'Unobserved. Disregarded.'

Bleauforth gazed out of the window at the uninviting sludge green water of the River Thames flowing beneath it, appearing to be considering the question in depth before framing a response.

Bishop Roger wasn't fooled. This, he was sure, was Bleauforth's way of avoiding the bishop's inquiring eye and was further evidence of him being in possession of information that would rock the game to its very foundations.

'Ignored. Unnoticed…'

'Yes, yes. I heard what you said.'

'Ditto.'

'Eh?'

'Let's just say that we're never as alone in this world as we might sometimes like to think we are.'

Bleauforth's face registered confusion morphing gradually into enlightenment. On this occasion the Bish wasn't talking about the omnipotence of the Almighty. More of that of his hand servants on Earth.

'A certain mobile telephone conversation not thirty minutes since?' added Bishop Roger to aid the Bleauforth enlightenment process. 'That's the trouble with that particular item of modern technology I always think. They're fine unless used… injudiciously.'

'Er…'

'Never know who might be 'privy', as it were, to the odd snippet of overheard conversation.'

'Eh? Oh. Oh, bugger. Sod it.'

'Mmmmm.'

'Ahem…er…so…ah…would I be mistaken in thinking that sounds like a fairly confident appeal for a caught behind?'

With difficulty, Bishop Roger managed not to vocalise the paraphrased biblical words that were chiming 'vengeance is veritably mine sayeth this particular lord' in his head.

'I see,' said the now ashen-faced Bleauforth, his usual bombastic delivery tempered by an uncharacteristically timorous tremor to his voice.

'So…er… I suppose the question is, what would be the intentions of the one who, hypothetically of course, may or may not be in possession of any snippet of any allegedly overheard conversation?'

'Speaking, as you say, hypothetically,' said Bishop Roger thoughtfully, 'one might not be able to say if any intentions were intended. It might be solely a matter of… confirmation, so-to-speak.'

'Strictly concerning the hypothetical umpires or the other hypothetical stuff as well?'

Other stuff? There was more? The time seemed appropriate for one of Bishop Roger's well-practiced 'I'm ready when you are' looks he used to great effect on lesser clerics called before him to explain congregational drop-offs.

'OK, OK. I give in, blurted Bleauforth. 'Fact is, I've been busting my britches at having to respect committee confidentiality over all this. But since you know already, I see no real reason why you shouldn't have chapter and verse to avoid any misconceptions… as Joseph might have said to Mary. Sorry. That just slipped out. But I'll only let you in on it if I have your hand-on-heart assurance that what I'm about to tell you goes no further than these four walls.'

'Scout's honour,' said Roger who'd never even been in the cubs.

'Right. Well…' and, with some relief at having someone to share his pain with, Bleauforth lurched into the tale of how the MCC was facing imminent bankruptcy unless it accepted the terms and conditions that came with the Chinese bail-out offer.

Now it was Bishop Roger who lost the power of speech. All he could do was blink in disbelief as Bleauforth unravelled the details behind the Ke-Ching offer to inject gazillions into the MCC and into English cricket in general if the committee would allow them a seat on the board and sanction the use of truly space-age technologies for the Double Tops competition. Technologies, Bleauforth explained, that would not only see the games umpired by computer but would ensure playing conditions never varied from one ground to the next.

In short, he went on, the Chinese company was convinced the game's very survival depended on taking the inconsistencies and uncertainties out of cricket and was making clear between the lines that its terms were a non-negotiable commodity. If the committee wasn't able to accept them, they'd walk.

'But…' said Bishop Roger after a moment's thought, 'this is

just for the Double Tops competition, right? It won't apply to test matches or any of the other competitions?'

'For the moment, yes. But you know as well as I do that certain aspects of the game once considered sacrosanct are now seen as quaint forgotten oddities. Remember how the Packer Series completely changed the face of the game in the seventies? Back then, coloured clothing was considered an unheard-of departure from the traditions. Now, pyjama cricket is the norm leaving whites the strict preserve of test matches and even that rule is being eroded with all the advertising on players' clothing.

'Then there's the use of floodlights. Was a time when they would NEVER have been employed when the red ball was in use. When you're fielding, it's like having a black bomb coming at you out of the sun. These days, to keep a test match going under bad light conditions and stop the crowd leaving, it's standard practice.

'I tell you, Roger, this is just the start. Once we give in to Ke-Ching's "technological revolution" it'll spread to the rest of the game. So bye-bye umpires and thanks for all the ducks.'

'So what's the committee going to do?'

'What it always does with difficult issues. Sit on it. Old Gainsborough wasn't blind to having an outright rebellion on his hands if he allowed a vote at the last meeting. With all the money men now on the board it stood every chance of being accepted there and then. So he declared it was raining and that we'd have to come off for an early tea. It was his only way of preventing the rest of us turning into a lynch mob.

'Gainsborough's compromise was to defer any decision until a detailed investigation's been carried out into the effects of the proposals and into the Chinese wallahs who're forcing them on us.

'But that won't put the day of reckoning off for ever.

Fortunately with the Christmas hols coming up we have a few weeks to look into things. But after that, unless we uncover something to strangle this mad idea with, it'll sail through.'

'So how's that going?'

'The investigation? To tell the truth, it's only just started and isn't exactly proving plain sailing. It's nigh on impossible getting anything of note on Ke-Ching out of China. They're a HUGE company with all the right connections and you know how tetchy the Chinese get about outsiders poking their noses into their affairs. All we're getting at the moment is the PR brush-off. Or, in this case, the PRC brush-off.

'But I know a rat when I smell one and I'm damned certain there's a whole rotten nest of 'em lurking in this particular compost heap. Just can't find it at the moment, and unless we do, we're sunk. It'll be chopsticks for cricket as we know it unless we get something on them soon.'

* * *

Bishop Roger missed the afternoon session of the Lords Spiritual convocation. He was there, but then again he wasn't. He was having an out-of-body experience which involved trips to St John's Wood, Hong Kong, Beijing and his boyhood holiday refuge, now his diocese, in West Cornwall. Somewhere in one of these places he knew he'd find something that would save the game he'd loved and cherished ever since being given his first bat and ball by his one-eyed, one-legged, fisherman uncle Sam whose passion for cricket drove him to continue playing until he lost the other eye in a freak sailing accident.

'Bleddy wind changed sudden-like,' said Sam. 'Boom caught I full in't face and buggered t'other eye. 'ad to navigate back to 'arbour like 'er were pitch black wi' no lights showing. That's when yer other zenses take over, zee. Caught the whiff o' a fishin' smack and knew by the stink on 'er she were fully laden so 'ad to be heading in to Newlyn. So I just followed 'er and found usself in 'arbour 'ventually. Bashed the poor old tub up a bit on the wall but gorr'in in the end. Story made the bleddy paper it did! Had to cry off playing the next day and 'aven't turned out since. Still 'oping though.'

Such events were just run of the mill to Sam whose body was now missing an assortment of key components thanks to a series of nasty fishing accidents he took as par for the course.

'Sometimes reckon the fish got more o' I than I got o' they,' he'd chuckle to anyone who'd listen.

Mostly it was the young Roger who spent many a school and college holiday with his accident-prone uncle helping maintain the battered old lugger moored in Penzance harbour which now served as Sam's home, his fisherman days a thing of the past.

On occasion, Roger thought he might follow Sam into the profession but his uncle would have none of it.

'Look at 'e boy. 'ave to be a big daft bugger like I fer the fishin' game, norra brainy little squib like 'e. No, boy, 'e knows as well as I you's more a fisher o' men than o' fish.'

And so it had proved. Roger had distinguished himself in theological studies at Christ Church, gone on to take holy orders and taken up his first 'living' in the Surrey parish where he'd met and nurtured the young Toby Tode.

Ah, Tode, Bishop Roger thought to himself as his fellow Lords Spiritual debated the ethical dimensions of a government White Paper proposing that voting rights be restricted to those able to pass an intellectual means test. Tode might be just the chap the MCC was looking for. Being part Japanese he'd know how the Oriental mind works – and how to gain an insight into the one the MCC was having trouble reading.

Yes. That was it. He'd give Tode a call. Better still, he'd pay him a visit. It was always a pleasure seeing how his protégés were faring in the parishes he'd dispatched them to.

… # chapter ten

Even by its own uncooperative standards The Beast was being especially unreasonable. The damned machine was resolutely resisting any attempt to start it and Toby Tode had resorted to giving it a word of advice in a language the clergy weren't supposed to know.

The Beast had been so-christened, if that was the right word, long before Tode had ever clapped eyes on it and was a name the then-trainee groundsman at Christ Church College had found especially appropriate.

Tode was convinced the cricket pitch heavy roller had been forged in the fires of hell and put on Earth as Satan's retribution on the faithful. If the machine had had an identification plate he wouldn't have been surprised to see 666 as its serial number and a maker's logo comprised of horns and tails. But since no such plate existed, The Beast remained wholly unidentifiable which did nothing to diminish Tode's suspicions regarding its true provenance.

Despite extensive enquiries, no one at Christ's could be found to provide Tode with any history of the thing or how it had come to be there and even a search of the college accounts going back to the twenties had revealed no trace of it. So far as anyone knew, it had just always been there and, before Tode, no one had queried its existence. A bit, Tode mused, like the relationship between the college theology students and God.

The only thing that was certain about The Beast was that

without Tode there to administer to it, nothing could be done to coax it into life. On his departure in 1989, the machine had gone into a deep, unremitting sulk and the college had eventually had to dig deep for a shiny new, more cooperative replacement with all the individuality and character of the grass and mud it was brought in to pound into submission.

Returning some fifteen years later to ask if he could take it to his ministry in the far west of Cornwall, the college authorities had only one question: why? What could he possibly want with such a stubborn, useless piece of junk whose dead, in all senses of the word, weight was threatening to take it back down to the place Tode was convinced it had originated.

In response, Tode felt able to supply no more than a watered-down 'my club needs a roller and you've got a spare one' version of the truth. He wasn't sure his former employers would fully understand his real reason – that he couldn't shake the feeling that a spiritual connection of sorts existed between him and it, that it would be fitting partner for the club mower known fondly to all as the Grim Reaper and that all three of them were meant to be together in perpetuity. It was The Beast, after all, that had provided him with his ride to vocational enlightenment one sparkling summer's day in the late eighties, the day that 5c beat, for the first time in living memory, the pros from Loughborough College.

* * *

Renowned as a breeding ground for county class cricketers, Loughborough always provided the season's toughest opposition and Tode had resolved to produce an especially placid wicket, one that might at least afford 5c with a reasonable chance of acquitting themselves with the bat.

To achieve the desired result meant beasting the hell, as it were, out of it, trundling the machine back and forth over the strip for a good hour, an exercise that always sent Tode's mind off on a journey to the furthest reaches of the mental cosmos.

Under normal circumstances, he found nothing especially out of the ordinary there but today was different. On this occasion, he'd had an unusual encounter. Cutting through Tode's mindless reverie came, quite distinctly, the voice of God. And the word Tode had heard him speak was 'priesthood'.

God's verbal apparition came as something of a shock to the young groundsman who'd never been one for exhibiting any great show of belief in deity in any form. But on this day, the big man seemed to have singled him out for special attention and Tode felt a great weight lift from his shoulders. He'd waited a long time for this day to come.

Something in him had always nagged that maybe there WAS something else, that 'this' wasn't all of 'it' and that some day some 'thing' would happen to reveal what 'it' really was.

The Australian in him kept intervening in such thoughts telling him to ignore such a heap of dingo dung but his Japanese side disagreed leaving Tode confused and conflicted and locked in a spiritual limboland from which there seemed no escape.

Now, an answer had finally arrived and in his exultation the newly-enlightened Tode rose up on The Beast to punch the sky and whoop with joy. Which was when, out of the corner of his eye, he spotted the Reverend Roger walking alongside the machine mouthing something at him over the din of the engine.

Tode froze, his fist in the air, his heart sinking to his ankles and his stomach contracting with a feeling he'd last had when a malicious childhood friend had purposefully burst his birthday balloon.

Just when his Japanese side seemed to have gained the upper hand, the light at last penetrating Tode's darkness, the Reverend

Roger of all people had switched it off thrusting Tode unceremoniously back into the void.

'Bugger,' mumbled Tode to himself. 'Thought that was it.'

'Pardon,' shouted the reverend over the Beast's engine cacophony.

'What? Oh. Nothing. Just thought…'

'What?'

'Thought you were… someone else,' yelled Tode.

'Who?'

'Just… Thought I heard…'

'What?'

'Another voice.'

'Whose?'

'Er… '

'You expecting someone?'

'Yes… No… Not really. Look, can't talk now. Got to get off the wicket.'

Five minutes later, as Tode was putting the machine to bed in its shed, Reverend Roger appeared at the door.

'Toby? Sorry to bother you old boy but felt I had to check to see if you were OK. You looked like you'd seen a ghost when you spotted me. Wondered if there was anything amiss.'

'No, not really. It's just that when I'm rolling the wicket with earplugs in I tend to drift off into my own little world. Intrusions come as a bit of a shock sometimes. Sorry. Didn't mean to offend.'

'None taken. I thought it might be something like that but you did seem mightily troubled. Did I interrupt some profound thought?'

'Profound? Not quite sure…'

'Not in any bother are you? Anything I can do?'

'Not bother exactly. Just a bit of mental conflict. Thought I'd heard something I hadn't. Probably a trick of the earplugs. Anyway, what brings you to this neck of the woods?'

'Don't go spreading it around but I'm playing truant. Taking a day off to see my old tutor who lives nearby and arrived a bit early. Thought I'd take a stroll around the ground, it being such a lovely day. Spotted you and couldn't help but notice you were giving the wicket a good seeing to. Must be flat enough to play billiards on after the beasting you were giving it. Passed comment at the time but don't think you heard me.'

'What was it you said, exactly?'

'Think it was something like "the worst thing that can happen on such a wicket is for 5c to win the toss, decide to bat and not make use of the conditions". Something like that.'

'Something like? Those weren't your actual words?'

'Might not have said "worst". Think the expression I used was "least good".'

* * *

Thinking back on that day some thirty years later, Tode had had to chuckle as he began the tortuous process of stripping The Beast's engine down... again. The Reverend Roger's remark had left him in need of a restorative libation in the local pub, which was where his road to the priesthood had really begun.

Leaving his fellow ground staff to finish off marking up the wicket, Tode and the reverend had repaired to a quiet corner of one of the more salubrious hostelries in the area where Tode had, after a couple of stiff ones, managed to vocalise his thoughts.

The reverend began by lending a sympathetic ear but as the story unfolded, he allowed himself a small smile which Tode found contagious and by the time he reached the punchline the pair were hugging one another in fits, much to the innkeeper's bemused consternation. He didn't get many pissed vicars in his establishment and wasn't quite sure how to handle the situation.

Fortunately, it was a quiet afternoon in the pub so the landlord beat a hasty retreat to the other bar leaving Toby and Roger to embark on the dissection of Tode's conflicted soul.

It was a painful and embarrassing process for the Australian in Tode but the reverend had learned a thing or two during his years in the ministry and Tode found himself offloading without really being aware of it.

By the time he had to return to the ground, he felt as if he'd been uncoupled from a great weight he'd been dragging around. The reverend was the only person he knew who might understand his dilemma and Tode had grabbed the opportunity with both hands, even going so far as to postulate that his mishearing of the reverend's words was in some way divine intervention.

Maybe 'priesthood', he suggested, was the word he'd wanted to hear but couldn't bring himself to vocalise without outside assistance.

'Hmmmm,' was the reverend's sole response.

'Wodjer mean "Hmmmm". You're beginning to sound like Winnie the Pooh.'

'Hmmmm,' said the reverend. 'Time to get back to the match, methinks.'

Back at the ground, things were going extraordinarily well for 5c. After losing the toss they'd found themselves in the field and, to their surprise, had Loughborough in trouble. The Christ Church bowlers had struck gold, making the ball talk on this wicket and their opposition had no response. Loughborough were all out cheaply and the 5c batsmen were steadily chipping away at the paltry target, serious inroads having been made by the time the semi-inebriate cleric and his erstwhile parishioner arrived.

In the end, they saw only ten overs, 5c accelerating and crossing the finishing line with thirteen overs to spare. As the celebrations began, Tode wandered out to inspect the damage to the strip, the Reverend Roger in tow.

'Blimey,' exclaimed the cleric. 'They've roughed that up a bit.'

'Not really,' said Tode. 'Looks much like it did this morning.'

'What d'you mean? It was pancake flat after you'd done it to death with The Beast.'

'That was THAT strip,' said Tode pointing at the wicket next to the one that had just been played on. 'The boys must have marked up the wrong wicket.'

'How on Earth could that have happened?'

'Divine intervention?' proposed Tode with a grin and a wink at his clerical friend.

* * *

Clarity of mind was a new experience for the Christ Church groundsman. A mishearing it might have been but the feeling that he'd been shown his true path wouldn't leave him. The word 'priesthood' kept resonating in his head and it wasn't long before he was knocking on Reverend Roger's door asking to continue the conversation they'd started in the pub.

Two years of theological training and a lot of deep thinking later, Tode's ordination allowed him to add the prefix 'Reverend' to his name and the newly dog-collared ex-groundsman sighed a huge sigh of relief. When you had a name like Tode and no one used the correct Japanese 'Toe-Day' pronunciation, anything was better than 'Mr'. From his first day at school, Tode had had to weather the sniggers the name prompted and not a day went past without him praying for release from his millstone.

God, it now seemed, had heard his prayers and intervened and the newly-anointed Reverend Tode revelled in his replacement epithet.

Which, in itself, was a new millstone. The wearisome weight of his old name had been replaced with an equally weighty new feeling of guilt over the possibility that faith alone might not have been solely responsible for bringing him to the door of the church.

It was a concern that, despite his prayers and best efforts, he never truly shook off and the worry continued to dog him throughout his clerical career.

It was there when he took up his first posting as parson to the vicar of a roughhouse parish in the industrial badlands of Tyneside, when he got his own first parish in the equally challenging docklands area of Plymouth, when he was sent to Liverpool on his most perilous mission yet and was still there when he took up his current posting in Cornwall's wild west.

In the church authorities' eyes Tode was a natural for the Liverpool posting for three specific reasons. He was still young and fit, he had experience – in spades – of inner city parish problems and he had Oriental blood.

For years, the church authorities had sought someone who might be able to connect with Liverpool's substantial Chinese community, most of whom lived cheek-by-jowl in an area of overcrowded squalor close to the docks where their forefathers had jumped ship generations earlier.

Despite the area's reputation for rabid godlessness, the church had never lost hope of gaining a foothold in Liverpool's Chinatown and of setting its residents on the path to redemption. It was just a matter of sending in the right person... as a missionary, so-to-speak.

In Tode, they thought they'd found their man and made him an offer he couldn't refuse. Give it a go for a few years and your next assignment will be substantially less challenging they'd said, it apparently not occurring to them that being part-Japanese would make Tode about as acceptable to the residents of Chinatown as the black death.

Missionary impossible, as Tode dubbed himself, in fact lasted just three, Tode slipping out of the area as quietly as he'd arrived the day his 'parishioners' decided they no longer had need of either him or his place of worship

The year was 2003 and thanks to China's insatiable appetite for raw materials to feed its rapacious industrial boom, the price of scrap metal had soared making no church roof safe from the opportunists, especially Tode's. In fact, his church seemed to have been singled out for special attention, every scrap of lead, copper, zinc and iron being ripped from the roof and shipped, probably that very night, to the People's Republic.

The irony of seeing the church that had been built on the proceeds of Britain's pillaging of China in the eighteenth and nineteenth centuries gradually being repatriated to its port of origin was not lost on the hapless cleric who'd had to stifle a manic laugh on being informed by the city building inspector that his house of God was no longer safe or fit for the purpose for which it had been intended.

Two days later, the building inspector's words came to prophetic fruition. Entering the building to recover his vestments before locking up until funds could be found to effect the necessary repairs, Tode found himself treading on the ceiling.

Gravity had had the penultimate word, the final one going to the diocesan authorities who'd phoned to say that perhaps, in view of the circumstances, it might be best if he suspended services for the time being.

'Perhaps,' chuckled the now-Bishop Roger in the next call Tode received, 'in view of the circumstances it might be best if you buggered off out of Liverpool and came to stay with me for a while. There's something I'd like to discuss.'

Arriving at the bishop's West Cornwall residence less than twenty-four hours later, Tode was greeted with open arms, a warm smile and a sumptuous dinner over which his mentor sounded him out for a new posting, one which Tode, he felt, more than deserved after serving so diligently on the ecclesiastical frontline for over a decade.

There was an opening in a small rural parish in his diocese he thought might suit Tode nicely. The vicar of St Ruth in the extreme west of the county was retiring and the parish couldn't be allowed to remain unserviced for long. Those pesky Wesleyans were always looking to lure the St Ruth flock into their lair.

Tode had only one question. 'When do I start?'

The arrangement was perfect for both men. Reverend Tode was being offered the chance of becoming the sort of parish priest he'd always dreamt of being and Bishop Roger was being handed an irresistible opportunity to indulge a wickedly playful sense of humour. Where better to send a priest with Australian blood than to a village known locally as Strewth?

chapter eleven

'Be there a match on today then, vicar?'

Reverend Tode knew better than to rise to Charley Pascoe's bait. Hardly able to hear the quarryman's tease over the clatter of rain on The Beast's shed roof, the St Ruth vicar just smiled a thin smile at his grinning tormentor and continued fiddling with the infernal machine's engine. It was mid-December and fish were swimming in the lake where the cricket pitch used to be.

Until today, the week-long deluge had forced Tode to confine himself largely to barracks where he'd been working on a sermon centring, appropriately enough, on the Noah story. It had been progressing nicely until he'd received a call that left him in need of a visit to The Beast's shed, the place he always went when there was serious thinking to be done.

What would his bishop be doing visiting him in the run-up to Christmas? Surely he'd have far better things to do at this time of year, thought Tode as he wrenched The Beast's fuel pump from its mountings praying that Bishop Roger wasn't coming to see how preparations for the festival of lessons and carols were going. The series of storms hitting the area recently had disrupted matters somewhat, the 'choir' – if that's what it could be called – having to abandon choir practice on more than one occasion to man the lifeboat and/or fire engine.

Whether the call-outs were genuine or not, Tode harbouring dark thoughts that the only alarms his choristers were hearing were those of the village pub's landlord calling time, they'd seriously disrupted preparations for the carol service leaving Tode with prematurely greying hair, a nervous twitch and nails bitten to the quick.

So it was with some trepidation that he opened the vicarage door to Bishop Roger a couple of days before the festival, relaxing only on being assured that it wasn't carols that were occupying the right reverend's thoughts.

'No, my boy,' he'd said reassuringly. 'I'm quite confident you've got that side of things well in hand. No, I'm here to ask if you might be able to provide me with a bit of assistance on another matter.'

Uh-oh, thought Tode. Here it comes. The diocese has run short on its flower budget and he wants me to ask the local growers to drop their prices so the cathedral isn't deprived of its usual extravagant floral display this Christmas.

'Thing is, Toby, I'm wondering if you'd make a few enquiries for me.'

'Subject of?' asked Tode cautiously, his mind wondering how to tell his bishop to politely bugger off. His flower-producing parishioners were in enough financial strife already thanks to this never-ending recession and now an unprecedented string of storms.

'Well, er, cricket as it happens.'

Tode wanted to speak but found his vocal chords refusing to cooperate. With the relentless December rain threatening to inundate not only Strewth but the entire Cornish peninsular, on Tode's chart of likely topics for discussion cricket ranked right up there with his contingency plan for coping with a sudden explosion in congregation numbers.

'Mmmm. Yes. Cricket. More specifically… er… Chinese cricket… Not as in French cricket, you understand. As in cricket as… er… played in China.'

Tode's mouth moved but nothing came out.

'Thing is, need to know a bit about China's... erm... perspective on the game. You being an "international", so-to-speak, thought you might have some... insight on the matter.'

'Insight.'

'Mmmm.'

Tode stared at Bishop Roger, his mind doing somersaults inside his head while thinking that his visitor might very well have gone off his.

'No HUGE rush, but wondered if you'd give it some thought over Christmas.'

Oh, no worries, thought Tode. I'll just cancel the festival of lessons and carols, the food distribution to the old and the infirm, the nativity play, the visiting of the sick, the Christmas Day services, Christmas dinner and the traditional Boxing Day football match and go and do something useful like finding out about Chinese bloody cricket. What is this man on?

'Grand. Knew I could count on you. Give you a call in the New Year then. Got to dash, my boy. Confirmation to do this evening.'

And with that he was gone leaving Tode with zero indication as to what had prompted this sudden obsession with Chinese cricket coupled with a mixed feeling of relief and dread. While his bishop hadn't asked him to rustle up some cheap begonias for the cathedral, his query had planted a teaser in Tode's mind he knew was going to cost him sleep.

This needed serious consideration and since there was only one place for that, Tode donned his Wellington boots and tramped off pensively in the direction of the village cricket pitch/temporary duck pond.

* * *

'Hello? Is that the Reverend Toby Tode?'

'Speaking.'

'Wonderful. Voice from the past here. Harry Wong from Christ's. Remember me?'

Blimey, thought Tode. He's tracked me down at last to wreak vengeance for allowing him to think I was a fellow student.

'Er… yes. Of course. The 5c scorer and scholar of all things cricket. How are you?'

'Oh fine, fine. Reason I'm calling is, well, I was up visiting the college a short while ago and your name came up in conversation. I was there to donate some equipment to the club to say thanks for all the good times there and noticed The Beast was no longer in its shed. They said you'd carted it off to your parish. Tell the truth, I didn't even know you'd been ordained so congratulations on that. A bit late I expect but better late than etcetera, eh?'

'Thanks. Much appreciated.'

'They said you're down in Cornwall now. That right?'

'Yes. Little place called St Ruth. Been here some fifteen years now.'

'Lovely. Passed through the area once a long time ago and all I remember about it was flowers. Flowers everywhere. Beautiful.'

'Yes. They grow them commercially here. Ship them all over the world.'

'I know, I know. Actually that's the reason I'm calling. I've got a small stake in a flower import business in China which needs a new supplier. Our regular one's gone bust. Well, busted actually.

'Anyway, with Valentine's Day and Chinese New Year virtually coinciding this year we need a replacement supplier double quick. Wondered if there were any growers down your way who might have some stock ready for shipping. I could get there sharpish if there's any looking for new business.'

Dear God, thought Tode. Without even praying for divine intervention to help dig his flowery flock out of their financial mire He seems to have decided to help out anyway. Wong was just the sort of person Tode and the village needed for more reasons than one. Besides throwing the flower growers a lifeline he might just be able to help Tode with a tricky little problem of his own. If there was anyone who'd have chapter and verse on Chinese cricket it'd be Wong and Tode found himself murmuring a little prayer.

With Christmas and all its ancillary events now out of the way, Tode had at last had time to give Bishop Roger's request some thought and wasn't making much progress.

Every search concerning China's involvement in cricket led him back to the Ke-Ching Double Tops competition which anyone with an interest in cricket would know about anyway.

Beyond that, he'd learned virtually nothing that anyone with an internet-connected computer wouldn't also be able to find and had started preparing himself for having to report the dearth of new information to the bishop. And now providence had brought him Wong, the one man he should have thought of asking straight off. Well God, thought Tode, one-nil to you I think.

'Hmmm,' replied Tode trying to keep the yelp of delight out of his voice at the thought of having the arrival of a new flower buyer to announce to the community. 'I think some of the growers might have some spare capacity. When were you thinking of making the trip?' Please God, he prayed, don't let him say tomorrow. He needed time to warn the village of Wong's arrival and to get his mind in order on the Chinese cricket issue.

Wong's answer allowed Tode to breathe again. His former Christ Church 'alumnus' was calling from Beijing and couldn't get to Strewth for a week or so.

'That should be OK,' Tode had replied in relief. 'Shall I make a reservation for you at the village inn? It's pretty accommodating and they'd welcome a guest this time of year. Not too many visitors in January so you'll get preferential treatment and a chance to rub shoulders with the locals.'

Wong had readily agreed knowing there was nothing like getting in with the residents of a community for gleaning titbits of information that might be to his advantage when it came to doing business in the area.

Tode's mind was working in precisely the same way but in exactly the opposite direction. Putting Wong at the mercy of the locals would be to no one's advantage except the people he was coming to do business with. If there was one thing he'd learned about the Cornish during his time in St Ruth, it was that they had no peer when it came to prising information out of newcomers whilst offering next to nothing about themselves.

It was a Cornish character trait, he'd decided, that had its roots in the county's infamous reputation for being the smuggling portal of Great Britain.

Ever since the word 'duty' had gained a second meaning, new arrivals in Cornwall's villages had had to be thoroughly vetted lest they turn out to be in the pay of His or Her majesty's revenue collection service. Hidden agendas didn't stay hidden for long in a village like St Ruth once the Dreckly Inn's inquisition team got started. If Wong had any ulterior motive for dropping in on Cornwall, the Dreckly boys would have it out of him 'faster'n a nasty pasty', as Daffy the local flower growing magnate might have put it, and without Wong even realising it.

Although Strewth's residents would have the decided upper hand when dealing with Wong on home territory, Tode thought it best not to allow them a completely free rein. Should any get it in their heads that Wong's intentions were anything less than honourable, Wong might end up like the pair from the West Midlands who'd found themselves suspected of being agents for a company looking to dump English waste down the area's disused mineshafts and Tode wanted no repetition of that unseemly incident.

The only way to make sure was to call a village meeting and for that there was only one place – the skittle alley of the Dreckly Inn.

Serving as anything from community hall to polling station to temporary mortuary and even as a skittle alley at times, the venue was perfect. Tode's news was for Strewthian ears only and privacy at the Dreckly was virtually guaranteed. It was difficult finding a pub whose proper name no one used, the Dreckly tag having been attached by the locals to the four hundred year-old St Ruth Arms the day the name of the current landlord first became known some thirty years earlier.

The moment the blow-in from England introduced himself, Derek Lee became an instant and unlikely hit with every man, woman and child in St Ruth.

For four long centuries the village had sought and failed to come up with an acceptable alternative to the pub's proper name, one which to every resident of the village had all the character and appeal of a pasty made in England.

Now, that long-cherished nickname had been found and the locals revelled in being able to drink in a pub run by a man whose name was as close as dammit to Cornwall's version of *mañana*.

* * *

The Dreckly's skittle alley was packed. Tode hadn't needed to put up notices announcing the meeting. The village grapevine had done that for him.

All he'd needed do was mention it in the village shop while Mrs Kneebone was within ear-wigging range and within hours Tode's phone was ringing off the hook with people asking if it was OK for them to bring their sister-in-law's cousin – you know vicar, the one with the hip from Marazion – who was staying for a few days while the rat catcher was in her house.

Fully half the turn-out was of the cousin of the sister-in-law variety whose only interest in being there was 'juz ter zee what's what like'. That didn't stop them contributing, of course, and a meeting that should have been done and dusted in an hour was still in session when Dreckly called time.

Nevertheless, the information Tode wanted disseminated had been and now it was up to those it affected to do with it as they thought fit.

For Daffy and the area's other flower growers it meant a frantic few days sprucing up their polytunnel products to look their best for Wong's arrival and sales of hairspray at the village shop going ballistic.

By the time the growers had finished with them, their blooms could have withstood a tempest without losing either a petal or a shade of the violent primary colours that no rose or tulip had ever been accorded by the great creator.

While the subsequent sensory-overload displays would have had any European flower buyer vomiting into the bedding plants, Strewth's blossom boys remained firm in their belief that what they had to show Wong was just what the Chinaman would be looking for.

Where he came from, their research had revealed, pastel shade blooms that drooped within hours of being unwrapped were about as acceptable to the average Oriental taste as a Penzance Chinese takeaway. No self-respecting Shanghai girl would give her suitor the time of day unless she was presented with a bouquet that challenged any LSD experience, defied gravity, could hold up a motorway and had all the seductive scent of an oil refinery.

When Wong eventually arrived to inspect the St Ruth floral product, he admitted privately to Tode to being both impressed and surprised by what was on offer so far from the 'real' world as he put it.

All he'd expected to find were polytunnels crammed full of the regulation ranks of roses, carnations, tulips and gladioli he'd seen in the growing sheds of upcountry England. Never had he expected to discover that tropical plants also thrived here, almost swooning over the quality of the bird of paradise blooms that were Daffy Dimmock's speciality. They were every inch the equal of the plants his former supplier in Kenya had produced before the changing climate and that producer's over-enthusiastic use of pesticides got the better of his operation and put him out of business.

While Wong was swooning, Daffy was crooning. What had done for Wong's Kenya supplier had made people like himself. Originally specialising in early daffodils, Daffy had been one of the first to spot a way of capitalising on Cornwall's rapidly warming climate. While everyone around him pooh-poohed the idea, he'd diversified into sub-tropicals and while his fellow growers struggled to bring their traditional flower crops on, Daffy's plants had thrived. Soon he was buying his competitors out and employing them back to tend polytunnels humming with exotics.

But then, as Daffy suspected Wong already knew, had come 2008, the year the banks crashed, recession and slump followed and flowers were the last things on the minds of cash-strapped former flower-fanciers.

A decade of slump later, with demand still in the doldrums, Daffy and the others were on the verge of admitting defeat, of giving up and going back to growing things you could actually eat. At least that way they wouldn't starve.

And now, out of nowhere, providence had brought them Wong, a man with a chequebook 'as big as missus Kneebone's mouth', as Daffy had so quaintly put it, and an offer that had left him and his fellow flowermen struck dumb.

So generous an offer in fact that all affected were of one mind on the matter. Wong was one of the few outsiders who deserved to be honoured with an introduction to the Dreckly Inn's most treasured of treasured possessions.

* * *

'Yer, me 'ansome, try a spot o' the local nectar,' said Daffy thrusting a schooner of the pub's best-ever mead into the Hong Konger's hand. 'Tiz yer proper job is that. None o' yer evil chemical brews like upcountry.'

'Nuthin' but the finest nachral ingregents in there,' added Charley Pascoe, 'an' all brewed local like. 'Tiz the pride o' Strewth is that. Well, that an' Daffy's bird o' paradise plants o' course.'

Not a big drinker as a rule, Wong had tried to hide his alarm on being given a tumbler three times the size of the little glasses the Chinese used to conduct toasts and he wasn't at all sure he could down it in one as you did in China. But since he was on foreign soil and knew the best way to ruin relations with potential – and much needed – product suppliers in their own backyards was to disrespect their customs, he cheerfully clinked glasses with Daffy and Charley, put his own to his lips and sank it.

Wong's two barfly companions stared at him, then at each other. Generally you sipped at mead. Especially one that had won the region's coveted Golden Nectar award. Here was a beverage that asked to be treated with almost reverential respect not woofed down like a shot of tequila. This Oriental clearly had little of that for their lovingly-brewed local product and under normal circumstances the two Cornishmen would, in no uncertain terms, have put him right on how to treat the St Ruth speciality.

But this situation, they both knew, called for a different approach. At all costs, Wong needed to be kept sweet if he was to come good on his offer and that meant not only grinning and bearing the insult but following the Hong Konger's lead. So Daffy and Pascoe shrugged at one another, lifted their glasses and drained them.

'Another?' croaked Daffy to Wong who, as polite custom demanded in his part of the world, was already holding out his glass for the first of two refills.

Duly replenished, Wong repeated the exercise, Daffy looked at Pascoe, shrugged again, followed suit and when his eyes cleared found Wong already indicating he was ready for a third.

'Bugger me', thought Daffy, 'this bloke's a reg'lar bleddy sponge.'

'Ugh,' thought Wong, doing his best not to grimace in pain, 'this stuff's an acquired taste. But to keep these two happy I'll just have to swallow their foul medicine. Don't want to go upsetting them.'

As the three were in the process of going through the nightmare exercise for the third time, another thought, mutual this time, crossed their collective mind: 'Thank God. Here comes the cavalry.' Tode had slipped into the bar to ask the two Cornishmen if they were coming to the meeting.

Daffy and Charley nodded enthusiastically saying they'd be there in a mo and Tode had strode off in the direction of the skittle alley.

'Sorry Mr Wong,' said Daffy. 'Gotter go in a minute. Important cricket club meeting tonight.'

'Clicket?' slurred Wong, horrified at hearing the pantomime Chinaman he thought had been exorcised at prep school making a reappearance.

'Yer,' said Pascoe. 'Gotter decide what sort o' cricket us is playin' next season. Prob'ly all foreign to 'e like but there's some who's fer changin' to that new form o' the game they's playin' in England now.'

'New form?' said Wong wishing his companions would stop swaying while they were talking to him and absentmindedly sipping from the replenished glass Maisie the barmaid had placed in front of him assuming the three empty glasses had been put there for a purpose.

'Called Double Tops,' chipped in Daffy lifting his own glass. 'Brought in a couple o' years back by some foreign company that's sponsoring it. Called Catching or zummat. Dunno much about 'em but they's gorrit in they's heads that two innings each o' twenty overs is bedder than the straight forty-over game us plays. Can't zee the attraction meself. Juzt gives the opposition two chances ter get yer out fer bugger all.'

'S'right,' chimed in Charley Pascoe raising his glass in agreement. 'Shouldn't think Mr Wong 'ere knows what us is blathrin' 'bout but you's right on, Daf. Don't do ter go messin' wi' zummat that don' need fixin'.'

'Oh, but I DO know what you're talking about,' interjected Wong proudly. 'I've been a clicket... CRICKET... follower for years and I'm well aware of the competition you're referring to. Introduced by some people I know as it happens,' he said before he could stop himself.

'Gerron wi' 'e boy,' said Daffy in amazement. 'You's a cricketer?'

'Abzlutlluly. Love the game. Bezt thing that ever happened to leather and wirrow.'

'Well bugger me,' said Daffy. 'If that don' call fer another round, I don' know what does.'

chapter twelve

'Ar'ernoon vicar. Nice day fer it.'

Tode glanced up from the depths of The Beast's interior with a look over his bifocals Daffy knew signalled a stinging metaphorical smack on the wrist. Missing a cricket club meeting, as Daffy was not unaware, was regarded by his club president as akin to missing both church and a catch on the same day. Which was why the St Ruth CC vice-captain had struggled out of bed to transport his hangover to the cricket ground where he knew Tode would be taking his annoyance out on The Beast.

'Sorry 'bout last night, reverend. Sort o' lost track o' time and 'fore us knew it, meetin' was done an' dusted. Charley akst me to pass on his apologies also.'

'Noted,' said Tode without smiling. 'I hope you're not feeling TOO conflicted over having to choose between a cricket meeting and entertaining our visitor. No hiccups with the supply contract I trust. Looked like it was a delicate issue you were discussing and he wasn't very communicative when I saw him off this morning.'

'Ah, no vicar,' said Daffy, opting to pretend that his club president's little jibe had flown over his head. 'Pretty much a done deal there. He were proper took with us flowers. Said they was 'ansome. Can't wait to get 'em off to China.'

'Glad to hear it. So if it wasn't flower-talk that kept you from the meeting, what was it?'

'Well, mattererfact, it were cricket.'

The message contained in Tode's single raised eyebrow in response to this apparently ludicrous claim really did go over Daffy's head. Knowing full well of Wong's predilection for the game, all the eyebrow was intended to convey was Tode's mild amusement at the thought of a cricket discussion being conducted in the bar of a Cornwall country pub between a man of Chinese extraction and a pair of dyed-in-the-wool Cornish nationalists intent on depleting the pub's stock of illicit liquor.

Had Daffy been in possession of all the facts re. Tode, Wong and cricket, Daffy might have received Tode's message in the way it was intended. But since he wasn't, it wasn't, leaving Daffy convinced he was being told he'd need to improve on that somewhat if he wanted to avoid filling the team's twelfth man slot for the entirety of the coming season. So…

'Swear to God, vicar,' Daffy protested, 'and Charley Pascoe will bear I out. Yer man Wong's a reg'lar cricket nut. Bin following the game fer years, he says. Knows all the rules 'n everythin'. Even tested uz on the number of ways a bloke can get out. Charley and me got nine out o' the ten 'tween uz. Forgot 'bout bein' timed out. Al'ers ferget that un.

'One thing us dirn't know though was that youm can't be run-out by a ball deflected onto the stumps off a helmet worn by a fielder. So's by rights youm shouldn'a given I run out in that match agin St Aggies when I flattened young Percy Penhalligon wi' a pull shot and the ball rebounded off his helmet onto my wicket. Law 38, section 2, sub-section c that is. Mine of information is yer Mr Wong.'

Tode raised his other eyebrow to make a pair. Daffy, somewhat to Tode's surprise, was indisputably telling the truth. There was only one man in Strewth who'd know that, the man who'd fled from the scene that morning before Tode could corner him on the subject of Chinese cricket.

After an evening spent in the company of Daffy, Charley and the Dreckly Inn's inexhaustible reserves of local hooch, the green-gilled Wong was hardly able to communicate his Newquay airport destination to the taxi driver let alone divulge the inner secrets of Chinese cricket. On noting that Wong's mind was clearly unable to focus on anything other than trying not to retch into the untouched Dreckly Inn full Cornish breakfast staring accusingly up at him from his plate, Tode had thought better of raising the subject.

As the taxi ferried the decidedly uncommunicative Wong away an hour later, Tode cursed his two cricket club colleagues for upsetting his carefully worked-out breakfast table ambush plan. Now he'd have to resort to badgering Wong with phone calls to keep his bishop from badgering him.

Or he would have had Daffy not come to the rescue.

'…so looks like the world 'ad bedder watch out,' Tode heard Daffy saying on his return to planet Strewth. 'If they's can get 'old o' cricket, they's can get 'old o' anything.'

'Er… specifically?' asked Tode, resorting to the technique he'd developed to avoid giving his parishioners the impression that he was never anything less than permanently preoccupied with the piddling problems they delivered to his doorstep daily.

'Well vicar, if they Chinese gets a seat on the MCC board, who knows what sort o' game 'er'll turn into. It'll be all kung fu chop suey shots wi' bamboo bats an' dim sum dumpling deliveries out'er the back o' the 'and if they gets they's way, won' it?'

'Will it?'

'Cert'n. Theys'll be right there messin' wi' the laws and changin' things so's us won' recognise the game us grew up with. Cert'n.'

'But what makes you so sure they'll get a seat on the MCC board?' prompted Tode, unsure as to how or when the custodians of the laws of cricket had made an entrance into the conversation or what the Chinese had to do with it.

'Well, 'tiz plain from what yer Mr Wong was sayin' after he'd had a few. Remarkable stuff is yer Dreckly mead. T'ain't called "Old Thumbscrews" fer nothin'. Nothin' like 'er fer loosnin' a man's tongue. Couple o' drops o' that and you'd 'ave Satan his self tellin' 'e the best route out'er purgat'ry. So wi' 'arf a bottle down 'is neck, us couldn't stop Mr Wong squawkin'. Seems this yer Ke-Ching mob's got bigger things on they's mind than jus' the Double Tops competition.'

* * *

A couple of hours later, Tode was to be found at his desk grinning like a Cornish pixie who'd just sent an English tourist down the wrong path.

Using the internet to add body to the jaw-dropping revelations Daffy had prised from Wong, Tode had been able to piece together a report on Chinese cricket that should keep Bishop Roger off his back for weeks:

27 January 2018

Dear Roger,

I trust this letter finds you well and that you'll forgive the tardiness of my response to your pre-Christmas enquiry concerning cricket in China. As I'm sure you'll fully appreciate, festivities to celebrate of the birth of our Lord took precedence over research into the matter.

Let me begin by saying that, as you'll see from the following, my research reveals there to be considerably more to China's involvement in cricket than at first meets the eye, so I crave your indulgence while I outline the results of my findings in depth.

As I'm sure you're already aware, cricket was played in Shanghai as long ago as 1858, the expatriate British community entertaining visiting teams there right up to 1948, the year before Mao Zedong declared China a People's Republic. At that point a waterlogged pitch, so-to-speak, forced play to be suspended, resuming only when Deng Xiaoping became party chairman on Mao's death in 1976. Deng's Opening-Up policies began attracting the expatriate community back to China in the early 1980s and cricket re-emerged in Beijing and Shanghai in particular.

Over the following years, native-born Chinese gradually became attracted to the game and, by 2004, there were enough of them involved for the International Cricket Council to grant China affiliate ICC membership status.

Two years later the country appointed its first national cricket coach – one Rashid Khan who played four tests for Pakistan in the early 1980s – and then, in 2009, a cricket ambassador in the form of the rather better-known Pakistani, Javed Miandad whose international career, as I'm sure you're also well aware, spanned a full twenty years from the mid-1970s.

To welcome Miandad to his job, the Chinese national team recorded its first ever international win, beating Myanmar in the 2009 Asia Cricket Council Trophy Challenge, a win which prompted some observers to attach a 'one-to-watch' label to the team.

The late Peter Roebuck, who you'll recall was a former English county player and prominent cricket journalist, even went so far as to put into print his expectation that China would be hosting the Cricket World Cup in 2023. After all, he said, cricket was being included in the 2010 Asia Games which China was hosting and, in his eyes, there seemed no reason why the country shouldn't capitalise on that experience and bid for the World Cup.

Roebuck went quiet on the subject after China failed to win a single match at the Asia Games but not coach Khan who confidently predicted that China would not only be at the 2019 Cricket World Cup in England but that it would be granted test match status by 2020.

To those rendered speechless by Khan's predictions, China's under-19 team had a response. Its one hundred percent home-grown side stunned observers by coming fourth out of eight in the 2011 Asia Cricket Council Challenge Cup, only losing to the likes of Kuwait and Saudi Arabia whose sides were one hundred percent NOT home-grown. In common with other Gulf States, these two wouldn't have had cricket teams back then had it not been for the hiring-in of cricket-in-the-blood nationals from various parts of the Indian sub-continent, Pakistan in particular.

The Chinese under-19s' narrow defeats against such sides attracted favourable comments from certain quarters, the general view being that if the country's 2011 youth team could get this far pitched against players imported from countries with strong cricket pedigrees, think what they might be able to achieve in the run-up to the 2019 World Cup. By that time the under-19s would have developed into fully fledged adult cricketers with years of international competition under their belts.

Events since then make such comments look somewhat prophetic. A string of good wins have moved China to within striking distance of a 2019 World Cup qualifying place, a not-inconceivable possibility in view of the current generous level of financial support provided by the Chinese state to the national team.

Certain interested parties of my acquaintance who maintain a close connection with Chinese cricket – acquaintances who must remain nameless so as not to jeopardise their ongoing activities in the country – believe the state has effectively signed a blank cheque made out to Chinese cricket for a reason the cricket world might find a trifle challenging.

The Chinese government, my acquaintances say, has unearthed yet-to-be-published incontrovertible evidence that cricket was being played in China centuries before the game emerged in England.

Reports from China suggest that Chinese archaeologists working at the two thousand year-old terracotta warrior site in Xi'an have not only found a group of figures arranged in the manner of a cricket field setting but with two of the figures holding implements the archaeologists have convinced themselves are archaic forms of the modern day cricket bat.

The find is said to have inspired Chinese researchers to conduct an in-depth study of the game, studies which, say my acquaintances, have led to high-level Chinese academics concluding that a sport of such complexity could not, in fact, have originated anywhere but China. No other socio-political order, they contend, has ever possessed the degree of sophistication necessary to produce a game of such staggering intricacy that it requires not one, but a whole panel of judges, to interpret the laws governing it.

To support their case, the academics are said to be of the opinion that the core values intrinsic to cricket emerged out of the political order of the time. The then-dynasty, they say, laid heavy emphasis on Chinese society being ordered by fair play, gentlemanly conduct and sportsmanship, core values the academics believe were embodied in a game specifically designed to help weave these values into China's social fabric.

As staggering as it will be if cricket – or something very much like it – is confirmed as having been the product of an ancient Chinese dynasty, one might well be prompted to then ask why today's communist regime would want to lay claim to it. Surely the whole ethos of the modern day Chinese political thought is based on correcting – indeed eradicating – past imperialist mistakes.

It is, say my acquaintances, because China's present-day leadership regards itself as heir to the very values the then-emperor tried to impose on Chinese society. And it is for that reason, they say, that a top level decision was apparently taken in 2013 to channel Chinese funds not only into domestic cricket but into cricket in any part of the world where the game's future was being undermined by severe financial shortfall.

As a game whose values and origins are traceable to ancient China, the regime is said to have concluded that, for reasons of 'face', cricket must not be allowed to wither on the global sporting vine.

During the course of government investigations conducted to identify likely recipients for China's support, my acquaintances report that Beijing was surprised to learn that the game in England was facing as many financial problems as anywhere and, in 2014, a decision was taken to inject Chinese money into English cricket.

But therein lay a problem. Pride and suspicion, Beijing knew, would prevent the English cricket establishment accepting undisguised Chinese charity. So a way had to be found to prop the game up without the funds being easily identifiable as money originating from Chinese state coffers.

At which point enter Ke-Ching, ostensibly China's answer to eBay but in effect a company as beholden to the government as any of the country's wholly state-run enterprises. Ke-Ching received a 'request' from Beijing to initiate and fund (with Chinese government money) a heavily-subsidised cricket tournament in England and thus the concept of the Ke-Ching Double Tops competition was born.

Ke-Ching, as is now well-known, was welcomed as a sponsor for English cricket by the England Cricket Board and has now run two full seasons of its heavily-subsidised Double Tops competition to some applause from cash-strapped followers of English cricket.

On a personal note, I would like to say at this point that despite its name – which, to my ear, could only have been dreamt up by someone who clearly has little or no understanding of the game – I've thoroughly enjoyed this competition, as have my parishioners, some of whom have even travelled as far as Truro for matches featuring the Cornwall county side.

But as enjoyable as it is, until this most recent information came to light there had always been one aspect of the competition which bothered me. Why would Ke-Ching choose cricket of all sports to sponsor? Surely there are better ways for an internet trading company to promote itself.

On being informed that Ke-Ching was just doing the Chinese government's bidding, that question has now been answered – only to be replaced by another. Are we really expected to believe that China's motives for injecting funds into English cricket are purely altruistic? It has no history of altruism. Everything it does is based on self-interest, period. To the sceptic, China's cricket-supporting activities plant the notion that an ulterior motive may be lurking in some dark recess.

This is confirmed to some extent by further information received. My acquaintances suggest that Ke-Ching, on behalf of the Chinese government, will shortly be asking the English counties to accept China's national players onto their books in order to give them experience of top flight competition – experience they'll find invaluable in the run-up to the final stages of China's 2019 World Cup qualification campaign. It's a request to which the company confidently expects a positive response given the level of financial support recently injected by Ke-Ching into the English game.

What's more, it's also reported to me that, in the event of the English counties failing to give their unanimous consent to the Ke-Ching 'request', the company is in the process of instigating a contingency plan for ensuring across-the-board compliance. My acquaintances suggest that in the near future we should not be surprised to learn that a Ke-Ching representative has been co-opted onto the MCC board and that that body has thrown its weight behind the Ke-Ching request.

Only one question remains to be answered – how Ke-Ching plans to gain that MCC seat. Although this remains open to speculation, my acquaintances are of the opinion that its support for English cricket at all levels will be 'unlikely to act against the company's best interests'.

Quite so. To all intents and purposes, it would seem from the information received that Ke-Ching and its political masters hold all the aces at this present time, not only regarding the inclusion of Chinese players in English county sides but also, possibly, regarding all future decisions made by the MCC board.

If you will allow me to offer my own opinion at this point, it would seem to me that English cricket is about to enter 'interesting times' as the Chinese might themselves put it. On the one hand it is faced with having to kowtow to Beijing, on the other to face continued decline of the game unless an alternative sponsor can be found – an unlikely prospect in view of the state of the British economy at this present time.

It is not a choice I would relish having to make and can but offer my prayers that those having to make it make the right one.

In conclusion, I would like it noted that although none of the above has been confirmed by any official source, the contents emanate from trustworthy interested parties and can be regarded as being at the very least extremely close to the actual situation pertaining. Should I become aware of anything that either adds to or detracts from the information provided here I'll let you know.

In the meantime, I'll sign off with the hope that my humble research efforts add to your sum of knowledge on the matter in hand and that the information provided proves of some use to you.

My very best wishes to you and yours for the New Year.

God Bless.

Toby

* * *

As he ploughed through Tode's report, Bishop Roger's bushy eyebrows rose and fell like two hairy caterpillars on a trampoline. To the bishop, the notion of China vying to take the game over was as preposterous as Beijing's claim that cricket originated some five thousand miles away from Broadhalfpenny Down, that somnambulant corner of southern England universally accepted by the world cricket fraternity as the undisputed mid-eighteenth century birthplace of the game.

On the other hand, though, if the Chinese really did believe they were cricket's true custodians and really had singled it out for special financial attention, Bishop Roger reckoned the rest of the world had better sit up and take notice. It was money that had won China its current dominance on the global economic stage and if cricket followed suit, one could quite easily see China emerging very rapidly as one of the game's major powers.

While Tode's information certainly did add to his sum of knowledge on the matter, he was left hoping the MCC and his noble 'friend' Lord Bleauforth wouldn't find it quite so enlightening. Their own research must surely have uncovered at least the same information if not a great deal more.

But just in case it hadn't, the bishop felt it his civic duty to alert Bleauforth to everything he now knew bar the name of his source. That, the bishop decided, was best omitted. Were it to become known that the information had been provided by someone of Japanese ancestry, questions might be asked in the Lord's Long Room regarding the credibility and impartiality of both the source and his findings.

* * *

At the very moment Bishop Roger's email was entering Lord Bleauforth's inbox, Harry Wong was entering his Woking mansion with but one thing on his fragile mind – a sumptuous soak in his sunken jacuzzi. It was the only thing he could think of to clear the fog that still shrouded his mental recesses, cleanse his system of the previous night's 'entertainment' and help him recall what it was, precisely, he'd said.

The last thing he could remember with any degree of clarity was embarking on an explanation of Law 38, section 2, sub-section c for the benefit of his drinking companions who, he was amazed to learn, were of the impression that you *could* be run out from a rebound off a fielder's helmet.

It was astonishing, Wong remembered thinking, how the average western cricketer took an almost perverse pride in displaying an ignorance of the laws governing the game he played. In China, the exact opposite was the case and Wong found himself musing that such ignorance and complacency was not only symptomatic of the decline of the game in the West but in part responsible for China's impending rise to the top of the world cricket tree.

While western child cricketers indulged themselves in reading – or, more likely these days, viewing in video format – comic book accounts of their cricketing heroes' exploits, ambitious Chinese child cricketers were learning the laws off by heart.

Unless they could pass a rigorous cricket exam, they'd never be allowed to participate in any form of organised cricket. And since in China there was no form of the game – or any other sport come to that – that wasn't organised, not passing meant only one thing. They'd never get the chance to play at all – a weeding-out process China's cricket overlords considered essential if the country was ever to be taken seriously on the world cricket stage.

Organisation? That word rang a bell. Now he thought about it, Wong vaguely recalled quipping about the world's cricket authorities needing the organisational skills of Emperor Qin to keep on top of all the various competitions being run worldwide.

With the quip drawing nothing but blank looks from his audience, Wong had been forced to elaborate, educating them about the man responsible for creating the China we see today and for the construction of the famous terracotta warrior army at Xi'an some two thousand years ago – an army, Wong had said whimsically, that Qin seemed to think could protect him using weapons looking not unlike antiquated forms of cricket bat.

But that was it. Where the conversation had gone after that remained swallowed up in the mists that still swirled round his befuddled brain and until they cleared, all he could hope was that he hadn't touched on the real reason behind Ke-Ching's arrival on the English cricket scene.

If he had ventured down that path and if, by some freak occurrence, word got back to Ke-Ching that he wasn't as ignorant as the company thought as to why they'd brought him in to act as the company's front man, the news would hardly serve to help him achieve his goal of turning an invidious situation to his considerable advantage.

But surely, he consoled himself, there was need to worry on that score. Apart from knowing that no amount of drink could loosen his lips on that particular issue, his companions on this occasion were hardly the most attentive or well-connected of folk he'd ever come across.

Stuck on the end of an under-populated peninsular jutting out into the North Atlantic, the only thing they'd be interested in would be ensuring they got his flower supply contract… wouldn't it?

chapter thirteen

Lord Vernon Drummond Quincy St John Bleauforth, seventeenth earl of the fiefdom of Crichester, extracted his forehead from the lamppost he was certain hadn't been there the day before and swore a vile oath. As if he didn't already have enough on his mind, he now had a sizeable dent in it courtesy of the Labour-controlled council which, he suspected, deliberately placed such obstacles in the paths of opponents of their idiot lefty policies.

Dabbing his bloodied brow with a handkerchief as he ploughed through the massed ranks of squawking Oriental tourists and shivering home-grown beggars accosting them on the Strand, Bleauforth finally reached the sanctuary of Simpson's and testily hurled his coat in the direction of the fawning toady bowing and scraping inside the door.

Sir Victor Turnball was already there, sipping a dry Martini and nibbling at a plate of potted shrimps and warm toast.

'Medicinal libation?' Turnball offered with smirk.

'Double,' growled Bleauforth. 'One for the gut and one for the nut. And send the bill to the bloody council!'

No sooner had Bleauforth received Bishop Roger's email than he was on the phone to Turnball, the one man on the committee Bleauforth knew to have as many reservations about the Ke-Ching proposal as himself.

'Lunch. Tomorrow. Simpson's,' Bleauforth had commanded imperiously, ringing off without offering any explanation.

None was needed. Having worked together for so long they'd almost reached the stage of finishing one another's sandwiches, Turnball knew from his noble friend's tone that this was going to be a full pudding lunch, the sort that required him to cancel all afternoon engagements, wear his larger waistband trousers and be prepared for a council of war.

It wasn't long before the enemy was identified.

'The bloody Chinese, of course,' was Bleauforth's pickled onion eyeball response to Turnball's enquiry as to who the hell Bleauforth was frothing about.

'They're at the gates. The Grace Gates, no less. And we are the gatekeepers. The last line of defence old bean. Get past us and the MCC is doomed. So stiffen the syntax, summon up the slings and arrows and prepare to fight 'em on the outfield!'

'Not sure the ground staff will appreciate that.'

'Won't BE any ground staff if no one does anything to stop the buggers. Well, not ENGLISH ones anyway. Wong and his mates will probably import boatloads of Shanghai coolies to do the job.'

Ah, thought Turnball, the noble lord has had some news.

By the end of the fish course all had been revealed and by the time the sorbet arrived Turnball knew as much as Bleauforth, Bishop Roger, the Reverend Toby Tode and Daffy Dimmock. Well, almost as much. Bishop Roger's involvement in the story was only known to Bleauforth, Tode's was only known to Bishop Roger and Dimmock's was only known to Tode leaving Turnball believing Bleauforth's information emanated from a place rather closer to the horse's mouth than its opposite end.

'So what's the plan, then?' asked Turnball, assuming he hadn't received a luncheon invitation just to be the audience for a Bleauforth rant.

'The plan, Turnball, is to stop the bloody chinks in their tracks and let them know in no uncertain terms that cricket is, and always has been, an ENGLISH game invented in ENGLAND by the ENGLISH and kindly lent to the rest of the world so that they might participate in something good and honourable and wholesome and the very embodiment of the meaning of the term "fair play" – something our commie friends in Peking would appear not to be acquainted with if this is a measure of the way they play the game.'

'So you don't have a plan then.'

Bleauforth just scowled into his platter of blood-oozing rare roast beef. Being stumped was an unfamiliar experience for a man who treated spin bowlers with the sort of contempt usually reserved for bed-wetting, tree-hugging, hand-wringing, social worker whiners intent on getting meat dishes banned from restaurant menus on the grounds that the fumes might contaminate vegetarian offerings.

Chinese spin, Bleauforth was discovering, was different. Countering it required the sort of finesse the English public school system thought not worth bothering its more robust pupils with. Which was why, in the end, Bleauforth had been forced to bite the bullet, admit defeat and promote his quicker-witted broadcast partner up the batting order.

If there was anyone who might have the answer to the Chinese attack it'd be Turnball, a man whose withering intellect had proved such an ideal foil to the Bleauforth battering ram bombast that the pair had been awarded long-term BBC commentary contracts and dubbed the Wallace and Gromit of the sporting airwaves.

* * *

As the Bleauforth imminent-Chinese-invasion rant continued through the rest of the main course and into pudding, Turnball's mind was working. By the time the cheese board arrived he, unlike

Bleauforth, HAD formulated a plan. At its core was the urgent need to hobble his noble friend *tout suite*.

To Turnball, Bleauforth's information sounded short-pitched and in need of a thorough factual accuracy stress test lest something had gone awry in the translation. Until they had chapter and verse in triplicate, it was crucial that Bleauforth was stopped from confronting Wong and Hu Nei over the channelling of Chinese state money into English cricket and the MCC via Ke-Ching. The very future of Lord's could depend on it.

The question was: how? The Bleauforth blue blood was up and Turnball knew that no amount of thinning agent would be enough to temper it. How many times had he pleaded with the man not to call him through for risky singles while the pair were batting together only to find Bleauforth charging towards him yelling for a run, the ball already in the fielder's hands? Too many.

So no, on this occasion, Turnball knew he'd have to stand his ground and let Bleauforth run himself out. Turnball had a bring-Bleauforth-to-heel blackmail card up his sleeve and now seemed a good time to play it. It was time to remind his noble friend of the debt he owed him regarding Bleauforth's impetuous flirtation with narcotics back in the eighties.

With connections in places higher even than Bleauforth could reach, Turnball had used all his influence to prevent the episode reaching the courts. So far as the world was aware, the case had been dropped for lack of evidence. Turnball knew better and it was to that knowledge he now turned to reel the noble lord in.

By the time the liqueurs arrived, the wind in Bleauforth's apoplectic sails had begun to flag and Turnball took advantage of a lull in the windbag to jump in.

'Well, old boy,' he said, 'that's quite a clamorous alarm you're sounding. If what you say holds water – and I'm not for one moment doubting its authenticity – doing nothing could well see our Chinese friends sneaking in through the back door and making off with the great game.

'Thing is, though, from what I'm hearing from certain other interested parties,' Turnball lied, 'confronting our new prospective sponsor with such an accusation at this moment in time might not be altogether to the benefit of certain other, more formal, inquiries currently being conducted into said sponsor's activities away from the cricket field.

'That being the case, might I suggest that the taking of a measured approach to the issue in hand might be the best course of action to adopt until advised otherwise? Just to make sure no sensitive toes or apple carts are in the way, so-to-speak.'

Bleauforth blinked. Although never publicly disclosed or discussed, suspicions over Turnball's connections with Britain's intelligence agencies abounded and Bleauforth was not at all sure he hadn't just become the recipient of an official hands-off warning from one of them. In fact, the only thing he could be sure about was that he'd never get Turnball to elaborate unless he couched his call for enlightenment in a language common to both men. Going the direct route would only lead to a miasma of coded insider-speak winks and nudges you had to be a top level Foreign Office operative to understand.

'So,' said Bleauforth after a moment's reflection to choose from the limited choice of comprehensible communication methods available to both men, 'from what you're saying, am I to surmise then that while this situation persists, the head coach, as it were, advises the setting of a defensive field until the batsmen's strengths and weaknesses have been fully assessed?'

'Let's just say that it's not unlikely that the captain has already set the field and wouldn't take kindly to having it messed with at this stage in the game… not kindly at all if you get my pharmaceutical drift.'

Bleauforth's flapping jaw indicated that he had… and that Turnball had his man. Although the narcotics episode had been placed in the legal deepfreeze, both men knew it could be retrieved and re-heated any time his 'protectors' felt like it. Unless all things Chinese conveniently slipped the Bleauforth mind until told he could remember them, Turnball was unequivocally telling him that the threat of the warming oven hovered.

'Jolly good,' smirked Turnball at the look on Bleauforth's face as the penny dropped. 'And the same goes for that excellent lunch,' he said, leaning back in his chair and dabbing his lips with his serviette to indicate he had as much intention of picking up the bill as he had of picking up a freshly-deposited dog's turd. 'Much appreciated, old boy.'

chapter fourteen

'Rory? Victor here. Wondered if you had a moment. Need to discuss something I think might tickle your fancy.'

'Got an editorial conference at eleven but could spare a few moments after that. Noon OK?'

Turnball arrived at a quarter-to. Being left alone in his former sports editor's office before Rory McDermott's return would give him a chance to scan McDermott's desk for anything that looked like evidence of cordial relations existing between Ke-Ching and the *Daily Grind*. If the Chinese had already got to McDermott and the paper he represented, he'd take the story elsewhere.

Unfortunately for Turnball McDermott was already in residence and the MCC man was left with no alternative but to spiral his way towards the nub of the issue.

'Sorry for the early intrusion, old man. Thought it'd take longer to get here. Trains packed with New Year tourists and all that. The sales seem to be a magnet for visitors from the Orient these days.'

'Hmmm.'

'Used to be the Yanks and Germans but not now. S'pose it's something to do with the Chinese being the only ones who can afford to travel. Did you know that Mandarin is now the most popular language in language schools? Incomprehensible if you ask me. And the names! It's as if every Chinese was called either John Jackson or Jack Johnson. God knows how they produce telephone directories.'

'They don't.'

'Say again?'

'There aren't any.'

'Really? Well, can't say I'm that surprised. Must make finding one another a challenge, though.'

'They seem to manage.'

'You sound very certain. You a bit of a China buff, then?'

'Got to be a bit slanty-eyed these days, old son. Helps spot insurgents.'

'Insurgents?'

'People thinking that the likes of this paper can be employed as a vehicle for the planting of subliminal messages.'

It wasn't often that anything McDermott had to say left Turnball lost for words but on this occasion the paper's former cricket correspondent found his jaw flapping.

Was that aimed at him?

Did McDermott think it was him who was in the pay of the Chinese while all the time he'd been eyeing the paper as a possible China lickspittle?

It was all so deliciously ironic that Turnball was unable to stifle his amusement, starting with a small snort of derision, building to a full-on, thigh-slapping guffaw.

'You think... I'm here... at the behest of... the Chinese?' he managed between spasms of barely controllable mirth.

'Aren't you?' asked an unperturbed McDermott. 'There's a not insubstantial rumour doing the rounds that the relationship between the board of which you are now a member and a certain Chinese company is getting too cosy by half. Isn't that why you're here? To work the old pals act to get them a bit of free publicity?

'Frankly, old son, if that's your game then I'd counsel a swift about-turn in the direction of the street if you want to avoid an even swifter descent to it from the window. Call us old-fashioned but there's those on this desk who view Ke-Ching's arrival on the cricket scene as the thin end of a bloody big wedge... one with test match cricket at the other end of it.'

'But...'

'No buts. Just state your business and bugger off. I've a meeting to get to... one at which we'll be discussing tactics for scuppering an attempt by another Chinese carpetbagger to take control of this very organ.'

'In which case, I might just have something to help the cause.'

'Eh?'

'A little snippet of news of some relevance to your case. But if you really think I'm a chopstick Charlie, I'll bid you farewell and be on my way.'

'OK. OK. You have my attention. Spill. But it'd better be good.'

Twenty minutes later, Turnball still had his ex-editor's attention.

Having finally discovered they were batting for the same side, sufficient trust had been established for the two men to form a wary Chinese cricket investigation alliance – one in which the *Grind*'s most recently-acquired foreign stringer was to find herself involved in a way she could never have imagined possible.

* * *

After an interminable shift on the *China Daily* in which the paper's writers had seemed determined to break all records for Chinese self-aggrandizement, Amber Middlethorpe found herself groping for the phone more to put an end to its drill-bit incursion into her pounding head than to participate in a sensible conversation. It was three in the morning and Amber was beginning to regret the mounting of a celebratory shift-survival attack on a handy bottle of *baijo*, a filthy Chinese brandy whose container, it was said, was the more valuable part of the package.

'*Wei*?'

'Pardon?'

'I said *wei*… yes… hello.'

'Oh, is that what it means?'

'*Wei.*'

'Well well. You learn something every day, don't you?'

Amber snarled. If this was her father playing a prank on her from his eight hour-different time zone, he was going to learn a few more Mandarin words, none of them with a polite translation.

'Is that Amber Middlethorpe? Got this number for her but not sure it's right.'

'Yeah. Whoozat?'

'Name's Rafferty. I'm on the sports desk at the *Grind.*'

'The what?'

'The *Daily Grind*. In London.'

Amber was suddenly wide awake.

'Oh… ah… *naihao*… I mean hello.'

'I thought "hello" was "*wei*".'

'It is. It's another form of… never mind… what's happ'nin'? I mean… what can I do for you?'

'Well, some writing would be good. Fancy crafting a little feature for us? Nothing especially onerous. Shouldn't take too long. Editor needs something from your neck of the woods. Subject cricket.'

Now she really WAS awake.

'Say again.'

'The editor needs something…'

'Yes. I got that bit. Did you say CRICKET? You sure you've got the right person? You do know where I'm based.'

'Yes. Beijing. Got your email right here offering your services as a local stringer. Sorry we didn't get back to you sooner but frankly, the editor thought he'd give you a bit of time to settle in before giving you a run-out, so-to-speak.'

Settle in? She'd had time to do that all right. That email had been one of several dozen she'd fired off to a range of editors offering her freelance services before boarding the flight to China over a year ago.

None had had the desired effect save for a response from *Crane Hire Monthly* asking her to provide regular updates on the number of cranes peppering the Beijing skyline.

At first she'd tried to get official figures but had finally given up on being informed that such information was a state secret.

This was the only other product of her freelance services promotional exercise and was about as bizarre as the cranes commission. Cricket? Had she heard him right?

She had. Rafferty of the *Grind* confirmed it. Twice. For reasons known only to the editor, Chinese cricket was on the paper's radar and the sports desk had been asked to find someone to look into it. What they were after was a back-grounder on how the game had developed in China and where it was headed.

'Look twenty years ahead,' Rafferty had told her. 'Where will China be on the world cricket stage then?'

Amber groaned inwardly. The thought of spending time with either 'c' word, let alone both, was about as appealing as a *China Daily* double shift but there was no way she was going to voice it out loud. Get this right and it could be her passport out of China and into a job on one of Britain's last remaining vaguely respectable nationals.

So, feigning an intense interest in both the subject matter and the assignment, she'd bitten Rafferty's hand off for the assignment, promised to file the requested fifteen hundred-word piece within the week and then, to prove this had been no *baijo*-fuelled dreamworld fantasy, had made herself a cup of strong coffee and sat down to ponder the raft of questions the phone call had thrown up.

Top of the list was how the fuck was she to tackle a topic about which she had no specialist knowledge, for which she had the utmost contempt and to which she seemed to be forever shackled? Her father's obsession had even followed her to China. How the fuck had that happened then?

* * *

Rafferty knew. Had it not been for a chance meeting with Simon Middlethorpe when their respective sides met on the cricket field the previous season, Amber's name would have remained as unknown to the *Grind*'s chief sports subeditor as her father's batting average and Rafferty would have been left struggling to fulfil his editor's command to find someone to look into Chinese cricket.

Under normal circumstances, approaches from proud fathers trying to get their media children a job on the paper he worked for were instantly consigned to the Rafferty memory shredder. On this occasion, though, the name Middlethorpe had stuck.

Only when McDermott issued his command did Rafferty realise why. Some months earlier, he vaguely recalled receiving a freelance stringership begging letter from someone of that name in Beijing.

Rafferty's retrieval of that letter was the moment he knew he'd been awarded a rare place on his sports editor's promotion prospects list.

McDermott's lips had morphed from their customary cynical curl into an unnerving, unheard-of smile on being informed of Amber's existence and he'd even done Rafferty the honour of allowing him to stand his boss a drink that night.

Sure, he could have called on the paper's regular man in Beijing to take the story on but that, Rafferty knew, was McDermott's last resort. The man's habit of filing nothing but poke-China-in-the-eye hatchet jobs had made him a marked man in authoritarian Chinese eyes and putting him on the job was almost certain to make those eyes narrow even further.

So no, what this story needed was someone whose inquiries wouldn't arouse suspicion. A rooky female reporter who'd already sold her soul to the Chinese devil was perfect and Rafferty congratulated himself on having found her.

Replacing the telephone receiver after his call to Beijing, Rafferty swivelled in his chair and gave his boss the thumbs-up. The paper had its man or, in this case, woman. Now all they had to do was wait for her to produce… and maybe nudge her along with the odd prompt or two.

Both McDermott and Rafferty knew Amber would need to be kept pointed in the right direction on this one. It was important she didn't get sidetracked into spending too much time on the history of the game in China. That, via Turnball, they had already.

Her job, McDermott had briefed Rafferty, was to get confirmation that China really was poised to colonise the cricket world by effectively buying a controlling interest on the board of the MCC. If true, the paper would have unearthed a story that would not only rock the sporting world to its roots but help pull the rug from under China's hegemonising feet.

Taking the drink McDermott allowed Rafferty to buy him, the sports editor toasted his own devilish artifice. The *Grind*, he crowed with barely concealed self-satisfaction, now had a listening bug in China's changing room – a turn of phrase McDermott felt especially pleased with in view of the double-edged meaning that could be applied to it.

By having an ear at the keyhole of the room in which China was plotting world sporting change, the paper would be able to trumpet its own involvement in helping scotch Beijing's dastardly ambitions.

OK, in return for Turnball's tip-off he'd agreed to first onpass his findings to his tipster so the MCC could incorporate them in its deliberations over the Ke-Ching sponsorship offer, but after that he was free to do with the information as he liked.

That *was* the understanding he'd reached with Turnball… wasn't it?

chapter fifteen

Five thousand miles away from the *Daily Grind* office, Amber Middlethorpe was doing exactly what Rory McDermott thought she'd be doing. Worrying.

This was the big one. Her chance to impress. Her chance to engrave her name on the minds of the *Grind*'s editors – and possibly others – forever. On the other hand, if she fucked up…

No. The possibility couldn't even be entertained. Positivity was the way to tackle this assignment. That and using every tool in the box to produce something that glowed in the dark, something that sparkled with such scintillating insight it DEMANDED her editors sit up and take notice.

Only one problem with that. She and cricket were sworn enemies. Having to sit through her father's interminable blow-by-blow accounts of his batting exploits to get the use of his car was bad enough. But having to WRITE about it! She'd rather undergo a full body wax.

There was only one thing for it. She'd have to assume a new persona until this onerous assignment was behind her, someone who was actually interested in the stupid game. It wasn't as if she hadn't done it before to get what she wanted. Last time it was to get on the right side of the slimy Chinese her father had cajoled into helping get her a job. This job as it turned out.

Simon Middlethorpe hadn't warned his daughter that Wong would be at the 2016 end-of-season Ousedon Cricket Club bash. To have done so would have been to invite rather more questions than he felt like answering. Questions like: 'Why are you telling me this? Not using your contacts to get me a job are you?'

Middlethorpe would've had trouble denying it. Amber could spot one of her father's deceits from the dark side of the moon and would not, on this occasion, be the least bit impressed. The pulling of strings to 'get on', in Amber's highly-principled estimation, was for the dim-witted, the weak-willed and the talentless and Amber had let her father know in no uncertain terms that she considered herself some distance above such nepotistic nonsense.

Sheer hard graft had put her in the top five of her journalism degree course and Amber KNEW it was just a matter of time before someone in Britain's rapidly failing newspaper industry saw sense and came knocking on her door.

OK, almost two years after graduating that knock was still awaited but that wasn't the point. It was the principle of the thing. She'd rather stack supermarket shelves with all the other embittered jobless millions than succumb to the leg-up option and Simon had been left in no doubt about it.

So Simon Middlethorpe's entreaty to Wong to 'help get the bloody girl a job' had been kept strictly between the two men with Middlethorpe's newfound business backer wholly in agreement over the need for secrecy. As a Chinese, he not only knew all there was to know about the preservation of 'face' but how important contacts were to anyone with ambition. No one where he came from got anywhere without a healthy list of *guanxi*. So central was the contacts game to everything you did in China that to lose your *guanxi* was to lose everything. Business. Reputation. Honour. Face. Everything.

So when Simon had broached the subject, Wong had had no hesitation in offering his assistance. Any addition to his own *guanxi* was welcome. In his world, the offer of help meant being owed one in return and although Wong couldn't immediately think of anything anyone in the Middlethorpe household could possibly do for him, you never knew. Something might turn up.

But that could wait. For the moment, the important thing was to come up with a way of engineering a meeting between Wong and Amber without raising her suspicions.

'Some celebratory event, perhaps,' suggested Wong.

'I know the very thing,' said Middlethorpe, a mischievous glint playing in his eye.

* * *

So far as Amber knew, she was at the cricket club function solely to work the bar. It was the price her father had demanded for upgrading her antiquated laptop and was the only thing that could have persuaded her to cross the cricket club threshold.

To Amber, cricket was the rough equivalent of religion – an insidious establishment invention designed to distract the general populace from the raft of social injustices inherent in the system. If the minds of the masses were kept occupied with hocus pocus rituals like church or cricket or football or Strictly Come Dancing they couldn't be hatching plots to overthrow the established order.

So no, attending a cricket function wasn't top of Amber's list of things to do on a Saturday night. But with a laptop in urgent need of her father's attention, she'd had no option but to agree his terms.

As she did so, she felt her initial grimace morph into a small, thoughtful smile. There was, the thought had just occurred, the chance of this disagreeable little task having an upside. Being in charge of the bar meant being in charge of the punch. And being in charge of the punch meant being in charge of what went in it and of the amount she ladelled into the glasses of the collection of dignitaries her father had invited to the bash.

Simon Middlethorpe was considering running for the council but before finally committing he needed an idea of the degree of support he might expect from local 'names'. Hence the inclusion on the invite list of a selection of people who'd rather be trapped in a lift with Jeremy Clarkson than go within a hundred miles of a cricket function. If they came, he'd know pretty much where he stood and whether there was any point launching an election campaign.

In the event, it was a one hundred percent turnout but Simon Middlethorpe wasn't fooled. The majority, he was savvy enough to know, were only there to protect their own interests. Should hell actually freeze over and the local community elect a Free Radical Party activist as their county council representative, not one of those he'd invited wanted to risk being remembered for not having attended one of his functions. Their next planning application could depend on it.

So, pretty much as Middlethorpe had predicted, his guests had held their noses and forced themselves up the cricket pavilion steps to universally make great shows of ensuring he knew they'd arrived. That done, they then proceeded to stand around wearing fixed smiles and trying to stay out of range of the club's cricket minutiae bores intent on regaling them with batting averages to five decimal places, the mysteries of reverse swing, the finer points of the LBW law and how they'd suffered at the hands of umpires who didn't fully understand it.

As with most bashes at the cricket club, this one had begun in the spirit of stiff, frosty, polite English decorum. But by ten o'clock, as Amber knew it would, the evening's early chill had thawed and the function had begun resembling a scene from a Breugel painting.

The punch Amber had privately named her 'Below the Belt Special' was doing exactly what it said on the tin and exactly as

Amber intended. As the level of fluid in the bowl dropped, the tastier became the titbits of local gossip and the more saleable they became as tip-offs to the local rag.

With no firm job prospects in the offing, dishing the dirt on the out-of-hours activities of local movers and shakers at least kept Amber in with the paper's editor. If she kept the tips flowing there was always the chance of replacing one of his more indolent hacks. In the economically bombed-out Britain of 2016 no one was above being shown the door if there was someone better and, more importantly, cheaper hammering on it.

Under normal circumstances she wisely kept her father and his closest cronies immune from prosecution but there were times when it was difficult to resist. Like the time she'd overheard him discussing the installation of listening bugs in the opposition's changing room with the local MP, the owner of the security systems supply firm which sponsored the club. That one had been noted down and filed for later use should her father ever stop turning a blind eye to her occasional 'business' trips to Amsterdam to supplement her meagre freelance earnings. She could see it coming once his election campaign got going in earnest.

As with the changing room bug story, she'd decided that anything gleaned from the cricket club function should also be kept in reserve as a hedge against her father's intransigence – with one exception. Her father would be only too pleased to see the lady mayoress exposed for what she really was and to Amber's considerable satisfaction, her primary target did not disappoint.

The woman who'd set herself up as the district's role model for moral propriety and upright citizenship seemed intent on gifting her the kind of embarrassing spectacle any local hack would kill for. As the effects of the punch took hold, cracks started appearing in the honourable lady's perfect finishing school persona until the chrysalis of self-righteous probity crumbled away completely and the inner devil woman was revealed.

One moment she was having an intense conversation with her finance director over how the imminent cuts in housing benefit would affect property prices, the next she was on the dance floor cavorting like a monkey to 'Jumping Jack Flash' and making the club statistician drool into his drink.

As she gyrated with wild, ape-like abandon, it wasn't just the odd lock from her expensively coiffed head that was being spilled. It was the equally expensive contents of her uplift superbra, clearly designed more for decorous dinner dates than for animal acrobatics.

An hour later, with the whole place jumping to 'Hi Ho Silver Lining', the punch bowl all but empty and the lady mayoress's boob job a very open secret, Amber declared her mission well and truly accomplished and awarded herself a celebratory tipple from her father's stock of good claret kept out of sight below the bar.

Emerging from its depths, Amber found herself confronted by a new face, one who must have just arrived or she'd most definitely have noticed. In place of her 'regulars' stood an exceptionally dapper, fifty-something Chinese man in a pinstriped suit.

'Might I sample that vintage too?' he'd asked in an accent that was unmistakeably Oxbridge and most definitely not recently acquired.

'Er, sure,' Amber had mumbled, not a little bemused. For a moment she'd had to pause to remind herself where she was. You didn't see too many Chinese in the small mid-Sussex village of Ousedon.

None in fact. This was a first for her and was as noteworthy as the appearance in the village of a couple from Texas a year or so back who'd sought Ousedon out having heard the name in the course of their travels and were keen to discover if the place resembled the city of the same-sounding name back home where nodding donkey oil wells outnumbered the city's lamp posts.

Just minutes after their arrival the couple had left, apparently satisfied with the information supplied by Old George, the Ousedon valley's fishing warden, that the area's local oilfield was located 'behind that there wood on t'far side of t'river', Old George assuming in all honesty that the pair must be looking for the Ousedon Estate's agricultural diesel storage tank. And, he'd assured them, there were definitely more nodding donkeys than lamp posts in Ousedon. Of that he was certain.

They'd thanked him as profusely as only Texans can, had stuffed a twenty dollar note into his gnarled old fist and driven off through the lamp post-less village en route to the Euston station cattle ranch to see if it measured up to anything their lone star home state had to offer.

That night, Old George had recounted the tale to the gaggle of early drinkers in the Ousedon Arms proudly exhibiting the dollar bill as evidence of the encounter which Barry, the pub's wide-boy landlord, had said was probably of the third kind. Even so, he'd offered to exchange the note for three pints of best bitter and the conversation had turned to things foreign.

'Today them Americanos. Tomorrow them Chinese,' contributed Billy the Pig in an attempt to convince the pub's regulars that his knowledge of global affairs extended beyond the breeding habits of Gloucester Old Spots.

Had Amber been aware of Billy's perspicacity she might have viewed him in a whole new light on being confronted by the first Chinese she'd seen locally beyond the vicinity of the Jade Gate takeaway on Uckfield High Street. If there were more in the area they kept a very low profile, bordering on invisible in the mid-Sussex countryside even though the rest of the country seemed to be being over-run by Orientals in the wake of the global financial crash eight years earlier.

* * *

'Hmmm,' said the Chinese sipping the wine Amber had poured him. 'A 2002 Burgundy I'd say. Probably a Morey St Denis. Your father keeps a good cellar.'

'You know my dad?' said Amber, astonished that her father hadn't mentioned he was in touch with a Chinese man who not only had a nose for a good wine but could say 'cellar' without mixing up the l's and r's.

'Through business. I'm Harry Wong from Hong Kong,' he'd said, oblivious to how this sounded to someone from the rural mid-Sussex heartland and holding out his hand to Amber. 'Pleased to meet you Ella. Your father talks of you often.'

Amber froze, staring at him open-mouthed, her hand in his. No one used her given name anymore. Especially complete strangers she'd known for less than a minute.

'Ah, sorry,' said Wong. 'I can see you're surprised that I know your proper name. I'm afraid your father let slip the charming story of how your sister Emma thought it amusing to prefix "Ella" with "Amber" when you were children and how it became such an embarrassment to you at school that you'd retaliated by prefixing her name with "Dil".

'I have to say I found the story so delightfully English it stuck in my mind. It's amusing little plays on words like these that puts the English streets ahead when it comes to linguistic gymnastics and makes foreigners like me envy you greatly.'

'My father seems to have told you a lot about me,' said Amber, grinding her teeth as she tried to control a rising fury over her father's inability to respect one of her most jealously-guarded childhood secrets.

'Not really,' said Wong. 'He just had one too many at a business dinner we had last month and I'm afraid he got a bit maudlin and emotional. Said how proud he was that you'd done so well at college but how worrying it was that finding employment in the mass media market was proving such tough going. Any progress on that front, incidentally? Have your talents been snapped up yet?'

Amber paused with the glass to her lips and took a long, slow sip of the full-bodied yet playful little vintage to allow time to think before replying. For all she knew, Wong could be the father of a fellow struggling freelance out on a fishing trip for the lowdown on potential markets for his offspring's work and the last thing she needed right now was competition.

Normally she could tell from someone's eyes if they had a hidden agenda but not with this bloke. His gave away about as much as any Tory bloody government and she decided to follow suit. So…

'I'm biding my time,' she'd said with the sort of nonchalant shrug she hoped signalled supreme confidence and self-assurance. 'Not sure which is the right direction for me at the moment.'

'Quite right,' said Wong, impressed by her talent for telling a blatant untruth with such conviction. 'Never a good thing to rush the fences, eh? I'm sure any editor worth his salt would jump at the chance of employing a girl of your obvious talents. But you don't want to end up on the wrong road, do you? That first real job can have an enormous effect on the rest of your career.

'No, if you ask me, you're doing the right thing playing the waiting game. Then you're ready to pounce when the right opportunity comes along. It's something I keep telling my own boy but he's too impetuous. Always wanting it now. Never willing to wait and think things through before diving into choppy waters.'

Amber warmed to him. Here was a man wholly unlike her father who kept pushing her to take the first thing that came along.

This bloke seemed to understand how she felt about not selling herself cheap for the sake of getting a start.

'The secret is to choose your moment,' Wong went on. 'Timing is everything, don't you think? Too early and you might find yourself in a dead-end. Too late, and you miss the boat. It was just like that with the dotcom explosion of the early 2000s. A lot of people jumped in without looking and lost their shirts. But like you, I waited til things had settled down a bit. Did OK out of it in the end.'

Amber wondered what 'OK' meant. He had the look and assured poise of a man who'd done considerably better than 'OK' and Amber didn't know quite what to make of him. She wasn't used to being confronted with obvious successes in post-crash Britain. Those who'd escaped the financial carnage of recent years – especially those who'd quietly done well out of it – tended to keep a low profile to avoid attracting the attention of the grudge-harbouring jobless millions who passed their empty days polishing the blade of the guillotine.

She'd have followed her journalistic nose and prompted a few more details but the statistician had materialised at the bar, leering down her cleavage and gesturing towards the punch bowl. As she drained the last of its contents into his and the lady mayoress's glasses, she could sense Wong sizing her up out of the corner of his eye.

'I know what you're thinking,' he'd shouted over the disco din once her customer had wobbled back into the mêlée. 'You're wondering what a nice chap like me is doing in a place like this.

'Truth is, I enjoy getting back to my roots,' Wong lied. 'I wasn't always "well-heeled" as you say in Britain. Had to fight my way up the ladder just like you. Learned a thing or two on the way and now I'm in the privileged position of being able to pass some of that knowledge on to those I think deserve a chance. People like you, for instance.

'I can see you're too busy to discuss things now, so I'll just leave one of these with you so you know who to call should you ever find yourself in need of a guiding hand.'

Without taking his eyes off Amber as he spoke, Wong had one-handedly flicked open a solid gold business card case with his thumb and deftly extracted a card with his index and middle finger, all without spilling a drop from the glass in his other hand.

As Amber took it, Wong smiled, delivered an almost imperceptible bow, turned and disappeared into the stomping throng leaving Amber struggling for words and wondering if she'd had more to drink than she thought.

* * *

While Simon Middlethorpe nursed a terminal hangover the next day, Amber remained securely locked in her room. It was her punishment on him for setting her up with Wong, was all Simon could think to think.

In fact, it was his daughter who was doing the real thinking. While clearly a set up by her father to get her on the employment ladder, Wong's appearance hadn't been received with as much disdain as Simon Middlethorpe had assumed. Although she'd never have admitted it to her father, Amber had secretly reached the point at which she was grudgingly prepared to bend her principles if it meant a chance, finally, to break into the media world proper.

By the end of the day, she'd virtually decided to give Wong a call but not to openly seek his job-seeking assistance. Since that would be an open invitation for weeks of insufferable told-you-so gloating from her father, Amber had decided she needed an ulterior motive and after agonising long and hard over the problem at last the answer had come to her.

The appearance of an obviously wealthy Chinese in the narcoleptic village of Ousedon was just sufficiently noteworthy to make a story for the local paper – but only if she could get Wong to let her in on the real, underlying reason for his visit to the UK. There had to be more to it than checking on her father's microscopic solar energy business.

Two days later, after dialling the number contained on the expensive plain white vellum card that offered nothing more than 'Harry Wong. Market Dynamics Analyst', Wong was buying Amber lunch and a month after that Amber was climbing aboard a China Airways flight to her first proper job in the media.

Wong had turned out to be nothing short of candid. She needed a job and some solid journalism experience. He was in a position to arrange it. No strings. He knew a few media people in the Chinese capital who were always on the lookout for bright young English-speaking journalists to help improve the quality of China's foreign language publications and if she proved a good worker, his friends would owe him one. So, as getting her to Beijing would help both her and him, if she wanted him to, he'd have a word.

She did, so he did and soon a whirlwind of email traffic had begun whistling back and forth between Beijing and the nether regions of the Sussex countryside culminating in a work visa and a firm job offer with the state-run *China Daily* newspaper.

It'd all been so swift that Amber had hardly had time to consult her principles over working for a government which executed wrongdoers at the drop of a chopstick, had no compunction in locking up even Nobel Peace Prize winners if Beijing reckoned they were too subversive to remain at liberty, treated the wholly state-owned media as an extension of the propaganda ministry and had never budged on its policy of placing an individual's rights solidly below those of the state.

She also hadn't made much progress checking out the working practices of the People's Republic. She just had to trust that they wouldn't retain her passport and ship her off to the nearest re-education camp until she'd been indoctrinated into the Chinese way of doing things.

She was pretty sure it wouldn't come to that. Western migration in the direction of China was hardly a recent phenomenon and word was that in many respects the country was now indistinguishable from parts of Europe and the US. It was becoming common knowledge that, to maintain the pace of its economic expansion, China needed western expertise as much as skilled western workers needed employment and that the government had revised some of its more radical policies to accommodate them.

And so it was that Amber Middlethorpe had found herself closing her eyes, humming loudly to drown out the voice of her principles pleading with her to walk away, and signing on the dotted line.

Wong had assured her she wouldn't regret her decision. She'd be joining thousands from the West now in respected positions throughout China and turning the country's position as the world's number one economic force to their own advantage.

And who knows, he'd said, maybe their paths would cross again once she got settled in.

'I hope so,' thought Amber. 'You still owe me a story.'

chapter sixteen

The moment she walked through the *China Daily*'s monstrous dehumanising plate glass doors Amber knew she and the paper were going to get along like fire and water.

While physics had never been her academic strong suit, of one scientific fact she was fairly certain. Put the two together and you got one of two things – a doused flame or steam.

It hadn't taken Amber long to discover which of the two her editors had in mind for her, a discovery that served only to generate super-heated jets of the other in abundance. The more China's prime purveyor of state-sanctioned news tried to bring their new idealism-driven worker ant to heel, the more she dug her own in.

The problem, it seemed, lay in lack of understanding. While her editors couldn't understand how anyone could get upset about the paper acting as a Chinese government poodle, Amber couldn't understand how anyone couldn't.

Running one hundred and eighty degrees contrary to every ideal she held about journalism, to Amber the paper had not one redeeming feature about it. From its core editorial policy of elevating fawning sycophancy to an art form to the editor's apparent determination to expunge the word 'why?' from the *China Daily* lexicon, everything about the paper stank and Amber knew her conscience would never rest easy if she just sat back and complicitly let it happen.

OK, as Amber knew only too well, there was an alarmingly

large and growing proportion of the western media that had succumbed to following a similar editorial agenda but that wasn't the point.

What was, was that in Amber's highly principled, undercooked estimation it was a given that a journalist's duty was to fight – and never stop fighting – for objectivity and impartiality. To root out all that was corrupt and rotten and evil and expose it to the light. Anything less, she steamed at her editors, negated one's right to apply the term 'journalism' to one's work. That was what she'd been taught, that was what she fervently believed and nothing was ever going shake her faith in the mantra. NOTHING!

Interesting, said the editors. And have you finished editing that piece on China's panda procreation programme?

For nine whole months Amber had banged her head against the Great Wall and all it had produced was a migraine.

All, that is, until the day enlightenment finally dawned. The day she realised this was like jousting with ghosts. With nothing she ever said or did making the slightest bit of difference to the paper's content, realisation at last struck that if she was to make any impact at all she'd have to come at the problem from a different angle. A Chinese one.

What would they do in her position? If there was one thing her time at the paper had taught her, it was that if the Chinese couldn't get what they wanted by knocking on the front door, they'd simply go round the back. So that's what she'd do. And the way to do it, she decided, was to stop ranting and start doing – starting with making subtle, reality-based changes to any story that so much as hinted at Chinese triumphalism. In other words, pretty much everything that crossed her desk.

If nothing else, such fifth-columnist strivings would at least give her the satisfaction of knowing her overseers would have to start working for a living. And even if none of her edits made it through to the final editorial cut at least she'd be able to return to the sanctuary of the Sussex countryside with a clear conscience.

To date, three months after the launch of what she'd dubbed Operation Shipwreck, that's about all her efforts looked like they would produce. With her eagle-eyed editors spotting every alteration she made and simply changing them back to the originals her new strategy had had about as much effect as her jousts with the paper's editorial ghosts and Amber could feel her resolve crumbling.

She'd even found herself passing the lesser triumphalist articles on with nothing added or taken away and despite trying to block it out, Amber could see the day coming when she awoke to find herself metamorphosed into just another of the paper's Orwellian zombies traipsing mindlessly to and from the *China Daily* word factory each day.

With Operation Shipwreck looking like it would claim but the single victim and its creator on the verge of giving in to the inevitable, Amber could already feel her blood turning to water when the phone rang.

Rafferty's call didn't just give her new life. It gave her pause for thought. Ruminating over its contents as she sat at her desk later that morning, Amber had had an epiphany. Operation Shipwreck was clearly nothing like any strategy the Chinese would have adopted in her position. It was way, way too obvious.

No, in her position they'd apply a far more devious strategy. Something like the Chinese martial arts technique of turning an opponent's strengths to one's own advantage.

Rafferty's call, she now realised, gave her the opportunity to do just that. Played with a certain amount of guile, her current employers' intransigence could actually be made to work in her favour. The *China Daily*'s fawning toady approach to journalism could, in fact, be immensely helpful in her drive to fulfil a long-cherished ambition – getting a foot in the door of one of Britain's last remaining quality newspapers.

* * *

Steeling himself for yet another battering ram assault from the barbarian virago hovering outside his door, the *China Daily* news editor grimaced inwardly as he reluctantly beckoned Amber in.

What would it be this time? A lecture on the responsibility of the press to stand aloof from government diktat? A full-frontal offensive on the importance of objectivity? A series of sneering jibes over the paper's pathetic record of investigating political malfeasance? It didn't matter. He'd heard them all and had learned that the only way to defuse this troublesome foreigner's bombasts was simply not to react.

It was a strategy that was forgotten the moment his editorial nemesis walked in and smiled a smile of such sweet coyness it made his teeth ache. How could you not react to someone who'd come to ask forgiveness for all her past mistakes? Someone who said she'd come to tell him that having deliberated long and hard over what the *China Daily* was trying to do, she'd at last seen the light. That it was abundantly clear to her now that what the country needed was more papers like the *China Daily*, not thorns in the flesh of China's drive to emerge from years of under-development.

'That being the case,' Amber went humbly on, adopting her most penitent, hangdog posture, 'I'm here not only to apologise for my earlier, wholly unforgiveable obstructive behaviour but to present something to you that I hope will help convince you of my sincerity – a story I believe might be just the sort of thing the *China Daily* is looking for…'

Between the time of Rafferty's call and her arrival at the news editor's door, Amber had been digging. Unable to sleep, she'd dived headlong into the web and within the hour had dug up enough for a modest backgrounder on the history and progress of Chinese cricket.

What she'd found would have intrigued even the most hardened of cricket cynics. From a virtual standing start just ten years earlier, China had not only produced a national cricket team of reasonable quality but one which was now beating sides with half-decent cricketing pedigrees and stood a better-than-even chance of qualifying for the 2019 Cricket World Cup. No wonder then that Chinese cricket had grabbed the *Daily Grind*'s attention. It was almost enough to grab hers, even prompting a trawl of her own paper's archives for articles about the team.

Answer came there none.

On inputting 'China cricket' into the paper's database, the only reference the search threw up related to a *China Daily* report of a police raid on an illegal cricket-fighting den in Shanghai – another sport that had failed to catch her eye.

The finding left Amber in a state of surprised deflation. She'd expected and hoped for at least something on a team that seemed destined for sporting greatness. Something that would help short-circuit her own story's research process. Now, it seemed, she'd have to do all the legwork herself. It was not an appealing prospect.

On the other hand, the more she thought about it, the more the dearth of cricket news in the *China Daily* worked to her distinct advantage and, to her disgust, Amber found herself internally vocalising one of the more despicable sentiments ever expressed by her scruples-challenged electrical contractor father.

'From every bomb crater, a tiny flower blooms,' he'd once muttered in response to a local press report of an entire family being burned alive in a house fire caused by faulty wiring.

Although some way short of her father's reprehensible

intention to cash in on another's catastrophic misfortune, the tiny flower sentiment also applied in the case of the *China Daily*'s under-reporting of the Chinese cricket team's successes.

Presented with a finding that fitted the paper's China self-glorification news agenda so perfectly, the news editor's subsequent inevitable commission for her to convert it to full-out feature would surely open doors closed to the regular foreign media.

Behind them, Amber's news nose told her, lurked the real, untold story of Chinese cricket – a story she was certain would speed her towards achieving her holy grail, a full staff position on the *Daily Grind*.

* * *

Once he'd recovered from the shock of being confronted by a somewhat reconstituted, decidedly more compliant foreign devil subeditor than of late, the *China Daily* news editor had, as Amber had confidently predicted he would, drooled over her findings.

Listening with rapt attention to her proposal, a light began to shine in his eyes and within moments of sending her off to put flesh on the story's bones he was on the phone to the paper's editor crowing about HIS discovery.

Back at her desk, Amber struggled to contain the smile of satisfaction that came with knowing things could hardly have gone better. Whilst being the proud possessor of full *China Daily* reporter accreditation she could rest assured that her integrity would be protected through the certainty of knowing that her byline would not be attached to the puff piece she planned to craft lauding the accomplishments of the country's cricketing heroes.

Thanks to the *China Daily*'s unwritten policy of never allowing non-Chinese writers' names to appear in the paper, that honour would undoubtedly be bestowed on her news editor – unless the editor himself stole it from him – leaving her journalistic credentials intact. She'd need them when the real story, the one that *would* bear her name, emerged in the columns of the *Daily Grind* enlightening its readers as to how Chinese cricket had come so far so fast.

As relevant as the speed of China's cricket development was to the whole China-rising issue, no amount of internet searching had shed light on the matter leaving Amber with the distinct impression that someone somewhere was holding something back. Get to the bottom of who and what, she told herself, and she'd have something that would see her name indelibly printed on the British journalism map forever.

But how? With no specialist knowledge of the subject matter nor any contacts to consult, any prospect of her turning up a scoop looked about as likely as China actually winning the Cricket World Cup. What she undoubtedly needed, she decided, was a guiding hand.

Guiding hand? A-ha!

chapter seventeen

Harry Wong was, unusually, in his office gazing thoughtfully out across Kowloon Bay when Amber's call came through. Assuming it to be Oliver Gainsborough calling back to resume the conversation cut off moments earlier, Wong casually answered it without looking to check the caller's identity.

'Look Oliver, so as to avoid descending to the level of tedious haggling,' Wong said without giving Amber the opportunity of announcing herself, 'I've been thinking that my associates could probably be persuaded to run to one point three percent tops. Really don't think two will cut the marmalade and custard, so to speak. How does that sound?'

Amber gave the phone in her hand a quizzical look.

'Hello? Oliver? You there?' she heard it say.

'Er... Mr Wong? Harry Wong?'

'Who's that?'

'It's Amber. Amber Middlethorpe. From the UK. Remember?'

'Good grief... Amber... Sorry... Thought you were... er... how are you?'

'Fine thanks. You?'

'Errr... yes... fine. Sooo... Amber...,' said Wong struggling to regain his poise, 'how nice to hear from you... To what do I owe the pleasure? Not here in Hong Kong are you?'

'No,' she purred back. 'Still deskbound in freezing Beijing and wishing I was somewhere warmer. No complaints though. Glad to be working. There's a lot of people I know who'd kill to be able to say the same and I owe it all to you,' she said with fingers crossed. Her gamble that Wong would fall for the old ego-massage ploy, no matter how disingenuous, was a risky one but it was the only one she could think of. Giving him an earful for landing her in such a dead-end, brain-withering, teeth-grinding job was hardly the way to encourage the spilling of beans on Chinese cricket.

'Hope you don't mind me calling but thought it was time I contacted you to say thanks for getting me into such an... interesting... organisation. The last twelve months on the *China Daily* has really opened my eyes...'

'Glad to be of service. How do you find Beijing?'

'It's amazing. Never expected it to be so... well... western. In many respects it's just like home. Well, except that there's not much countryside round here... and village cricket clubs in need of volunteer bar staff are a bit thin on the ground.' The little giggle Amber purposefully injected into the premeditated afterthought would, she hoped, jog Wong's memory of how they'd first met and ensure the hated 'c' word got an early mention.

'Ah. Do I detect a hint of nostalgia?'

'Mmmm. A bit, perhaps,' said Amber capitalising on the cue Wong had unwittingly provided. 'Never thought I'd miss the world of English village cricket but some things are just ingrained in us, aren't they?' Amber lied through her gritted teeth.

'It's not having access to the familiar that makes them special when you're away from home. When I'm there I hardly give it a thought. But now I'm not, I've realised how much cricket played in my life, mostly through my dad.'

'I know how you feel. Cricket is like a drug. Without a regular fix, withdrawal symptoms set in.'

'As it happens,' replied Amber quickly, anxious not to let the fish off the hook, 'that's exactly what I've been telling the *China Daily*. After all, the paper *is* aimed at an English-speaking audience and there's a lot of readers out there who think the same as you and me. An English-language paper without the cricket scores in it just isn't the same, is it?'

'What's their reaction?'

'Well, after a bit of badgering it would seem they're finally getting the message. They've even agreed to allow me a bit of time to work up a proper proposal for them.'

'What? About cricket? Good heavens. Well, congratulations. That's splendid news. The *China Daily* could do with a breath of fresh air. So how's that going?'

'The proposal? Early days yet but I am turning up a few things that might catch their interest. The progress of China's national side, for instance. Hadn't realised just how far they'd come in such a short time.'

'Yes. That's a good angle. Nothing like a bit of home-grown success to spur the interest of the country's media authorities.'

'Trouble is,' said Amber, 'I reckon the story needs a bit more than is already in the public domain to tip the balance. It needs a peg to hang it on to win them over.'

'Surely the governing body could help you out there. Have you made contact with them? I'm sure they'd be more than happy to give you a few pointers.'

'Not as yet. As I said, it's early days. Need to do my homework first so I can ask the right questions when the time comes.'

In the absence of any immediate response to her questions nudge, Amber assumed Wong must be considering the matter thoughtfully before offering his advice.

She was right, just not in the way she'd imagined. The words 'homework' and 'questions' from a western journalist in the context of Chinese cricket had caused Wong's bodyclock to skip a beat, his saliva glands to dry up and alarm bells to start ringing in the middle distance.

The anodyne, rather comforting news that the *China Daily* was considering running a puff piece lauding China's cricketing successes had suddenly offered a glimpse of a more menacing side, one in which the phrase 'witch hunt' made a surprise and not especially welcome appearance.

At a time of delicate, secretive discussions over the very future of China's place in the world of cricket, the last thing Wong needed right now was a proper journalist poking around muddying the waters. Especially a young ambitious one with a nose for a story, a name to make and a string of convictions for acting against the best interests of her Chinese employer.

Unbeknown to Amber, her *China Daily* copy-wrecking exploits had not only not gone unnoticed by Wong but had rebounded on him in the worst possible way for someone of Chinese extraction.

It was the subliminal hiss in the voice of the paper's politburo-appointed editor that had left Wong in no doubt as to the predicament he faced through having landed the paper with the unexploded journalistic bomb that was Amber Middlethorpe.

Unless he found a way to defuse it, he'd effectively been told, another was primed to go off under the one thing Wong and every other Chinese valued above all else: his *guanxi* – his connections in high places.

'If you want to remain on the Christmas card list,' was the message implied in the hiss, 'you might consider giving some thought as to how the bomb might be made to work in China's favour.'

Not unconversant with China's current policy for dealing with unstable ordnance, Wong knew exactly what was being asked of him. He was being 'advised' to formulate a strategy which accorded with a diktat the *China Daily* had received from on high to revise its methods of dealing with ticking explosive devices like Amber Middlethorpe.

No longer were they to be summarily dismissed. Instead, such weapons of mass distraction were to be put to work to further China's own ends, manipulated to ensure they blew up in their makers' own faces.

Under the strategy, the likes of the *China Daily*'s troublemaking foreign employee were to be fed a diet of wholly erroneous Chinese 'secrets' they'd be certain to onpass to media friends in the West.

When such easily disprovable 'secrets' were inevitably revealed to the world, China would be gifted an opportunity to crow about the extent of hypocrisy running the length and breadth of an increasingly China-hostile western media.

So often accused of having no interest in printing the truth, Beijing would be able to show beyond doubt that it was in fact the West which stood so indicted thereby destroying at a stroke all trust the western public had in its media's reporting of contentious Chinese issues.

Having shown herself to be without peer when it came to unbridled displays of contempt for an organisation that had been good enough to take her out of the ranks of the unemployed, Amber's name, as Wong wasn't wholly unaware, was in the top ten of ingrates singled out to receive the diet.

She was, in the *China Daily* editor's estimation, the perfect choice for ensuring highly explosive, barely credible, anti-China fabrications reached a western media so desperate for China-bashing stories it would publish anything she sent them without so much as a quibble. All that remained was the identification and planting on her of a sufficiently irresistible fiction.

As total recall of China's revised method for dealing with the likes of Amber returned to Wong, the Hong Konger felt the bells of cricket investigation alarm transform to peels of celebration. Here, Wong realised, was the perfect opportunity for providing the *China Daily* editor with just the sort of Amber-trapping fiction he was looking for. If that didn't remove the threat of losing his *guanxi* status, Wong was at a loss to know what would and within milliseconds Wong's convoluted mind had contrived a plan for achieving that exact end… and then some.

Should Amber, in the course of rummaging around in China's cricket bag, stumble upon a black box stuffed with wholly-fictitious China-damning evidence, its subsequent inevitable appearance in the foreign media would have the authorities and his editor friend grinning like loons.

Not only that, but when the news broke it would send the western newshound pack barking up every tree except the one that contained the real Chinese cricket story, the one Wong was rather keen didn't see the light of day until the time was right.

As the perfection of the scheme dawned on him, Wong's lips curled into a smile of malevolent satisfaction. Even by his own conniving standards this was good. But for it to succeed, he needed to pay close attention to what Amber was saying and set a field to initially frustrate her stroke play.

'Fact is,' he heard her continuing, 'I could do with your expert knowledge to put the game in a local context. I've got the basic background covered. But what I'd really like to get at is what makes the game attractive to the Chinese. I mean, it's not really a Chinese sort of thing, is it?'

'Hmmm,' hmmm-ed Wong. 'That's a pretty big question, Amber. I'd have to give it some thought so I don't send you down the wrong track. Tell you what. I'll be in Beijing over Chinese New Year. I could give you a couple of pointers over dinner if you like.'

The invitation exceeded Amber's expectations by several decimal places. The most she'd hoped for was a couple of names to get the ball rolling. But here was Wong not only offering her the chance to pick his brains face-to-face but to sample the Beijing

New Year good life at his expense. If there was anyone who'd know the right places to eat, it'd be Wong and Amber's mouth began to water at the prospect. China's one saving grace was its food.

She was still salivating at the thought as she went to bed that night to dream, oddly, of Oliver Twist demanding seconds of the house special – marmalade pie with custard.

chapter eighteen

Between her phone conversation with Wong and meeting him for dinner, Amber had hoped to be left to get on with the Chinese cricket familiarisation process.

It was not to be. Within minutes of her call to Wong, Amber had received an urgent memo from the news editor rescinding his earlier command to shelve all other work and concentrate on the cricket story. In his enthusiasm to get the piece in the paper, he'd forgotten that half the *China Daily*'s subediting staff would shortly be taking their Chinese New Year holiday. To continue getting the paper out, it was all remaining hands to the pump, Amber's amongst them.

It wasn't a lie as such. The paper would be shorthanded during the holiday period. It was just that the news editor hadn't thought to mention the call he'd received moments earlier from the editor relaying the guts of an 'advice' call the editor had received from Wong. Bringing Amber to heel, Wong had told him, might not go exactly according to plan if she was allowed free rein to prowl China's cricket outfield before Wong had had time to set the snares.

With better things to do than bother with wearisome Wong explanations, the editor had unquestioningly rubber-stamped Wong's petition leaving Wong a relieved man. It wasn't just the regaining of his *guanxi* status that was at stake. It was the whole Ke-Ching/MCC deal and with it Wong's chance of ultimately clinching the biggest prize in world cricket.

Everything hinged on Amber being kept off the story until the MCC had voted on the Ke-Ching bail-out offer. If, in the course of her research, the offer somehow came to her attention prior to the vote, the news was bound to be splashed all over the western press and the whole deal could founder.

Being about as enthusiastic as the Chinese Communist Party over seeing its internal affairs exposed to daylight, the MCC's reaction to finding its name publicly linked with a company the press might discover was a lackey of the Chinese state wasn't the best way Wong could think of for encouraging the committee to vote in Ke-Ching's favour.

That worry looked to be behind him now he had the *China Daily* editor's assurance that Amber would be distracted long enough for his plan to take effect.

He might not have been so sanguine had he known that all his call had done was to spark a train of events which would culminate in Wong being left with the impression that someone up there didn't like him.

Thanks to Wong, Amber found herself so bogged down in *China Daily* subbing work that she'd been forced to plead for a *Daily Grind* deadline extension.

Permission grudgingly granted, Rory McDermott had then lost no time informing Turnball of the delay. The interests of all concerned, he advised, would be best served through a postponement of the MCC's decision on the Ke-Ching proposal until the *Grind*'s contacts in China had had time to check out Turnball's information.

Knowing Turnball would never call for a delay without good reason, MCC chairman Sir Oliver Gainsborough had subsequently agreed to his committee colleague's postponement request and when the news reached Wong, the Hong Konger's blood pressure went critical. Now he'd have to dream up a new raft of distractions to keep Amber's attention focussed elsewhere until the MCC had voted.

Although none of the participants in this cycle of foot-dragging was to know it at the time, this was a vicious circle whose only hope of being broken was through one of its links cracking.

The smart money was on Gainsborough. It was his job on the line if Ke-Ching got tired of waiting and abandoned ship.

That money would have been lost.

In the end, it wasn't Gainsborough, Wong or any of the other chain participants that ended the impasse. That responsibility was directly traceable to the overheated libido of one who was even more ignorant of the circle's existence than those who were unwittingly caught up in it.

* * *

Never one to pass up a chance of grabbing a sly look down Amber's top, Bo Ling had sneakily manoeuvred himself close to his co-worker's shoulder as her attention was fully engaged on the contents of her screen.

What he saw astounded him. Up on the screen was the home page of the Chinese Cricket Association.

'You like clicket?' he gasped, his bulging eyes ping-ponging between the screen and Amber's very un-Chinese-like bosom.

'With a passion I can't describe,' mumbled Amber without looking at her slobbering admirer.

'Me too!' exclaimed the drooling Bo not getting it.

'Yeah, right,' drawled Amber back. It wasn't the first time her creepy colleague had fired a blatantly obvious pick-up salvo across her bows. Every time he passed he offered something clearly designed to entice Amber into conversation. On the few occasions she'd fallen for it, it'd always ended with Bo making some slimy, suggestive remark and Amber now knew better than to encourage him.

It wasn't that he was repulsive. He wasn't. It was just the oily, lecherous, adolescent way Chinese men – all of them in Amber's experience – tried to pick up foreign women. It was like being chatted up by Benny Hill.

Usually, her rebuffs had the desired effect but this time he stood his ground.

'Tluly!' insisted Bo. 'Clicket is very special game. I get best tickets to Chinese games. Cousin Ding is assistant national team trainer.'

'COUSIN Ding?' Amber's attention was suddenly all Bo's. It wasn't just that Bo had a relation who offered a back door route into the world of top flight Chinese cricket, it was the mention of a word rarely heard in China these days. The country's forty year-old one-child policy had effectively rendered the words 'brother', 'sister', 'uncle', 'aunt' and subsequently 'cousin' redundant leaving Bo something of a rarity in modern day China. He was undoubtedly the last of his line to still have need of them.

'Yes,' said Bo not getting this either. 'I can ask him to get tickets for you also. We could go together. Then after... maybe we can play together. You could hold my balls,' he slimed.

'The ones near the stump?' yawned Amber witheringly back in the hope that her allusion to the average Chinese man's deficiency in this department would embarrass her suitor into abandoning this line of conversation and retreat to the relative safety of cousin Ding's background.

All it did was prompt a toothy, lascivious leer. Amber's prospective suitor had got that one all right and wasn't about to let the opportunity of managing to engage his quarry in a risqué exchange go to waste.

'Only stump til it gets out,' was Bo's surprisingly urbane, surely unwitting, cricketing riposte and Amber only just managed to stop herself responding with an appreciative 'Bravo!' for his delivery of this most English of smutty double entendres. If he'd really meant it that way, she'd be tempted to allow him to show her the contents of his cricket box.

Amber felt bile rising in her throat at the very thought but fought it back, clear in the knowledge that the priority at this stage was keeping Bo sweet.

Without knowing it, this slavering Chinese wretch was holding open a door through which Amber could glimpse the wide open expanses of the promised land. If cousin Ding was as susceptible to the allure of western women as Bo, breaking into China's inner cricket circle was a done deal.

He was.

Instead of summarily sending Bo off with his ears ringing, Amber had forced herself to play up to his slobbering advances and accept his after-work drinks invitation – but not before making it conditional on a chaperone of her choice being present. Ding, perhaps? The Chinese Cricket Association would hardly employ someone of an irresponsible disposition.

It was the transformation of Amber 1.0 into the flame-haired temptress that was Amber 2.0 that had proved the clincher.

For two whole hours Ding's stalk-mounted eyes hardly wavered from their exploration of a cleavage made so enticing by Amber's most seductive, low-plunging top and uplift bra that he'd have given Amber the Party chairman's private cellphone number had he known it.

He didn't, but what he did know was the inside track on Chinese cricket and by the time Amber relievedly made her excuses and left, she was in possession of a sufficiently intriguing snippet of news concerning the country's cricket team to warrant the making of a meeting reminder call to Wong.

With just a couple of days left until Chinese New Year and no call from the Hong Konger it was time to jog his memory. Thus far she'd forced herself not to badger him on the grounds that to do so would be to risk antagonising him into withdrawing his valuable contact-providing assistance.

But that was before the name of the Chinese cricket team's assistant trainer had been added to her own *guanxi* and before Ding had been seduced into gifting her a sizeable peg on which to hang her story.

With a crucial World Cup qualifying match in Namibia imminent, he'd told her with a snarl, Chinese New Year for the country's cricket squad would consist of extra training at the practice ground and rebellion was in the air.

New Year being sacrosanct to all Chinese, Ding said, there was every chance of the issue becoming something of a *cause célèbre* amongst the country's dissenters. Once the news got out, he wouldn't be at all surprised to see people defying the authorities and taking to the streets in support of the cricketers' cause.

Amber wasn't slow to realise what that meant. If the cricketer rebellion really did spill over, the eyes of every diplomat and foreign correspondent in China would be focussed on the issue.

To get the jump on all of them, it was critical that Wong was cornered without delay for his reaction to both this bit of news and to the additional, scarcely credible, tip-off she'd just received from Jonquil Rafferty.

chapter nineteen

Amber had had some jaw-dropping moments in her time but her first sight of the Beijing Hotel's interior was right up there with the best of them. The hotel lobby's towering palatial elegance left her rooted to its polished marble floor and feeling very small as she gazed up at its gilt-adorned cornices oblivious to the arrival of Harry Wong at her elbow.

'When it comes to unabashed ostentation,' he murmured conspiratorially in her ear, 'China has few equals… and, it would appear, no shame.'

Amber's jaw dropped again. She didn't know whether to protest or smile knowingly back.

On the one hand, opulent hardly did the hotel's décor justice. On the other, here was her host astoundingly echoing her own thoughts. Modesty, her time in China had taught her, wasn't the first character trait that came to mind with the Chinese. If you've got it, stick it in the world's face was the watchword of twenty-first century designer-China where mammon worship was the one religion not only not frowned on by the state but positively encouraged.

The thought brought a wry smile to Amber's face as Wong led her in the direction of the restaurant.

The hypocrisy of the man! Complaining that the Chinese had no shame while flaunting his own good fortune by showing he could get a table in the most expensive eatery in town on the one night of the year when getting a table in any restaurant was tantamount to winning the lottery.

Getting one in the Beijing Hotel on Chinese New Year just smacked of brazen, egotistical exhibitionism and she wouldn't be in the least surprised if he ordered the whole menu and left it there to rot just to show he could do it.

It hadn't come to that but only, she suspected, because the nearby bunch of shrieking shiny-suited Chinese *nouveau très très riche* loudmouths with connections in all the right places and the manners of farmyard animals had beaten him to it.

As Wong and Amber scrutinised the restaurant's almost limitless tableau of fine Chinese fare, their screeching neighbours were engaged in a trial of loutish financial one-upmanship, the winner pipping the others at the post by ordering a dozen bottles of the finest, most expensive wine on the menu and mixing it with Pepsi Cola. Not even Wong could top that.

Instead, he restricted himself to directing Amber's gaze to dishes at the top end of the price range while muttering oaths concerning the obvious absence of a restaurant policy covering clientele acceptability.

'The least they could do is restrict entry to those who know not to wipe their chins on the table cloth,' Wong griped.

'Wouldn't that be a bit like restricting cricket club membership to those who know that the spirit of the game requires them to walk when they know they're out?' countered Amber with a sly grin. The sooner she turned the conversation to the guts of the reason for the dinner, the sooner she could dispense with the business end of the meeting and focus on the Beijing Hotel's truly astounding selection of food. It wasn't every day she got to feast on the finest cuisine China could offer at someone else's expense.

'Hmmm. Good ball, Amber. HowZAT!' returned Wong with a smile, delightedly accepting the invitation to lapse into cricketese. Opportunities to practice a language heard about as frequently as general election announcements in China were not to be missed.

'Missing off and missing leg, methinks. Well bowled that girl!'

'Not going over the top then?' Amber retorted. 'Thought that one might have pitched an inch or two short,' she added without any real understanding of what it was she was saying. The combination of being incessantly subjected to cricketese by her father and her innate resistance to it had left her in a state of blissful educated ignorance – a bit, she thought, like being able to regurgitate nursery rhymes you never remembered learning and never really understood but which stayed with you forever.

If Wong had any inkling that Amber was doing no more than mindlessly reciting cricketing parlance to appear to be *au fait* with the game he showed no sign of it. The only thing his eyes revealed was admiration for Amber's unplayable delivery.

'Don't think so,' he beamed. 'That one was spot on. Hitting back pad plumb in front I'd say... not that you'd ever get anyone from the "home team" to accept such a decision, of course,' he added with a flick of his eyes in the direction of the neighbouring table. 'It'd be taken as an accusation that they didn't always play with a straight bat.'

'Bugger,' thought Amber, struggling to translate this into plain English. 'Wish I'd never started this.' Had he just used the cryptic cricket code to impart a criticism of the Chinese system? Was he saying that admitting to guilt and fallibility isn't really a Chinese thing? If he was, this flash of open disloyalty to his political masters might be an opportune moment to confront Wong with the fantastical tip-off just in from Rafferty concerning Ke-Ching's real reason for launching a cricket tournament in England.

On being treated to Rafferty's tale of how China, he'd learned, was using Ke-Ching as the front man to displace the MCC as the guardian of world cricket on the grounds that it had unearthed –

quite literally – solid evidence that cricket was being played in China centuries before it was ever heard of in England, Amber was left with but one thought. Rafferty had clearly gone off his trolley.

While it was well known that Beijing was convinced that the origins of anything of any importance to the world could be traced back to China, surely it wasn't so desperate for new additions that it needed to include cricket on its list of Chinese inventions.

But the *Grind* man sounded serious and needed Amber to check his information out. Was China really trying to steal the game – maybe even Lord's – from under the MCC's nose?

The only person she knew who might be able to corroborate the finding was Wong. But getting him to do so was going to require a degree of cunning that would put the Chinese themselves to shame. As the man who'd spearheaded the Ke-Ching Double Tops competition, Wong was about as likely to verify the information outright as he was to order beans on toast.

On the other hand, he had dropped several hints that as a Hong Konger he was no institutionalised Chinese, a standpoint Amber might exploit by approaching the issue via a circuitous route – one whose signposts were all written in cricketese. Wong had given her a way in. All she had to do was guide him down the right path. So…

'And don't they?'

'Don't they what?'

'Always play with a straight bat.'

Wong thought for a moment.

'Let's just say it's the bat that isn't always straight.'

'Wouldn't that send the ball off in unexpected directions?'

'I rather think that might be the intention.'

Wow, thought Amber, this is working better than expected. If I read him right, he's confirming what everyone knows but never talks about – that what you see with the Chinese isn't always what you get. Including China's involvement in cricket? It was time to probe a little deeper.

'That would keep the fielding side on its toes.'

'And make it difficult to set a field in the first place.'

'Especially when you have to take the slope into account as well?' she proffered with a narrow-eyed glance at Wong. If there was one thing Amber knew about Lord's it was that the playing area sloped a full six feet eight inches from its north west side to its south east and that playing there meant having to take it into consideration. Her father was always banging on about it giving the home side an unfair advantage.

Wong's eyes were suddenly polished black pebbles and at that moment Amber knew she'd hit a nerve. A year in China had taught her that no Chinese ever reacted defensively to being confronted with damning evidence. They just clammed up and adopted the reflective sunglass look. Westerners new to the country usually found this so disconcerting that they generally backed off and changed the subject. Those who weren't knew that the only way to prompt a verbal response was to meet stone with stone. After a great deal of practice, Amber had her own pebble-eye visage down to a fine art.

It was Wong who cracked first. Pretending to turn his attention back to the menu, he muttered one word: 'Quite.'

Gotcha, thought Amber. Now he knows I know what he knows and that the time has come to talk turkey. It was time to bowl him a few easy balls and see if he was willing to take the bait.

'Of course, it helps if you're the "home team", as it were,' said Amber smiling her sweetest, most disarming smile.

'Naturally,' said Wong without taking his eyes off the menu. 'The more you understand of a ground's idiosyncrasies, the more likely you are to know how to accommodate them into your playing strategy.'

'And how would you "accommodate" them if you were the "home team"?'

Wong's eyes drifted up from the menu to meet Amber's as he considered his response.

'By making sure I was always the "home team" on this specific ground,' he said finally with an enigmatic smile.

'Mmmm. And how would you ensure that?' It was time to hit him with the jaffer delivery.

'Probably by bowling the ball that's right on the money.'

'Money can't buy love.'

'Oh really? Time, as they say, will tell.'

'Old Father Time by any chance?' prompted Amber. If Wong didn't baulk at her reference to the famous Lord's weather vane, that would clinch it. It would be indisputable proof that the subject under discussion was the spiritual home of cricket.

'Only when he's facing East,' said Wong, clearly enjoying the game of hide and seek Amber had initiated.

'And is he?'

'Looks that way,' he mumbled into the menu.

Bloody hell, thought Amber. That, if she was not mistaken – and if the mixed sporting metaphor could be excused – was game, set and match.

Unscrambled and decrypted, Wong had surely just confirmed that China's plan was to hijack the home of cricket – and subsequently the game itself – for its own. She had it from the horse's mouth itself, even if it was full of hay.

The story and undoubtedly a job on the *Grind* were hers. Or they would be if she could just nudge Wong along one more notch and put a bit of flesh on the bones.

'So the "home team" is up with the run rate and on course for victory...?'

'Maybe even the championship... but that,' said Wong emphatically, 'is another story – one best left for another day, I think. And my advice to you in the meantime is that you might find pacing your innings brings the greater chance of nailing the total you're chasing. You might find it's rather bigger than at first appears and that patience reaps the greater reward. Always best to block the good balls and score off the wayward deliveries, don't you think?'

Amber nodded. Wong was clearly offering chapter and verse on a story that went way beyond her original information and had let her know in no uncertain terms that jumping the gun could have only one possible result – the loss of his cooperation.

Message received, her nod had indicated. She wasn't about to be bullied by the *Grind* into going after the ball before it was there to be hit. Whatever the real story was, Wong's tone told her it knocked spots off Rafferty's information and for that she was prepared to test her editor's patience and bet the pot.

'Good,' said Wong. 'So now that's settled, let's order. Might I suggest we start with the pickled bat? Under the circumstances it would seem an appropriate choice.'

* * *

Wong smiled a smile of satisfaction as his head hit the pillow that night. That had all gone rather well, he thought. From being pinned on the back foot by the opposition's prime strike bowler, he'd managed to frustrate her deliveries sufficiently to get her taken off, preserve his own wicket and win time to get his eye in.

Not only that, but by purposefully giving the impression that he could be tempted into hooking at the bouncer he'd given her hope that she could penetrate his defences when she came back on for a second spell.

But by that time it'd be too late. His team's score would already be insurmountable. Even if his hook was caught on the boundary, victory would already be in the bag.

Or it would be if the MCC got off their butts and bloody voted. He'd still received no word that a vote was imminent and the longer they buggered about the longer he'd need to distract Amber from her quest.

It was clear that the *China Daily*'s instructions to her to drop the story until told otherwise were being ignored and that somehow she'd managed to get a glimpse of the bigger picture. If she was anything like her father who'd turned out to be a dog with a bone when it came to the main chance, that glimpse would be enough to have her peering in through the window until she got a sneak preview of the whole thing before its official unveiling.

It was only the 'promise' of a private viewing of an even bigger picture that was keeping her at bay but that, Wong knew, wasn't going to keep her out of the attack forever. Sooner or later, she'd lose patience and sell what she already knew to some western rag or other and it wouldn't be long before news of the MCC falling under the control of the Beijing body snatchers was splashed all over the front pages.

The priority now wasn't stopping that happening. That eventuality was inevitable. It was ensuring it happened after the event, not before.

* * *

When news of the unmitigated success of his delaying tactics reached him a week later, Wong's shoulders un-tensed for the first time in months. The committee had finally met, narrowly voted in favour of the Ke-Ching proposal and nothing had appeared in the press to spoil the party. Wong almost danced a jig of delight around his office. Now he could devote his time fully to his *guanxi* recovery scheme.

He might not have been quite so quick to celebrate had he been in possession of all the facts in the sequence of events sparked by the call Amber made to the *Daily Grind* moments after returning from her dinner with Wong.

In pleading for another deadline extension in return for what she was sure would turn out to be a world exclusive, Amber had found herself backed into a corner by Rafferty. Such a request could only be considered, he told her, if she was at least prepared to justify it with a summary of what it was she'd discovered.

Amber had had no option but to cautiously recount the essence of her meeting with Wong minus one or two of the more salient points, the source of her information in particular. When dealing with commissioning editors, bitter experience had taught her to take the words of a well-known Arab proverb seriously. Ignoring the advice to 'trust in God... but tether your camel' was, she knew, absolutely *the* best way of ensuring your work saw the light of day without your byline attached.

After listening attentively to Amber's bare bones presentation of the story so far, Rafferty's inclination was to approve the extension but knew that doing so without first consulting his editor would be to risk tweaking the tiger's tail.

Putting Amber on hold, Rafferty had then passed what he'd heard up the line to McDermott who'd received it with greedy ears and permission to grant Amber's request. From what she'd told Rafferty, Turnball's information could now be reclassified as fact and returned to Turnball for inclusion in the MCC committee's considerations of the Ke-Ching proposal.

Duly onpassed, McDermott then sat back to think what to do with what he knew. While yearning to get the story into print before someone else beat the *Grind* to it, his instincts were screaming 'sit on it'. His newfound fledgling China correspondent, some far away inner voice was telling him, seemed to know what she was doing and that on this occasion he should listen to the voice and hold fire.

From what he'd heard, it sounded like there was enough in the promised bigger story to see it elevated from the back to the front page and for that, McDermott finally decided, he was prepared to wait. The more ammunition he had to embarrass the *Grind*'s grasping, prospective Chinese owners with when the time came, the better.

* * *

'Lunch. Tomorrow. Simpson's,' was Bleauforth's reaction to Turnball's call. A brief précis of his colleague's investigations was enough to convince the noble lord of the need for another urgent summit meeting.

'My God! So it's true,' Bleauforth spluttered into his soup. 'The bloody chinks really do think they've a right to the great game! The bloody impertinence of it. I can't believe they've got the balls. What d'you think they'd say if we laid claim to the Great Wall? About the same as the committee will say to Ke-Ching once they get wind of this, I'd warrant.'

'Possibly. It's quite a bombshell, that I'll agree,' said Turnball. 'But we mustn't lose sight of the fact that not everyone on the committee thinks as we do. There's a sizeable proportion whose vision extends no further than the bottom line. As long as it isn't written in red ink, they're happy. And you can bet your bottom order batsmen that'll be the deciding factor when it comes to the vote. Reject Ke-Ching and we're back where we started, they'll say – stuck solid in the dudu and sinking rapidly towards an innings defeat.'

'But they can't. They just CAN'T! That'd be like handing over the keys to the Tower and murdering all the ravens. Surely they'll see that!'

'They might. But reason suggests it isn't something that can be relied on. All most of them really care about is seeing Lord's remaining in existence so they can impress their corporate chums in the hospitality boxes. They couldn't care less whether those boxes serve roast beef or chicken chow mein as long as they're there to do deals in. Most of the time they're hardly aware there's a cricket match being played the other side of the window.'

'So it's the end then,' said Bleauforth, his eyes visibly watering, 'is that what you're saying? That come the next meeting, the committee will effectively vote itself out of existence and pass responsibility for overseeing the great game to a bunch of slitty-eyed Beijing bureaucrats?'

'Not necessarily.' It was time to reveal the lifeline Turnball had been hiding behind his back. 'There is an alternative.'

By the end of lunch Bleauforth's tears of anguish had turned to droplets of admiration for his fellow committee member.

Turnball's plan was, by Bleauforth's standards, sheer genius even though he'd never be able to bring himself to admit it. Achieving, as it did, the saving of the game from the Chinese while putting the MCC back on a firm financial footing, the plan was worthy of any dreamt up by Machiavelli. And like any great plan it had simplicity at its root.

'What we have here,' said Turnball, 'is a situation in which we could do worse than do what the Chinese themselves would do – match sneakiness with sneakiness.

'Our sneakiness in this case, I would venture, should revolve around not letting on to our Chinese "saviour" that we're aware of its darker motives for coming to the rescue of the MCC.

'What seems absolutely clear to me is that if Beijing gains any inkling that its underlying reason for coming to the club's aid has reached ears beyond those in residence at the Great Hall of the People, there's every chance of our "rescuers" simply changing tack and deciding its funds might be better spent elsewhere.

'In such a situation I wouldn't be at all surprised to see them withdrawing their MCC bail-out offer, sit back and await the outcome.

'If, as now seems likely, the bank decides it can't be held responsible for the hacking of our account, I think Ke-Ching's – or rather China's – response will be predictable. It'll simply allow the MCC to go to the wall and jump into the vacuum with a rival cricket custodian operation once that's happened.

'If I'm right then it's clear that the priority here has to be getting Ke-Ching's funds into the MCC account before it and its masters in Beijing realise they've been rumbled... as they inevitably eventually will.

'But by the time it does it'll be too late. The club's financial situation will have been resolved, the MCC will be back in control of its own destiny and there won't be a thing Ke-Ching or whoever's pulling its strings will be able to do about it.'

Sitting back smugly to assess his audience's reaction to the plan he'd presented, Turnball smiled at the irony of the MCC being saved by funds provided by the very people who were effectively trying to take it over.

If he expected to see a similar smile spreading across the florid face of his dining companion he was to be disappointed. In its place was a furrowed-brow look of consternation.

'Hmmm,' Bleauforth mumbled. 'A cunning wheeze indeed, old fruit. But haven't you forgotten something? What if the Chinese decide they want their money back and instigate legal proceedings? If the MCC winds up in court accused of breach of contract, we'll probably end up even deeper in the financial dung heap than we already are.'

'Not necessarily,' retorted Turnball, disgusted that Bleauforth could assume he might have neglected to take such an eventuality into account.

'For one, such an action would have to be based on an accusation that the club was dishonouring a contract in which it had effectively agreed to be Ke-Ching's patsy in the running of MCC operations. Somehow I can't see Ke-Ching daring to even allude to such a requirement in any bail-out contract.

'For two, going the litigation route would inevitably be to risk exposing such a requirement in court – not the best way I can think of for attracting the world cricket fraternity to China's cause.

'Nevertheless, let's suppose for a moment that our "saviour" feels it has no option but to sue. That, I feel sure, is when our Chinese friends would come to realise that the British legal system can't always be relied on to be as sympathetic to the plaintiff's case as said plaintiff expects it to be.

'Were it to become apparent to the court that an excessive reparation amount would force the MCC into bankruptcy, I think there's a case for arguing that that's when national interest considerations might find themselves elevated above legal argument.

'When it comes to the preservation of national treasures like Lord's, no British jury would dare find in favour of an infidel invader like China. And even if it did, there's not a judge in the land who'd impose a crippling financial settlement. There's not one of them who isn't an MCC member.'

chapter twenty

Down at the Ousedon Arms the early evening drinkers were gathering, Simon Middlethorpe and Dinsdale Stewart-Krabbs amongst them. There were important things to discuss and where better to do it than over a pint of Barry's best.

'I suppose what it all comes down to is tradition,' muttered Stewart-Krabbs into his beer. 'Changing the form of the game we play isn't going to be to everyone's liking.'

'But it's not as if we're changing anything that hasn't been changed before,' argued Middlethorpe. 'We only started playing the forty-over game when we joined the league.

'Before that, if you recall, the club would have nothing to do with limited-overs cricket. Far too loutish for the likes of us. All the league is recommending is that we shift to the Double Tops format. The only real change is that the forty overs are split into two lots of twenty. I reckon it's a turn for the better. Gives you a second chance to embarrass yourself.'

'Speak for yourself,' grinned Stewart-Krabbs who, in 2017, had pipped Middlethorpe for next-to-last place in Ousedon CC's batting averages for the first time ever.

Middlethorpe frowned at his drinking companion. That wasn't in the script and if Stewart-Krabbs was going to go off-road on him and start ad-libbing, their carefully-prepared plan for bringing Baroness DeWitt to book was headed for a ravine. His aberrant co-conspirator needed to be brought to heel and quickly.

'NEVER... THE... LESS,' Middlethorpe responded firmly, his

voice raised a notch to accompany the meaningful scowl being cast in Stewart-Krabbs' direction, 'if the Double Tops format is good enough for the MCC, it's good enough for me!'

Stewart-Krabbs grinned again but this time returned to the prepared script with all the aplomb of an accomplished actor.

'What's the MCC got to do with it?' he responded with perfect timing. 'It was the England Cricket Board who agreed to let Ke-Ching launch Double Tops.'

'Correct. But from what I'm hearing, that's just the start of it. Through its sponsorship of English cricket Ke-Ching's got its feet under the MCC table and word is it's about to go one better. There's a pretty solid rumour doing the rounds that the company's using its financial muscle to gain itself a seat on the committee.

'You mark my words, if we don't see the MCC effectively being run by Ke-Ching in a couple of years then I'm a Chinaman, as it were.'

* * *

On the other side of the screen that separated the Stewart-Krabbs side of the bar from the DeWitt side, gamekeeper Twist was smiling a crooked smile into his pint. If played right, what he was overhearing could well save him from a visit to the Job Centre. His MCC committee member employer might yet be persuaded of his usefulness and grant him a stay of execution.

Five years, that's all he was looking for. Once he reached the newly-increased pension age of seventy he'd be free of the bloody DeWitt woman forever and be able to drink on his preferred, Stewart-Krabbs, side of the screen.

The screen hadn't always been there. Barry the landlord had seen fit to have it installed the day after the long-running

DeWitt/Stewart-Krabbs feud had finally spilled over and blood had been shed on the pub's not-inexpensive carpet.

Like all small settlements Ousedon had its fair share of family feuds but that ongoing between the DeWitts and the Stewart-Krabbs was legendary, dating back as it did to the English Civil War.

When Charles I lost his head to Oliver Cromwell in 1649, many of those who'd supported Cromwell found themselves rewarded with the estates of those who'd rather too flagrantly left their royalist heads peaking above the ramparts.

One such was the ancestral home of the current Baroness Daphne DeWitt whose monarchy-supporting predecessors, on the decapitated king's demise, had received a less-than welcome visit from the Cromwell-leaning forebears of Dinsdale Stewart-Krabbs.

The Stewart-Krabbs' first tenure of Ousedon Hall lasted just eleven years – the exact time it took for the British aristocracy to replace Cromwell with Charles II and to restore all confiscated property to its rightful owners – but the Stewart-Krabbs were nothing if not persistent.

Having become accustomed to the Hall's lordly pleasures, they simply decamped to a close-by manor house to plot their return and be a continuing thorn in the DeWitts' flesh.

A hundred years later and that return had been accomplished, the Stewart-Krabbs' capitalising fully on the DeWitts' failure to move with the times during Britain's eighteenth century agricultural revolution.

By converting early to mechanisation the Stewart-Krabbs plan to undercut the antiquated DeWitt operation and put it out of business had proved a complete success. Seeing their profit margins slump to the point at which they could no longer afford the Hall's upkeep, the DeWitts had been forced to put the estate up for sale.

With their roles now reversed, it was now the DeWitts' turn to plot revenge. Learning from past mistakes, the current baroness's forebears took a leaf out of the Stewart-Krabbs' book and pounced the moment it spotted a weakness in the Stewart-Krabbs estate management operation.

Buying into coal mining during Britain's industrial revolution the DeWitts quickly established a local coal supply monopoly for one reason and one reason only – to ensure fuel for the Stewart-Krabbs' steam traction engines never got beyond the farm gates.

Within months, ownership of the Hall changed hands yet again and over the next century-and-a-half it seesawed in direct proportion to the warring factions' capacities for ruining one another – much to the delight of the area's lawyers, estate agents and removal companies all of whom looked gleefully on, rubbing their hands over the prospect of firing hugely-inflated invoices off to one or other of the parties or both.

Their most recent fleecing had been that of Dinsdale Stewart-Krabbs, Baroness DeWitt returning to the Hall within months of Dinsdale falling for the beguiling advice of a highly-placed city contact to bet the family silver on the Lehman Brothers banking group just weeks before the 2008 financial crash.

When Lehman's collapsed and Dinsdale's contact was unmasked as a DeWitt stooge, the baroness re-took the Hall courtesy of the tidy settlement that accompanied her marriage of convenience to a title-chasing Afrikaner of the same name who'd cashed-in handsomely on the sale of blood diamonds to people with an even more despicable sense of ethical behaviour than himself.

In line with all previous changeovers, this one fanned the flames of the ongoing feud to maximum intensity but with one major difference.

In the past, the feud's primary skirmishes had been confined to the elegant portals of the House of Lords, the 'club' to which both parties held hereditary membership.

But with both clans' membership having been revoked under the Blair government's 1999 House of Lords Reform Act an alternative battleground had had to be found and there was only one other option – the sweeping, horseshoe-shaped bar of the Ousedon Arms.

Although there'd always been something of a sectarian divide between camps of pub regulars owing allegiance to one family or the other, successive Ousedon Arms landlords had ensured that no civil war re-enactments had been staged on their premises and in the feud's three hundred and fifty year history no aristocratic blood had ever been spilled within the pub's confines. That perfect record came to a violent and abrupt end the day Dinsdale Stewart-Krabbs handed over the keys to Ousedon Hall to Daphne DeWitt.

Along with the keys had come open accusations of market manipulation and the brandishing of a cricket bat under the baroness's nose, an action which only served to leave Dinsdale's leaking claret onto his shirt.

'Had it been anything but a cricket bat,' the secretly cricket-despising, MCC card-carrying baroness was quoted by the local paper as offering in mitigation to the charge of grievous bodily harm, 'I'd have gone easier on him.'

On walking free from the court courtesy of the Justice of the Peace baroness's connections on the bench, DeWitt had returned to the pub to make a derisory bid for the scene of her famous family victory only to find the screen now in place and Barry the landlord in no mind to sell up.

With the court case putting Ousedon firmly on the map the pub had become the focus of coachloads of aristocracy-obsessed gawkers dribbling with anticipation over the prospect of glimpsing the pub's roped-off section of bloodstained carpet.

Had they been allowed to take samples for analysis, Barry might have had his own set of charges to answer.

Following the incident, it had taken him precisely one pint to recognise the commercial potential of the section of carpet that had been the recipient of a dropped bottle of ink some years earlier and the resultant insolent stain had found its stock rising sharply in value.

From embarrassing blot it had become the nobility fixated's equivalent of an appearance of the Madonna to the spiritually simple-minded. Pilgrims flocked to the scene to worship at the altar of indisputable evidence proving beyond doubt that the blood flowing in the aristocracy's veins was indeed blue. Or, in this case, blue-black.

The screen too had been a stroke of commercial genius. Whilst serving its primary purpose of shielding the warring factions from one another's antagonistic glare, it provided extra wall space for the mounting of publicity material advertising the pub's neat, if rather tacky and over-priced, blood-feud brochure.

Containing photocopies of as many feud-related press clippings and historical documents as Barry had been able to lay his grubby hands on, sales of the brochure were keeping the Ousedon Arms' opportunist landlord amply supplied with S&M equipment and assorted lubricants.

* * *

As he sat under the pub's garish brochure-advertising displays on the DeWitt side of the screen, neither the feud nor the unsavoury out-of-hours activities of the pub's landlord were gamekeeper Twist's primary concern.

Right now, all he cared about was keeping his job, the cottage that went with it and Barry's drink dispensing cooperation.

Twist's credit, along with the patience of every other landlord in the vicinity, was exhausted and the storm clouds looming over his continued employment on the Ousedon Hall estate weren't helping.

But as he sat drinking in the contents of the conversation underway on the other side of the screen Twist felt an unaccustomed feeling of elation replacing his more customary utter dejection.

Sold in the right way to his MCC committee member employer, what he was hearing could yet save him from having to bed down with the birds he reared and rummage in the pub's waste bins for unfinished bottles of Spanish cooking sherry. And since it might even elevate him from estate wastrel to valued asset he forced his addled mind to concentrate and note down the bullet points.

* * *

When Twist stumbled from the bar some thirty minutes later, Simon Middlethorpe cast a satisfied glance at his drinking companion. Was that a smirk of smug self-satisfaction on the DeWitt estate gamekeeper's face?

He rather thought it was and if it was there for the reason the Ousedon Cricket Club co-conspirators thought it was, it was mission accomplished. Phase one of their ruse to get the baroness to shoot herself in the head through the broadcasting of a wholly fictitious horror story to the MCC committee was a complete success and it was all thanks to having a daughter unable to prevent herself crowing about a tip-off she'd had concerning the MCC and Ke-Ching.

'Can't say much about it at the moment,' Amber had teasingly told her father in her weekly phone call home, 'but it's big. Very big.

'Unless I'm very much mistaken, it concerns the very future of Lord's. But that's strictly between you and me for the time being. PLEASE don't go casting it around! Nothing's confirmed yet. I'm only telling you 'cos I thought you might be worried that a year of working for the "system" here might have fried my brain.'

Although he'd never dream of saying so to his darling daughter, it wasn't something that had occupied Simon Middlethorpe's thoughts greatly. To him, all media operations and all media folk were worthy of equal contempt regardless of whether they were private or state-run. In Middlethorpe's mind all worked to an agenda of some sort anyway and it seemed self-evidently clear from their content that none was above censoring news which ran counter to their own best interests.

So no, his daughter's tussles with the system that employed her hadn't interrupted his slumbers greatly.

What had, after Amber had rung off, were his imaginings of what, precisely, it was his daughter had uncovered.

On hearing the MCC, Lord's, Ke-Ching and China mentioned in the same breath, Middlethorpe's mind raced with possibilities.

It had long been rumoured that the MCC had hit a financial rock. Had they discovered in Ke-Ching a financial saviour prepared to do for Lord's what it'd done for county cricket via the Double Tops tournament? Surely the MCC would never open itself up to the humiliation of having to go cap in hand to the Chinese. But then again...

Middlethorpe's dreams that night were full of surrealistic images of dragons with cricket bats cavorting on an outfield littered with large denomination Chinese currency bills and when he awoke he knew he needed to see Stewart-Krabbs post haste. The dream had prompted the outline of a scurrilous subterfuge for settling the Ousedon Hall ownership issue in the Stewart-Krabbs' favour once and for all.

* * *

On being made privy to his friend's scheming stratagem, Stewart-Krabbs had had difficulty restraining himself. If it had the effect Middlethorpe imagined it would, not only would the return of the Stewart-Krabbs clan to the Hall be assured but it might even result in the English establishment chasing the clan's arch-nemesis from the shores of England itself.

Once the DeWitt gamekeeper had alerted his employer to the Middlethorpe/Stewart-Krabbs-implanted news that Ke-Ching was planning to use its financial clout to gain full control of the MCC specifically to eliminate opposition to its grand plan for turning Lord's into the biggest Chinese theme park in the western world, the MCC committee's reaction to hearing the news from DeWitt would be predictable.

Incensed, it would undoubtedly vote to have nothing more to do with the Chinese company and might even pass a resolution thanking the baroness for her unearthing of this crucial piece of information.

It was a resolution likely to be rescinded once the baroness's 'finding' was ultimately discovered to have all the substance of a waterlogged wicket and it was too late to win back either Ke-Ching's cooperation or its funds.

Without either, the MCC would find itself back in the financial hole the rumour mill said it had dug for itself and the noble baroness would find herself blackballed from polite society for having been responsible for losing the funding that would undoubtedly have saved one of Britain's national treasures.

OK, if the plan succeeded, it would also mean the MCC and Lord's probably facing an eventual visit from the official receiver but in the joint Middlethorpe/Stewart-Krabbs mind such an eventuality might not be amongst the worst of possible outcomes.

Having set Lord's test match ticket prices so high that only investment bankers and their crooked political friends could afford them, the MCC had not endeared itself to the grass roots cricket community and Middlethorpe and Stewart-Krabbs were not alone in thinking that the time had come for Lord's to be put in the hands of those who truly appreciated the game.

Seen increasingly as a body of men operating oblivious to the fact that the only flat caps to be seen at Lord's were those attached to the wheels of the hedge fund manager-owned Ferraris clogging the ground's car park, the MCC had become something of a cricketing pariah amongst the game's rank and file.

Unless they changed their ways, thought both Middlethorpe and Stewart-Krabbs, the time was rapidly approaching when the game's citizen cricketer wasn't going to take it anymore, rising up to reclaim the game on behalf of those who oiled their own bats, cut their own wickets and got their wives to make their own cricket tea sandwiches.

Ke-Ching had started it with the Double Tops competition. Now, thought the pair, it was time for the masses to build on their lead and oust those who kept them from the game and the ground they cherished.

It was time, they thought, for Lord's to become the people's ground and if the bailiffs did come knocking on the MCC's door, then that would be a mighty fine start.

With the club in receivership the way would be clear for a cooperative to take it off the receiver's hands and Lord's could be brought into collective grass roots cricketer ownership. Cromwell, thought Stewart-Krabbs, would approve.

* * *

He might have had Middlethorpe and Stewart-Krabbs done their homework properly.

By assuming not altogether accurately that DeWitt's membership of the MCC committee made her a cricket enthusiast of some distinction, they'd not only ensured their scheme's ultimate undoing but the baroness's wholehearted support for the Ke-Ching proposal.

The fit the baroness had had when appraised of the Lord's re-development plan by Twist was not of indignant outrage but of the giggles.

She'd always wondered why the Chinese had singled cricket out as a sport worthy of their support. Now it all gelled into place and DeWitt could not have been happier. She'd needed something to cheer her up after realising that Harry Wong's technology-use revelations weren't going to achieve the desired cricket-wrecking end product.

In the cold light of day once Wong had departed from her drawing room, DeWitt had had second thoughts about Ke-Ching being able to get its computerisation plans for the game rubber-stamped.

The more she thought about it, the more she could see her scheming fellow committee members smiling sweetly as they pocketed the Ke-Ching cash, welcoming Wong onto the board then closing ranks to ensure that everything he suggested was subjected to the infamous MCC foot-dragging consultation process. If it could be responsible for making Lord's the last major ground in the world to install floodlights thus losing it substantial day/night match revenue, it could certainly be employed to frustrate Ke-Ching's lofty ambitions.

So no, while frustration would undoubtedly be Ke-Ching's only reward for pumping millions into the MCC, the company would not be getting the baroness's vote. There was a very real danger that by giving it, she'd actually be helping save the one thing for which she had less time than the ban on hunting.

This ground redevelopment bit of news, on the other hand, was a very different matter. Not unaware that Stewart-Krabbs kept his ear close to the ground on world cricket issues, Twist's tip-off had been received with scarcely a hint of doubt as to its authenticity leaving Baroness DeWitt in jovial mood.

Knowing what she now knew, she could now throw her full and very considerable weight behind the proposal completely confident in the knowledge that its approval would ultimately achieve what she'd striven all her adult life to achieve. And what tickled her most was that should the Ke-Ching proposal get the committee's nod, it would have been the committee itself which would have effectively voted both itself and Lord's out of existence. DeWitt could hardly wait for the next committee meeting to convene.

When it did, a week later, she almost fainted with joy when committee chairman Sir Oliver Gainsborough announced that, by the slimmest of margins – casting a glance in the baroness's direction as he said it – the committee had grudgingly decided that it had little option but to accept the Chinese shilling.

The tipping point, he inferred, had clearly been the latest bit of news from the MCC's bank informing the committee that its investigations into the account hacking issue were proving 'more complex than at first appeared'.

Knowing bankspeak for 'don't hold your breath for an early reunion with your lost funds… if at all' when they heard it, most had held their noses while voting in favour. Most, but not all. There were three who'd had to stifle little yelps of delight, all of them certain they were privy to information that would ultimately seal Lord's fate.

While DeWitt was convinced she was sitting on Ke-Ching's

dirty little Lord's-wrecking secret, Lord Vernon Bleauforth and Sir Victor Turnball grinned in the satisfaction of knowing they were in possession of information which could ultimately prove the answer to the Lord's prayer.

Harry Wong's reaction to the news was equally ebullient. Now that his campaign to gain Ke-Ching a seat on the board of one of England's most prestigious bodies had reached a successful conclusion he could concentrate fully on his other two primary preoccupations – restoring his *guanxi* status and winning the Cricket World Cup.

Since achieving the second was heavily dependent on a successful outcome to the first, it was first things first. It was time to cast more spurious bait on Amber's water, feed her a wholly fictitious tissue of fabrication of his own making then reel both her and the western media establishment in.

* * *

For reasons that would ultimately become abundantly clear to Amber, Wong's choice of meeting place for the start of the reeling-in process was somewhat less conspicuous than the opulent setting of the Beijing Hotel, a place you only went if you wanted to be seen.

This time the rendezvous chosen was the vast, teeming entrance hall of the Beijing Central Railway Station.

'Come carrying a travel bag,' were Wong's instructions to Amber. 'Look for me and ask if the seat occupied by my own bag is vacant.'

Intrigued, Amber had followed Wong's cloak and dagger instructions to the letter and had found herself seated next to someone she barely recognised.

Wong's transformation from dapper, Savile Row-suited

business tycoon to unshaven clerk in the Ministry of Works was uncanny and, for Amber, slightly unnerving. Was what he had to tell her so sensitive it required him to abandon his true persona in favour of such an effective, nondescript disguise? Apparently so.

On the pretext of offering her a share of his plastic container of egg fried rice, Wong first muttered an instruction to just eat, not talk, followed by another to wait ten minutes then take the train shown on the ticket that was now in her pocket. Then he packed the container and disappeared into the heaving throng of equally shabby, equally nondescript Chinese travellers pushing and shoving their way to and from the platforms.

It was as well that Wong had said ten minutes. It took nine for Amber to match the Chinese characters shown on the ticket to the destination characters displayed on the departures board. As she boarded the train, she hoped to hell it hadn't said 'Tibet'. Not only did foreigners need a special permit to go there but she'd only brought one spare pair of knickers with her.

Fifteen minutes into the trip, Wong materialised next to her seat transmitting a 'follow me' message with his eyes.

She found him puffing on a cigarette in the smoking prohibition-ignored area between the carriages and not looking at her.

After a moment, in appalling English he offered her a cigarette, his expression pleading with her to take it despite knowing her to be a lifelong non-smoker.

'Oh, OK,' she yawned silently back, rolling her eyes in mock exasperation over what she saw as a wholly pointless exercise in furtive subterfuge. All they were going to discuss was cricket, not a top secret government plan for expanding Chinese influence around the world.

Or so she thought.

Writing up her mental notes later that evening after disembarking at a local station just outside Beijing and catching the next train back, Amber had had trouble keeping a straight face.

It wasn't just what he'd said, it was the way he'd used pantomime Chinglish to say it, deliberately mixing up the l's and r's presumably to put as much distance as possible between his real identity and that of the persona he'd adopted.

All this did, thought Amber, was to make it more intelligible to any secret service drone who might be listening in. It was Wong's affected Oxbridge accent they'd have had trouble with.

There were times when she'd struggled to understand it herself and the added layer of Chinese coolie-speak hadn't helped. All she could do was hope it hadn't led to any misunderstandings on her behalf. She had a story to write exposing Ke-Ching's sponsorship of English cricket as the vehicle the Chinese government had chosen for worming its way into British politics and somehow she had to write it so Rafferty didn't do what she was doing and cover the screen with a fine spray of incredulous spittle as he was reading it.

chapter twenty-one

The smile that spread across Harry Wong's face as he watched the China Central Television news a couple of days after his train ride with Amber would have lit up a small town. The commentator's furious denunciation of the Daily Grind story as a despicable British government conspiracy designed to discredit China was surely the moment he'd see his China Daily guanxi status fully restored to him.

Presented with such a golden opportunity to put the West firmly in its place for having had the audacity to print such a laughable, barefaced calumny about China, the authorities had gleefully grasped it with both hands and turned the issue to China's very distinct advantage.

By printing such an eminently unsupportable story, the western press had gifted China a rare chance to thumb its nose at a West more used to putting China's out of joint. If that didn't defuse the bomb that was Amber Middlethorpe and bring him back into favour with the authorities when it became known who'd engineered the story-planting ploy, Wong was at a loss to imagine what would.

While the commentary had Wong waltzing round his office, some five thousand miles away Rory McDermott was feeling rather less dance-inspired. As the man who'd not only commissioned the story but had fought to get it on the front page, the *Daily Grind*'s sports editor wasn't unaware of the consequences that would ensue should the apoplectic CCTV blowback sway the paper's publisher into believing McDermott had jumped the gun somewhat.

'Rafferty!' McDermott bawled. 'Gerrin here you idle bastard.' If McDermott was going down, he wasn't going down alone.

'Boss?'

'I'm expecting incoming from the top floor any moment re. THAT,' McDermott boomed, a quavering finger pointed at the CCTV English news channel playing on his screen. 'Comments?'

Rafferty focused on the screen from a standing position. You never sat down in McDermott's office unless invited and Rafferty knew from his editor's tone that he was more likely to be asked to a Buckingham Palace garden party.

'Isn't that what we'd expect them to say?' offered Rafferty hesitantly once the CCTV commentator's rant had run its course. 'Sounds like a standard non-denial denial to me.'

'It does, does it? You don't detect a whiff of gun smoke in the air?'

Rafferty thought for a moment.

'If there is, it's from the firing of blanks, I'd say. I mean, did they actually say in so many words that the story was wrong? That phrase "prejudiced reporting" sounded like something you'd get from any ministry caught with its pants down and trying to wriggle out of it by deflecting blame back on the media.'

'Hmmm. So if you were me you'd stand by the story?'

'Unless someone comes up with something concrete to rubbish it with, yes, I think I would.'

'Even if the Foreign Office issues "advice" to us that by not retracting it, we risk setting Sino-British relations back decades thereby losing substantial Chinese investment and the jobs that go with it?'

'Is it our fault that China didn't close the toilet door properly?' offered the subeditor timorously, resorting to something he vaguely recalled his ethics of journalism tutor offering during a class discussion on restrictions imposed on journalists embedded with the royal household.

'I don't know where you get this crap from,' growled McDermott, 'but something tells me you've a distance to travel before you get to sit where I'm sitting. It's both our necks on the block here so here's what I want you to do while I fend off the editor whose call should be coming in just about... now.'

Right on cue McDermott's phone rang and the sports editor snatched it up without giving it a chance to ring twice. As he did so, he waved Rafferty out of his office with a grabbing motion of an upturned clawed hand – the internationally-recognised news desk signal to lowly male operatives that two highly sensitive parts of his anatomy were at risk should there be any sign of leakage in a seriously contentious story.

Rafferty knew precisely what was being asked of him. To preserve his manhood, he needed to drop everything and measure the CCTV commentary against the *Grind* story's headline point, the one which openly accused the Chinese government of using its financial muscle to insinuate its way into the Marylebone Cricket Club's inner circle specifically to use the MCC's political connections to infiltrate Britain's seat of power.

Half an hour later he was back in McDermott's office bearing a sheaf of notes containing a verbatim transcript of the commentary with the primary issues highlighted and a brief summary of his own conclusions.

'So, lad,' said McDermott, this time indicating the chair to his subeditor, 'do we stand or fall?'

'Stand,' said Rafferty sitting. 'From what I can see, amongst the CCTV blather there's not one phrase I can spot that categorically refutes the story. It's just a mishmash of froth-at-mouth rhetorical bollocks designed to bark not bite.

'Take this one for example. The commentary says the Chinese government, quote, "condemns without reservation the British media's malicious attempt to subvert the truth by printing wicked calumnies". That's nothing but bureaucratic fart gas. There's nothing in it that actually denies the story's content.

'Likewise the part that says the government "wholeheartedly and absolutely rejects such scurrilous allegations". That's nothing more than defensive posturing if you ask me. And the bit that says the story "not only insults the integrity of China but shows the British media to be less than honest in its claim to be independent of government influence" isn't what I'd describe as fighting talk. Its aim is just to deflect attention away from the primary issue which, in my humble opinion, has not been denied. I still maintain that the story's got legs and should be allowed to stand without apology.'

'Even if it costs you your job?'

Rafferty felt the blood drain from his temples. His wife, newborn child and bank manager weren't likely to find journalistic principles as compelling as himself when it came to keeping bread on the table. Suddenly Rafferty was confronted with the real world staring him full in the face – the one that chewed principles up and spat them into the nearest bin the moment the bearer walked in through the newsroom door.

On the sports desk, Rafferty had always reckoned that ethical dilemma would extend only so far as deciding whether to print that picture of Tom 'Dreamboat' Daley on the diving board with one testicle hanging out.

While certain to improve sales it would never leave him facing a decision of this magnitude. Were the testicle test ever to arise he'd just do whatever his editor told him to do. Perhaps now, Rafferty thought, might be the time for taking the same tack and was just about to voice his thoughts when McDermott grinningly intervened.

'Relax, lad. If anyone's for the chop it'll be me. Deputy heads will roll and all that since you can bet your boots the editor's got his own neck covered even though it was him who had the final say on running the piece.

'For the moment though, it would seem that no blood is to be spilled. Both the editor and me agree with your assessment that the CCTV commentary was mostly bluster designed to put the wind up both us and the government.

'The government can do what it likes but for the *Grind* the story stands… and if you want my personal opinion, I reckon we've done the country a favour. Imagine cricket as run by Beijing. The very thought is enough to send a chill up your sporran.'

* * *

While McDermott and Rafferty were in conference, three others were either planned or in session. A meeting between the British Foreign Secretary and his top aides was shortly to be followed by a gathering of members of a slimmed-down MCC committee followed in turn by an assembly of departmental chiefs at the *China Daily*.

There was only one item on the agenda – what steps now to take in the light of China's vehement refutation of the *Grind*'s startling allegation.

To Foreign Office permanent secretary, Sir Xavier Ffawcett-Pugh, the answer was simple. The government should do what governments always did on such occasions – avoid saying anything that said anything.

The priority at this stage, he advised, was not to antagonise China lest Beijing erect obstacles to the import of British goods and services and withdraw its substantial support for the country's industrial sector.

With that in mind, Sir Xavier counselled, until firm evidence emerged to either support or demolish the allegation, the Foreign Office's response should be one of considered obfuscation and committed non-committal.

'As is standard operating procedure in such circumstances,' Sir Xavier advised his minister sagely, 'there's a case for initiating the helium option.'

'The what?' asked the permanent secretary's flustered minister.

'The *helium* option minister,' replied Sir Xavier's desiccated assistant Jacinta Crum with a barely concealed sigh of exasperation. Having to explain the shorthand Foreign Office code for one of the first principles of diplomatic procedure to a man charged with overseeing Britain's relations with the rest of the world wasn't something she'd expected to have to do at such a high level briefing.

'The one, minister, whose primary function is not only to make speech barely recognisable but to propel the balloon of controversy into the stratosphere of uncertainty, destination place or places unknown.'

'Ah,' said the minister. 'You mean subject it to an inquiry.'

'Couldn't have put it better myself,' responded Sir Xavier with the sort of supercilious insincerity that came with having 'served' thirteen ministerial chiefs during his Civil Service career.

'And, if I might be so bold minister, the more open-ended the better…?'

***

On being made privy to the Foreign Office's chosen response for tackling 'the Chinese question', the MCC committee – or the twenty-two members of it who'd been deemed suitable for an unscheduled gathering of the clan – decided to follow suit.

Convened in the private meeting room of the chairman's exclusive country club well away from Lord's lest the two deliberately left off the invite list got wind of the gathering, the coterie of invitees positioned themselves squarely on the fence.

'Fact is,' Gainsborough told the entire committee less Baroness DeWitt and the committee's newly-appointed Ke-Ching representative Harry Wong, 'what we have here is a decidedly sticky wicket. This, if I'm not mistaken, is a damned-if-we-do, damned-if-we-don't situation.

'If we accept the *Grind* story as gospel and opt to annul the Ke-Ching approval vote on the grounds of match fixing, so-to-speak, I'm sure I don't have to remind you that the Lord's balance sheet, well, won't. The promised Ke-Ching funds have yet to be credited to the MCC account.

'On the other hand, declare the story a shoddy fabrication and chances are we'll be accused of an even more heinous crime than that of bankrupting Lord's – the crime of colluding with the enemy.

'Take this course of action and we run the considerable risk of being seen to have taken China's thirty pieces of silver in return for promoting them up the metaphorical batting order as it were. Not only that but it could be taken as the MCC having no quibble with the Chinese view that the British media is no more than a runner for government batsmen.

'So, gentlemen,' continued the chairman after a moment's pause to let his assessment of the predicament sink in, 'the way

I see it, it's not unlike finding oneself halfway up the wicket with the ball already on its way in. Which end do we make for? Try to complete the run or scramble back to safety? We've all been there, so which is it?'

The extended collective scratching of follicly-challenged heads was eventually interrupted by Sir Victor Turnball who'd remained aloof and impassive throughout the Gainsborough state-of-play assessment.

'If I might offer my thoughts Mr Chairman...? Thank you. Well gentlemen, you might find it of some comfort to know that it would seem we are not alone in facing this unwholesome dilemma. Information has reached me that, until this morning, there were certain sections of government who found themselves in an equally perplexing position. They too found themselves stumped by the Chinese question until it was realised that they had four hundred years of experience of dealing with such problematic situations to draw upon.

'That being the case, might I suggest we take a leaf out of the book of some of the best brains in Whitehall and approach this issue in like fashion?'

A general and highly relieved nodding of approval ensued. Thank God, the nods said, for Turnball and his highly-placed connections, ones whose ears would most definitely be targeted for the fitting of Chinese hearing aids if the *Daily Grind* story was to be believed.

'Thank you. Well, to strip the Whitehall stratagem down to its jockstrap, they've effectively declared play suspended due to bad light and come off until it improves. My suggestion is that we follow suit and do the same.

'While some sort of response is expected of us, until evidence emerges to either support or refute the allegation it does seem that the only response possible at this stage is the issuing of a statement to the effect that the committee is studying the issue closely. That, at least, should hold both China and the British media at bay until the shine goes off the new ball.'

***

Over in the Chinese capital the *China Daily*'s editorial mandarins sat around the conference table grinning like the stone lions standing guard outside the paper's Beijing headquarters. The UK Foreign Office and MCC statements hot in from London provided just the escape route they were seeking to extract themselves from a ticklish dilemma of their own.

After dutifully running Beijing's immediate response to the *Grind*'s allegations word-for-word, the paper's editor knew western eyebrows would arch knowingly if the paper/ government left it at that and opted not to follow it up with a similarly apoplectic opinion piece accusing the western press of gross hypocrisy. Of being only too willing to breach the code of journalism ethics they so often accused China of breaching and of descending to the depths of printing wholly erroneous alarmist sensationalism for the sake of sales.

Duly crafted, the editor had presented the piece to the paper's editorial 'trustees' for rubber-stamping only to have it returned with a rather surprising 'advice' note attached.

The trustees, the note said, were minded to 'advise' the editor to 'consider' postponing publication of the piece on the grounds that drawing further attention to the British press allegations at this stage might not be in China's best interests.

As perverse as the advice sounded in view of China having gained the decided upper hand with its denunciation of the *Grind*'s allegations, the editor wasn't unaware of the consequences that would ensue should he disregard said 'advice'.

Following that course of action wasn't likely to be in his own best interests and, presumably, his 'advisors' in the Great Hall of the People had their reasons for not pressing home their advantage.

Could it have something to do with ongoing negotiations concerning China's impending takeover of certain oil production facilities in Britain's sector of the North Sea? The editor rather thought it could and for that reason alone he took the decision to spike his lovingly-crafted piece and turn his attention elsewhere.

But only until the arrival on his desk of a dispatch from the paper's London correspondent reporting the UK Foreign Office/MCC's limp-wristed response to China's apoplectic refutation of the allegations.

This dispatch changed everything. In the editor's opinion, by not denying outright that it was being helped out of a financial hole by a Chinese company, the MCC had tacitly confirmed it was, thus providing the perfect opportunity for a follow-up regulation China self-glorification piece, the only sort of news not needing to be cleared by a power higher than the editor himself.

An hour later, the editor's re-crafting of his correspondent's dispatch read like something straight out of China's propaganda ministry.

Topped with the headline *China Races to Cricket Rescue* the piece took the form of a chest-puffing diatribe trumpeting Ke-Ching's altruism in offering to come to the assistance of financially-troubled western cultural icons like Lord's, an icon in which, the editor said, China could have no possible self-interest.

On revealing the piece to his editorial colleagues, the editor beamed contentedly knowing the piece achieved three things in one. It satisfied everything the paper's overseers expected of a *China Daily* story, it told the *Daily Grind* and its ilk where to get off and it helped justify his decision to keep his most troublesome foreign member of staff where he could see her.

* * *

No one was more surprised than Amber when no one came for her. With her byline all over the *Daily Grind* piece, the dreaded dead-of-night hammering on her door wasn't only expected, it was, thought Amber, a racing certainty. So much so, in fact, that as soon as she'd filed the story she'd begun packing. There wouldn't be much time when the secret service goons arrived to ship her off to the airport.

To her sleepless amazement, no knock had ever come and, even more astoundingly, the *China Daily*'s security chief wasn't lying in wait for her at the paper's gate the next day. Waved through by the guards with hardly a glance at her ID, Amber's emotions turned from contented resignation-to-the-inevitable to worry.

For some time now she'd suspected her time in China might be having an effect on her psychological well-being. Had she now finally gone over the edge and started having hallucinogenic delusions? Had she just imagined she'd written the *Grind* story shortly after filing the promised puff piece on Chinese cricket for the *China Daily*?

If she had, what was it doing there right in front of her eyes on the *Grind*'s website? Was that the product of paranoid delirium too? She dearly hoped not. Its existence, she was certain, was her ticket both out of China and into a dream job on one of Britain's better nationals.

***

While Amber was trying to work out why she was still in the country, Harry Wong was smiling to himself in response to the cooing tone coming down the line from the *China Daily* editor. It was a tone which told Wong his *guanxi* status had not only been returned to him but restored with interest.

'Ah, Wong,' purred the editor, 'as one who's spent time in the United Kingdom, I'm wondering if you've been keeping abreast of recent events concerning that country and China?'

'I think I might have seen something,' said Wong vaguely, fingering the print-outs of the *Grind* and *China Daily* cricket stories that never left his possession should the editor call at an inopportune moment.

'Some garbage concerning China taking control of the game of cricket in order to gain access to British politicians, wasn't it? A story China has subsequently roundly demolished.'

'Exactly so,' said the editor not fooled by Wong's vagueness for a moment. Wong's earlier plea to the editor to get Amber taken off the Chinese cricket story until, in Wong's words, 'the moment was right' had returned to the editor in upper case bold the moment he was alerted to the *Grind*'s scurrilous allegations.

While, for reasons of 'face', the editor knew Wong could never openly admit to being the source of a story that turned a problem into an opportunity for the paper, he also knew the Hong Konger would still be expecting some sort of show of recognition for his part in bringing Amber to heel and was only too happy to oblige. His name was also on Wong's *guanxi* list and was rather keen it remained there.

'As I'm sure you're more than well aware,' he continued in a tone intended to convey that recognition, 'the story was a complete fabrication and one which has now come back to bite the running dog imperialist British media in a very delicate place. They couldn't have done a better job of humiliating themselves if they'd tried.

'But what really puts the chilli in the hotpot is the fact that the story was written by someone of both our acquaintances. A certain troublesome foreigner who, until this incident, was seen as something of a liability to the *China Daily*...'

Wong smiled to himself. With the word 'until' issuing from the editor's own lips, Wong knew all his *guanxi* worries were over.

'Now,' the editor went on, 'it would seem, you have actually brought us an asset – one whose talents are just what we've been looking for. If said asset can be persuaded to report one fabrication to those who would seek to do harm to the People's Republic, who's to say that a repeat performance might not be achieved given the right encouragement...'

Wong smiled again and once the editor had rung off, sat back in his chair and breathed out for the first time in months. With the tiger he'd sought to tame now having a tracking device fitted and a team of dedicated handlers guiding it down paths of their own choosing, what could possibly go wrong?

* * *

The tiger's thoughts, meanwhile, were running along similar lines. What HAD gone wrong? By now she should be halfway to the UK dreaming of sinking a bottle of expensive wine with her friends to celebrate the offer of a job on the *Daily Grind* and the addition of a *persona non grata* stamp across her Chinese visa.

Instead, she was still at her *China Daily* desk doing exactly what she'd been doing before her piece had hit the *Grind*'s front page. It was as if the piece had never appeared.

The absence of any reaction from Bo Ling seemed to confirm it. Apparently oblivious of any untoward story having appeared in the British press, her would-be suitor was not only not ignoring her but behaving absolutely normally, slithering up to her desk on the pretext of checking the drivel that covered her screen and lingering longer than he needed to.

Only on being called away to assist another colleague did she discover the real reason for his visit. Along with the garlic, ginger, fish sauce and spring onion stench he left behind was a note poked under her computer keyboard.

'Call Ding from a public phone,' it read. 'Important.'

chapter twenty-two

Mixed emotions hardly described Sir Victor Turnball's feelings the day he found his tip-off splashed all over the *Grind*'s front page without warning.

While the piece could hardly have done a better job of demolishing China's devious cricket takeover plan, the timing of the demolition could have been better. Exposing China's true intentions was supposed to happen *after* the MCC had banked the Ke-Ching cheque, not before, and as he read through the article Turnball saw his whole Lord's preservation strategy unravelling before his eyes.

His mistake, it was now clear, was trusting McDermott to keep his word that he'd refrain from running any story concerning Ke-Ching and the MCC until Turnball had approved the final version.

By inserting the condition and not mentioning the plan he and Bleauforth had cooked up for relieving Ke-Ching of its cash, Turnball had convinced himself all his bases were covered. Should it look like McDermott was getting ready to print the piece before the Ke-Ching funds had landed, Turnball could play the delay card.

Unfortunately, Turnball was now realising, expecting the worker ants of today's sales-obsessed, reptile-infested media world to remain faithful to unwritten agreements and to ensure their stories were watertight before going to press was yesterday's thinking.

With scoop now trumping accuracy on all fronts, fact-checking had become as outdated as the wearing of whites on a cricket field, the end result of which was the appearance of a piece in the *Grind* which blew Turnball's whole strategy out of the water.

Not only that, but when, not if, Ke-Ching withdrew its MCC sponsorship offer on being unmasked by the *Grind*, and when, not if, he was eventually revealed as the source of the guts of the story, he'd have a very painful decision to make – either take it on the chin and lose everything he'd worked for or sell Bleauforth down the river.

It hadn't taken long to decide which of the two wickets was the more valuable and Turnball was on the point of initiating Operation Run Bleauforth Out when suddenly an alternative hit him.

Of course! Every contentious article had its Achilles heel – a failing that could be played on to 'encourage' its publisher into printing a retraction.

This one's was the very angle on which the story's primary news point was based. By venturing down the path of political interference, the piece left itself wide open to a bit of political interference of Turnball's own making.

Once McDermott had been made aware of the shaky ground on which he'd chosen to set up camp, the *Grind*'s sports editor might not be so dogged in his determination to stick with the story and Wong and Ke-Ching might yet be prevented from walking.

* * *

McDermott wasn't altogether surprised to see Turnball weaving his way through the newsroom en route to the sports editor's office just hours after Amber's article appeared. The greater surprise would have been *not* receiving a visit from the man who'd sparked the *Grind* investigation in the first place.

'So? Where is it?' demanded McDermott with a gleeful grin.

'If it's champagne you're referring to, I have to inform you that it's still on ice,' replied Turnball in a tone of similar temperature. 'The time for the popping of corks has had to be postponed for the not indeterminate future.'

McDermott stared blankly at his visitor. That wasn't in the script. Turnball should surely be hopping around in jubilation over the publication of a story that went way beyond the information Turnball had supplied and surely put paid to any sort of Chinese interference in MCC activities.

'Fact is,' said Turnball, frost forming on every syllable, 'word on the street suggests that the article in question has left certain official toes feeling a trifle trampled-on.'

McDermott's grin went the same way as his hopes for a rejuvenating mid-morning glass of Veuve Clicquot. Turnball's solicitor's-clerk-in-possession-of-a-writ face told the *Daily Grind* man to prepare himself for a rather less palatable mouthful than the one for which he'd been hoping.

'Fact is,' Turnball went glacially on, 'I'm getting hints that certain influential figures in the Whitehall firmament are less than worshipful of your story. From what I'm hearing, the mandarins are more than a little miffed at having had the wind taken out of their sails.

'Not that they're saying the *Grind*'s contention is *completely* wrong, you understand, it's just that it doesn't *completely* tally with their own understanding of the matter in hand. Information received suggests they're showing concern that the contents of the piece as it stands might conflict with the general interests of those most closely appraised of said matter's full implications.'

'Mind if we have that in English?' snapped McDermott who'd been looking forward to a celebratory snifter, not an editorial enema.

'Well, to put it in *Daily Grind* language,' said Turnball, 'the stiffs on the hill think you might have over-cooked the goose a tad and that by so-doing the likelihood of any golden Oriental eggs being laid in Britain in the foreseeable future has been rendered somewhat improbable.'

'Let's try again,' said McDermott with a snarl. 'What you're trying to say is that *their* mandarins have told *our* mandarins that *their* administration isn't altogether impressed at having had their little game rumbled and that there'll be repercussions unless *our* mandarins don't lean on *us* to withdraw the allegation. That it?'

'Partly,' replied Turnball. 'As I understand it, the government is in the middle of a series of delicate negotiations with Beijing re. inward investment and the *Grind* story hasn't exactly served to engender a relaxed atmosphere during the coffee breaks.

'Between you and me though,' continued Turnball with a conspiratorial air, 'I think there might be rather more to it than that. Word is that once the discussions are concluded, the Foreign Office is planning to ask our Chinese friends to explain themselves re. an even more worrying development than the one that's central to the *Grind* story.

'Indications are that said development makes the *Grind* story look both anaemic and misleading and that the paper's interests might be best served through revisiting the piece in the near term with a view to making certain adjustments to its content.'

'Fuck me, Turnball,' exploded McDermott. 'I've had some warnings-off in my time but that one not only takes the jaffa cake but serves to reinforce what I've always thought. You really are in the pay of the Chinese. What you've just said isn't a million miles from the rebuttal of our story carried by Chinese TV earlier this morning. A more suspicious mind than mine might be tempted to conclude that some collusion is ongoing between Beijing and London.'

'Since I've yet to see China's response, I couldn't possibly comment,' lied Sir Victor, staring out of the window to avoid meeting McDermott's glaring eye as he geared up for the casting of the final piece of wholly imaginary bait he was certain the *Grind*'s sports editor would find impossible to resist.

'All I can say at this point is this. Whilst not being privy to precisely what it is the Foreign Office has up its sleeve, I *am* persuaded that its significance is such that were the *Grind* to retreat from its current position and await developments, not only would it not be disappointed in the outcome but that certain disappointments caused by said article's premature publication prior to it being checked for discrepancies might be overlooked.'

'Look Turnball,' said McDermott, his voice rising in irritation over his uninvited visitor's apparent inability to get beyond the flirtation stage, 'even if I was tempted by your – or should I say the Foreign Office's – "suggestion" it's too late to retract the piece now anyway. In the light of China's pitiful non-denial denial, the editor has already decided to stick with what we've said. The story stands and I don't give a toss what your spooky Foreign Office chums are offering to get us to cave in to their "advice". You can go back and tell 'em the *Daily Grind*, unlike this country it seems, is not for sale. End of.'

On his way out of the *Grind* building, Turnball's lips twisted in bewilderment as he tried to take in what had just transpired.

Unable to recall the last time one of his carefully thought-out ruses had been so comprehensively chewed up and spat back in his face, he felt yet another layer of emotion added to the stratigraphy of unaccustomed feelings that had begun weighing on him since first spotting Amber's article.

Despondency was now jostling for pole position with astonishment, exasperation and despair. Was he losing his touch? If he was, he'd better get it back sharpish before that afternoon's meeting of the MCC committee's inner circle. Getting his star chamber colleagues not to over-react to the *Grind* article was vital if his Ke-Ching fleecing plan was to stand any chance at all of being put back on the rails.

As Turnball strode stiff-backed in the direction of the *Grind* exit en route to Gainsborough's country club, McDermott slumped in his chair to reflect on what he'd just heard and on what he was grudgingly prepared to admit might not have been the most profitable way of responding to it.

What he'd said, he decided ruefully, wasn't an altogether accurate depiction of what it was he felt.

Contrary to his spluttered denunciation of Turnball's Foreign Office offer, he did give a toss about it. He gave a very substantial toss. If it was something that would consign Amber's story to also-ran territory, he wanted it. Badly. But, on behalf of his editor, he'd just burned that particular boat so there seemed little point in crying about it. Unless…

'Rafferty! Get Middlethorpe on the phone. Tell her her story's got new legs and that the *Grind* is relying on her to get them perambulating…'

* * *

While Turnball was on his way to the MCC inner sanctum meeting trying to work out how to win his colleagues round while distancing himself from a story that could leave the club penniless, Amber Middlethorpe was also in motion.

Sitting in a taxi on her way back from the Beijing Central railway station, Amber was also trying to work something out.

Was it was purely a coincidence that Ding's choice of venue for a clandestine rendezvous was the same as Wong's? From what she'd just heard, she wouldn't have been in the least surprised to learn that the tale Ding had just imparted had come straight from the clerk in the Ministry of Works persona Wong had chosen for his own covert meeting with her. It was certainly delusional enough.

So delusional, in fact, that Amber was at a loss to imagine what any sensible editor might make of it. If the contents of her first piece sounded like something Lewis Carroll might have dreamt up, this one was pure Kafka and it was only the fact that the *Grind* had printed her previous offering that she was even thinking of filing it.

It was her first story's front page position more than anything else that finally convinced her that fact really could be stranger than fiction. Not only had it propelled her from obscurity to the outer fringes of B-list celebrity status overnight but had served to remove any doubt that the story was nothing more than the crazed product of her own, China-activated, psychological derangement. Seeing her name on the story was proof, surely, that she had yet to succumb to China's best efforts to unhinge her.

But as she frantically transcribed her recording of her conversation with Ding into note form on the way back to her apartment, the notes told her not to be so hasty. China, they seemed to be saying, hadn't finished with her yet and Amber felt the spectre of derangement rematerialising at her shoulder.

Go on, it whispered in her ear, file it… and see what reaction you get from an editor who must already be suspecting you're one chopstick short of a pair.

Thus preoccupied, Amber might have done better than to snatch up the ringing phone as she stepped in through her apartment door. In an eerie pre-emption to the call she knew she'd eventually have to place to him, Rafferty was on the line squawking unstoppably about there being more to this story than first met the eye.

Dig deeper, he'd commanded, and when you have, file a summary of anything you turn up *tout* bloody *suite*. And with that he was gone, leaving her staring at the receiver and replaying the conversation in her head, a conversation to which she'd contributed just three words – 'hello', 'right' and 'oh' in that order.

It took two cups of strong coffee for the message contained in Rafferty's Gatling gun delivery to dawn on her. If she was going off her trolley, she wasn't going off it alone. From Rafferty's skeletal account of events transpiring subsequent to the appearance of her story, it sounded like it was contagious.

It had even infected the 'powers-that-be' he'd mentioned in his call, powers that had all but confirmed the existence of a political dimension to the story that went way beyond the scope of her earlier piece.

'Well,' she thought as she finally took her coat off, 'at least that gives me *carte blanche* to file Ding's delusions,' and with that she sat down to muse on how much of the atomic bombshell he'd just dropped in her lap she dared include in her report. Should she, for instance, make reference to the reason Ding had given for deciding to drop it?

* * *

It wasn't for the reason she'd supposed. Yes, he was still fuming over his manager's decision to keep the cricket team at its training base over Chinese New Year but that wasn't the half of it. To compound the felony, Ding had discovered that should China qualify for the 2019 Cricket World Cup, the management had decided that the country's squad would contain not one home-grown Chinese player.

It was while Ding was checking the International Cricket Council's book of World Cup rules and regulations that he'd come across the incriminating evidence. Picking up the book from the team manager's desk while the manager was in a meeting, a piece of paper had fluttered to the floor.

Although Ding had tried not to look, it had been difficult not to notice that the paper contained some twenty names, all of them of Pakistani origin, arranged under the heading 'World Cup Visas Acquired'.

After every name the same date had been added – 17 May 2015 – four years to the day before the Chinese team would, if they qualified, be arriving in London to play a series of warm-up games in the run-up to the World Cup finals.

Ding hadn't needed a translator to tell him what was going on. The management was playing the foreign mercenaries game to make sure China didn't lose face through being humiliated in the competition's group stage.

It was all quite legal. ICC rules on player eligibility for its competitions allowed affiliate ICC members like China to field as many non-nationals as they liked provided those non-nationals could show they'd been residents of their adopted ICC affiliate country for four years prior to the start of any ICC competition.

Few countries had ever taken full advantage of the dispensation but there were precedents and this slip of paper convinced Ding that China was on the verge of following the lead the United Arab Emirates had set a quarter of a century earlier.

With no cricketing pedigree or history of its own, the petrodollar-flush UAE had decided to effectively buy the 1994 ICC Trophy – a competition devised by the ICC for the world's economy class cricketing nations – by hiring-in a squad of quality players from the Indian subcontinent for the duration of the tournament.

Despite the bad taste the UAE's victory left in the mouths of the likes of Kenya who'd organised the competition and had high hopes of winning it, the rules on player eligibility for ICC competitions had never been tightened and now it seemed that China was about to do a UAE at the World Cup proper.

Ding was not amused.

As much as he wanted China to impress the world with its cricketing prowess, he knew that what the management was intending wasn't only unnecessary but could backfire badly on his motherland.

Ding had seen how his fellow countrymen's skills had developed to the point at which they wouldn't look out of place in any competition featuring the world's top cricket nations. By sidelining them in favour of a group of imported mercenaries with questionable resident visas, China was in danger of losing all the face it might have gained by fielding a one hundred percent Chinese side.

But there was nothing Ding could do about it. Any approach to China's cricket management on the issue would be tantamount to a confession of having intruded illicitly into the management's private affairs and he valued his job and his neck too much for that.

So, taking a leaf out of the management's own book, he'd decided to co-opt a bit of outside help for himself. Help which took the form of the western media's current China correspondent of the hour – one Amber Middlethorpe. It was time, he'd decided, that the world should know what REALLY lay behind China's interest in both English cricket and the MCC. It was time to relay to the rest of the world the full story as told to him by a drunken uncle whose job it had been to collate important politburo documents for the government archive, one of which had left him scratching his head over where to file it.

Where on Earth, the uncle had slurred with derisive mirth to his nephew at the old man's retirement day feast, would you file a government strategy paper detailing plans to employ the game of cricket as the means for implanting Chinese politics in the White House?

Ding knew, and it wasn't in the archives. That'd teach the bastards to stitch his cricket mates up.

chapter twenty-three

Amber Middlethorpe sat staring at a computer screen that remained as stubbornly blank as her mind.

No matter how she tried to present it, the end-product of a story that had more corners than a geodesic dome and all the credibility of a political party's election manifesto refused to read as anything other than the manic gibberings of one recently returned from an hallucinogenic voyage to the furthest reaches of a parallel universe.

Having spiked every attempt at writing it, Amber was rapidly coming to the conclusion that whatever she produced, its contents would still leave her mentors on the *Grind* snorting with dismissive derision and wondering what it was she'd been smoking.

It was the slurred, disembodied voice of her dipsomaniac Glaswegian journalism ex-tutor which finally broke the logjam.

'Stop fooking aboot,' she heard him commanding out of the ether. 'What was it I counselled the news-confused to do in such circumstances? Take a dram. Then another. Then just write the fooking thing.'

In desperation she decided to follow his advice for once, uncorked a bottle of surprisingly palatable Chinese burgundy and plunged in with hardly a thought for form or structure.

Twenty-four hours, a trawl of the internet, a brief nap and another bottle of wine later, the result of her labours – intended to resemble the closest thing to an extended investigative feature as she could manage under the circumstances – stared accusingly back at her from her screen.

'Nice try,' it seemed to be saying, 'but who in their right mind is going to believe *that*?'

'Not my problem!' she screamed at the machine. 'Who am I to question the content? I'm just the messenger!' And with that she closed her eyes, conjured up the image of a pair of hands washing one another and punched 'send'.

* * *

Rafferty's eyes did the exact opposite on discovering Amber's copy in his inbox several days before anything was expected.

'Hi,' the contents read. 'Is this the sort of thing you had in mind?':

FINISHING WHAT GENGHIS KHAN STARTED
EXCLUSIVE – CHINA'S SECRET WORLD DOMINATION MASTERPLAN REVEALED
by Amber Middlethorpe

Beijing, 26 February 2018 – A shadowy Chinese plot to infiltrate to the heart of western politics and spread Beijing's growing global influence westwards goes way beyond anything previously suspected, the *Daily Grind* has learned.

Sources close to China's leaders have told the paper that Beijing's plan for gaining a foothold in Britain's Parliament – as earlier revealed by the *Grind* – is just a stepping stone to getting China-friendly politicians elected to the highest offices of US government.

Thwarted in its original aim of infiltrating US politics through economic means, China is said to have turned to using America's allies to help it penetrate the US citadel by the back door.

European countries who accepted Chinese support to help them recover from the 2008 financial crash are about to be presented with Beijing's bill for the service. Starting with Britain, China plans to coerce them into having no alternative but to assist Beijing with its US infiltration scheme.

Speaking on condition of anonymity, the *Grind*'s sources say internal Chinese government documents they've seen reveal that Britain's 'special relationship' with the US has made it China's number one coercion target and that China has already hatched a plot to ensure full UK compliance.

British government ministers will shortly find themselves coming under Chinese pressure from inside the Houses of Parliament themselves, entry to which Beijing is fully confident of gaining thanks to the good offices of a wholly unlikely, highly improbable and totally unsuspecting intermediary.

Without knowing it, the intermediary selected to act as China's conduit into the Westminster corridors of power is, bizarrely, the English cricket establishment, a choice one can only begin to comprehend by first understanding how the UK and the rest of Europe found itself in Beijing's financial pocket following the 2008 global financial crash.

Although never officially disclosed, documents seen by the sources reveal that China played a pivotal role in helping European countries recover from the crash.

According to the documents, not only did Beijing effectively save the euro but channelled billions into European economies facing collapse in the wake of their crippling bank bail-out programmes, the UK economy in particular.

China is said to have been only too happy to help out. Europe's impending financial collapse gave it the perfect opportunity to do to Europe what it had already done to the developing world – colonise it economically.

China started the process by buying into companies European governments were determined should not go to the wall.

Between 2008 and 2012, European companies coming under Chinese control included carmakers Volvo and MG Rover, France's GDF Suez oil and gas concern and Portugal's state power supply utility EDP and once Europe's governments saw how China's presence was helping stabilise these companies' fortunes, Beijing found itself being actively courted to invest further.

The powers-that-be in Beijing's Great Hall of the People were quick to take up the invitation, reacting by spreading China's investment net wider to encompass targets deemed less financially vulnerable.

Buoyed by the successful takeover of the likes of London's Thames Water, French carmaker Peugeot-Citroen and even British cereal maker Weetabix, Beijing's buy-out confidence soared. With nothing apparently proscribed from receiving Chinese funding, the pace of China's inward investment into Europe rocketed.

Although total public and private Chinese investment in western enterprises since 2008 is difficult to quantify, it's now certainly well in excess of the $1.5 trillion understood to have been injected into the West's industrial sectors by the Chinese Investment Corporation, a state body set up to utilise the $5 trillion currently in China's bulging foreign exchange reserves.

Once China had gained Europe's confidence with its commercial sector bail-out programme, Beijing moved swiftly into phase two of its western influence-grabbing scheme – the offer of clandestine financial assistance to governments hit hard by the crash.

Officially, China's only help to Europe came through the channelling of European economy rescue funds through the International Monetary Fund.

That, say the *Grind*'s sources, is some distance from the truth.

Ever since 2010, they say, Beijing had been using a complex web of intermediaries to secretly snap up European sovereign debt specifically to protect the euro and thus its own foreign exchange holdings, a quarter of it held in euros.

China's secret intervention in the Eurozone crisis – said to have been kept from becoming public knowledge lest news of Europe having to go cap in hand to Beijing sparked a further weakening of the euro – worked. By late 2013 the euro had recovered lost ground and financial analysts changed their tune from Eurozone doom to one of survival.

It was the moment China had been waiting for. With Europe now heavily in debt to China, the *Grind*'s sources say Beijing felt the time had come for making recipients of its funds an offer they'd have difficulty refusing.

In return for a modest involvement in running the economies it had helped save, China was prepared to write-off a proportion of those countries' Chinese debts.

Beijing never got to make the offer. Just as it was about to, Europe's mood changed.

With rumours circulating over just how big China's involvement in the European economy had grown, analysts who'd earlier lauded Beijing for riding to the rescue of European industry at last woke up to the parallels between this intervention and China's earlier economic colonisation of the developing world.

China's response was short and simple. Its only interest, it insisted, lay in achieving win-win outcomes for all concerned. By helping save western economies China would, by association, be saving its own. As an export-orientated nation, it said, China needed its traditional export markets to thrive in order to survive.

The critics weren't fooled. If win-win was really China's motivation, they argued, might one not expect to see recipients of Chinese funds 'winning' more than one goal to China's five?

The reaction came as a surprise to a Beijing – but only until it discovered who was behind it.

Europe, its investigations revealed, was being leaned-on by the US.

Alarmed by what it perceived as China's attempt to do in Europe what it had done in Africa, Asia and Latin America – gain political influence via the economic back door – the administration of the then-president Barack Obama had begun urging Europe to remain resilient in the face of Chinese pressure.

Despite the size of the Chinese-owned US debt mountain – then totalling some one trillion US dollars – Obama had always remained mulish in the face of China's determined economic arm-twisting. In 2012 he'd even gone so far as to invoke national security consider-ations to block the takeover of US oil major Unical by the Chinese National Offshore Oil Corporation and to limit the activities on US soil of Chinese telecoms giants Huawei and ZTE.

By the middle of his second term in office, Obama's resistance to the Chinese economic invasion had not only hardened but had become positively hostile. So much so that when China declared that the US dollar should be replaced as the world reserve currency by REDYs – a basket of currencies combining China's renminbi (more commonly known as the yuan), the euro, the dollar and the Japanese yen – the then-president embarked on a campaign of persuading US allies to oppose the move.

Coming on the back of seeing its economic colonisation plan for the US effectively blown out of the water, this slap in the face, say the *Grind*'s sources, was the last straw for China's hardliners.

With the yuan already in common usage in international trade transactions, Middle East-China oil trades in particular, China's leaders were persuaded by politburo hawks that the US action warranted a 'reprisal-with-Chinese-characteristics'.

The time had come, they said, to launch Operation Dragon's Breath, the official name for China's contingency plan for infiltrating US politics.

Based on the Chinese martial arts principle of turning an opponent's aggression back on itself, Operation Dragon's Breath had been devised as a twin-pronged strategy for using the US electoral system to defeat itself.

While the US government was being distracted by pleas from America's China-coerced allies to soften its anti-China stance, China would be using its financial muscle not only to get Beijing-sympathetic Chinese Americans elected to high US political office but to ensure that two contest the 2020 US presidential election, one for the Democrats, one for the Republicans.

As devious as the plan was designed to be, its designers were realistic enough to recognise that, in the final analysis, its success hinged on gaining the confidence of the American people themselves. Beijing was never going to get one if its stooges elected to the White House if it didn't first win the hearts and minds of the electorate and for that to happen the US voter had to be won over to the prospect of seeing ethnic Chinese occupying high political office.

To achieve that outcome Beijing built a crucial soft power confidence-winning element into Operation Dragon's Breath.

Known as the Global Institutional Support Scheme, the GISS initiative was designed to achieve two goals in one. Apart from blurring the edges of China's political ambitions in the West, GISS was established to replace a pair of earlier, wholly counter-productive Chinese charm offensives which hadn't charmed anyone.

As contentious as the opening of some five hundred so-called Confucius Chinese cultural institutes around the world had been, the suspicion accompanying their arrival paled into insignificance next to the furore that greeted Beijing's proud 2014 announcement that it intended to launch a programme to help save a panoply of financially-threatened western cultural icons.

When it emerged that Chinese state funds were being earmarked for the saving of the Eiffel Tower, the Acropolis and the Colosseum western commentators reacted with outrage. Hijacking the minds of western students attending the Confucius Institutes was one thing. But pocketing some of the West's most treasured national symbols? That, they ranted, could simply not be allowed.

The West's reaction, say the *Grind*'s sources, caught Beijing on the hop. Expecting gratitude, not outright hostility, for its generous western icon preservation offer, China's leaders met in urgent session to deliberate on how the programme had gone awry and what, if anything, could be done to salvage it.

The outcome, say the sources, was pure Chinese political fudge. With the preservation of face uppermost in the leaders' minds, rather than simply scrapping the programme outright, the decision was taken to recalibrate it and, in mid-2014, China's GISS initiative was born.

At its heart was the application of the Confucius Institute funding model to the western icon-saving scheme.

Like the Confucius Institutes – financed by channelling state funds through the Chinese non-governmental educational organisation Hanban – money for the icon support programme should, said China's soft power strategists, be channelled in future through an intermediary with no obvious links to the state apparatus.

By presenting the scheme as the product of the honourable altruistic intentions of the Chinese people themselves, the strategists' view was that western suspicion towards China itself would be assuaged thereby fulfilling the scheme's original, confidence-winning, goal.

With the strategic adjustment winning the approval of China's central executive, GISS was officially launched headed by a relative newcomer to top flight Chinese politics.

Promoted from her middle-ranking position in China's propaganda ministry, GISS director Hu Nei lost no time selecting a company through which state funds for the icon-saving programme would be channelled.

After careful consideration of the options available, Hu and the rest of the GISS board chose the Chinese internet shopping giant Ke-Ching to act as the GISS intermediary on the grounds that Ke-Ching's continuing status as a private sector enterprise was heavily dependent on it retaining the goodwill of the Chinese government.

While she had no doubt that Ke-Ching's offers of 'sponsorship' to threatened western icons would mask the state funding connection, just to make sure she proposed that a state-trusted non-state functionary be engaged to act as Ke-Ching's front man and that she herself should masquerade as Ke-Ching's promotions director to oversee that functionary's activities. In this way GISS would be permanently on hand to guide the functionary and he or she would be prevented from suspecting that his or her client was anyone other than Ke-Ching.

That decided, all that remained was the selection of the right front man, someone, said Hu, with a reputation for being openly critical of Chinese government policy. The presence of a known Chinese detractor would undoubtedly help allay suspicions as to the actual origin of the funds.

Given these requirements, in the GISS board's estimation there was only one man for the job. Chosen for the assignment was one Harry Wong, one of Hong Kong's richest men who'd already proved his worth to Beijing by helping channel state funds furtively into western economies during China's Eurozone bail-out operation.

Wong, said the board, was perfect on two counts. Not only did he have a reputation for being vocally hostile to China but, as a Hong Konger, he would always put profit ahead of principle. As every Chinese knew, Hong Kongers were businessmen first, nationalists second. National identity would undoubtedly be viewed by Wong as a negotiable commodity when it came to hard cash.

That decided, Wong was approached for the job by Hu in her Ke-Ching capacity and, to no one's surprise, Wong is reported to have wavered. Regardless of the size of treasure chest on offer, the board knew that, for the sake of face, Wong would feel obliged to put up at least token resistance. Being seen to be acting openly for a mainland Chinese company with suspected links to the government could be viewed in Hong Kong as selling out to the People's Republic.

So as to preserve a façade of respectability, Wong's reaction was to counter the offer with one of his own. He could only take the job on if he was accorded responsibility for selecting the icons for Ke-Ching support.

After considering Wong's counter offer carefully, GISS via Ke-Ching responded with a counter counter offer. Wong would be allowed first icon choice only.

When, after some deliberation, Wong accepted the compromise, his services were duly engaged by Hu and the GISS secretariat finally breathed out… but only until Wong revealed his choice of icon.

It was a choice which, as Hu is reported to have commented to her GISS colleagues, was 'as loathsome to China as the filthy British habit of adding milk to tea'.

Wong's choice was English cricket, a game viewed by many in China's politburo as the very embodiment of the British class system and home to the worst excesses of British imperialistic nostalgia.

Worse, Wong stipulated that the prime beneficiary of the funds should be Lord's Cricket Ground, the spiritual home of the game whose owner, the Marylebone Cricket Club, owed its eighteenth century origins to fortunes amassed by British aristocrats through getting the Chinese hooked on opium.

Two hundred years on, Wong is said to have told the horrified, yet intrigued Hu, the future of the MCC, Lord's and English cricket as a whole was coming under serious financial pressure. All three were feeling the full effects of the never-ending economic downturn and rumours were rife that Lord's might even be sold to private developers.

'To the English,' Wong is understood to have told Hu Nei, 'an England without a Lord's would be like a body without a soul and any entity acting to save the ground will undoubtedly win the undying gratitude of the British public... and their support for that entity's product.'

As persuasive as Wong's argument was, the bad taste the proposal left in the mouths of the GISS executive would have rendered it wholly unacceptable had it not been for a startling discovery that left Lord's being the perfect choice.

In the course of her investigations into Wong's proposal, Hu found herself in contact with a group of cricket-playing Hong Kongers with connections to Wong. Their reason for taking up the game, they told her, rested solely with the connections they stood to make from it – up to and including the British nobility itself.

If they ever got the chance to play at Lord's, they told Hu, they might even find themselves rubbing shoulders with British politicians since Lord's was, as Wong had once confided to them, the unpublicised sporting extension of the House of Lords, the British Parliament's upper chamber.

Stunned by this revelation and knowing Wong would never make such a claim without sufficient grounds, the GISS board accepted the information as inalienable, self-evident fact and gleefully inked-in the name of Lord's Cricket Ground as its number one choice of western icons designated to receive Chinese financial support.

By using its power of financial persuasion to gain entry to the Lord's inner sanctum, the board was not slow to realise that China would, in effect, be infiltrating *the* Lords. And having infiltrated that, China would have gained itself a parliamentary platform from which Chinese influence could be brought to bear on UK government ministers overseeing Britain's special relationship with the US.

If those ministers could then be 'persuaded' to lobby US politicians on China's behalf, the US infiltration value accruing from the saving of Lord's Cricket Ground would render all other considerations meaningless.

Thus decided, Lord's became GISS's primary funding target and Wong was asked by Hu to approach the England Cricket Board with a sponsorship offer.

As predicted by Hu, it was the presence of Wong which had tipped a suspicious English cricket establishment in Ke-Ching's favour.

After research revealed him to be a prominent China critic, the ECB and the MCC accepted his word that no link existed between Ke-Ching and the Chinese state and duly approved the Wong-initiated, Ke-Ching-sponsored, Double Tops cricket tournament whose first games were played across the English counties in mid-2016.

Following two highly successful Double Tops tournaments, the *Grind*'s sources say Wong then received an order from Hu to approach the MCC board with an offer of direct sponsorship to the club. Word had reached her that the MCC was suffering a short-term financial shortfall and Ke-Ching was wondering if it could help.

In fact, say the *Grind*'s sources, responsibility for that shortfall was not traceable to any fault of the MCC but to a direct intervention by the GISS executive itself.

To get a foot in Westminster's door GISS knew it first needed to get one in the MCC's. But with infiltration of the MCC inner circle proving more challenging than GISS expected, its board had put an MCC persuasion plan into effect, one in which Chinese financial grease was being applied to the infiltration wheels.

The upshot, say the sources, was the MCC board's alarming discovery of a substantial black hole appearing in its financial reserves.

Not only that but that its bank – one whose survival of the 2008 crash is said by the sources to have come courtesy of a sizeable injection of Chinese cash – was taking no responsibility for the MCC's loss.

This surprise announcement from a bank with which the club had had erstwhile good relations left the MCC little choice but to accept Ke-Ching's timely 'sponsorship' offer, one that's said to be being provided with but one string attached. To ensure Lord's benefits fully from its funds, Ke-Ching has made its financial support conditional on the company being given a seat on the club's board.

With that seat now obtained, GISS is said by the sources to be fully satisfied with the outcome of its 'investment'. By being privy to all decisions made by the top echelons of a club the GISS executive believes to be an integral part of the British Parliament, Hu and her colleagues are convinced that China is now within an ace of seeing a friendly face installed in the Oval Office.

The MCC is reported to be equally content with the arrangement. Unaware that its strings are now being pulled by Chinese bureaucrats who're effectively using the MCC's own money to bail the club out, the MCC board is understood to have declared giving Ke-Ching committee voting rights a small price to pay for seeing Lord's saved from extinction.

With the true provenance and motives of all parties involved now revealed, one can only speculate as to the respective parties' likely reactions.

In China's case, say the *Grind*'s sources, the exposure of its plot to gain access to US government via Britain's Parliament via the MCC will be received as little more than a temporary setback.

Knowing it to be only a matter of time before China regains its rightful place at the top of the world supremacy order, China's leaders will simply switch tactics again to achieve the same result, something they feel is no more than their ancestral duty to achieve.

After seeing China's global dominancy usurped by Europe and then the US in the nineteenth and twentieth centuries, the sources say China's leaders feel under obligation to regain that dominancy for the man who, more than any other, was responsible for seeing China rise to become the world's original and only true superpower.

Although it's taken successive governments longer to accomplish than expected, once China is again in full global control Beijing will finally have completed the job Genghis Khan started eight hundred years, almost to the day, ago. ENDITEM

* * *

'What's up Rafferty?' said McDermott. 'You look like you've seen the ghost of cricket past.'

'Worse,' the wide-eyed, ashen-faced subeditor mumbled into his computer. 'The future.'

chapter twenty-four

Even by McDermott's snarling standards his mood was murderous and as the afternoon wore on the *Daily Grind*'s sportsdesk staff began glancing nervously at one another. Sooner or later someone would have to brave the lion's den to remind its rampaging occupant that deadline was approaching and that his sign-off was still needed on the back page splash.

'Fuck the fucking lot of 'em,' McDermott growled at the walls, stomping round his office fist-thumping his temples as if they were personally to blame for his predicament.

'Fuckfuckfuckfuckfuck...'

Unfortunately for Rafferty there was no way of avoiding it. Drawing the short straw had left him the one wishing his quavering hand was holding a chair and a whip rather than the splash hard copy his seething boss had yet to approve.

'WHAT? Oh fuck. Right. Yes. Give it here.'

From seething tempest the *Grind*'s sports editor was suddenly all professional concentration and manic, old-school editorial intensity, blue pencil ripping through the copy until what had started life as a relatively mundane sporting misdemeanour had been slashed, burned and reconstructed into a read that would have left Mickey Spillane gasping.

Rafferty could only gawp in admiration and wonder. Faced with what McDermott was facing, could he have risen to the challenge? If, like McDermott, he'd found himself having to choose between surrendering professional principles or his position, would he have been able to switch from hair-tearing tyrannosaur to iceberg editorial axe-man as seamlessly as McDermott? Probably not. McDermott was right. Rafferty had a way to go yet before he could even think about sitting where his boss now sat.

But think about it Rafferty now was. Such an eventuality was looking increasingly likely in the wake of the highly public stand-off between McDermott and the *Grind*'s set-jawed management that morning. Nearby staff had seen the blood visibly drain from McDermott's purple-veined temples on being roundly informed that the only way his Beijing stringer's piece was going to appear in the paper was over McDermott's own dead body. No named sources, no story they'd categorically told him.

'NAME THE FUCKING SOURCES!' McDermott had raged at Rafferty. 'I'd stand a better chance of getting a creationist fundamentalist to accept his ancestor was a monkey. If they had ANY understanding of the way things work in China, they'd know there are only two sorts of Chinese who'd ever go on the record with such a story – the irredeemably mad and the death wish-afflicted.'

But then, seethed McDermott to himself, the management DID know that. You didn't need the IQ of a Mastermind contestant to work out that while negotiations over the injection of a life-saving amount of Chinese money into the *Grind*'s parent company were ongoing, mission impossible was their way of telling him that sports editors should stick to sports and leave the serious thinking to the big boys.

* * *

Such an insult to a man who'd done time across the newsdesk board had his staff queuing up to pick a number in the hurriedly-organised sportsdesk sweepstake predicting how long McDermott would last before the dam broke and he stormed out leaving a wrecked office in his wake.

Had they known what was really on their tormented editor's mind they might have had second thoughts. It wasn't principles McDermott was beating himself up over, it was principals.

Principal one was doing what his tortured news sense demanded of him – ensure that a story that HAD to be told somehow got out into the public domain.

Principal two was finding a way to get it there without finding himself out there with it. A job was a job to McDermott and as shite as this one was, having reached an almost palaeontological age by modern era news game standards the forty-seven year-old news hack wasn't unaware of what awaited him on the wrong side of the employment/unemployment divide.

Leaking it to a competitor paper or posting it anonymously on the web had been considered but rejected out of hand. His fingerprints would still be all over it and no one wanted a snitch for an employee. So what to do? 'Accidentally' leave a copy of the story on a train or in a pub? But then he'd undoubtedly be facing the same fate for acting negligently when the news eventually broke.

Negligent? Me? The only ones who could be accused of that, McDermott fumed inwardly, were the paper's bloody management. THEY were the ones ensuring that a story that was so clearly in the national interest remained in the media deep freeze.

'Hmmm,' he murmured to himself as the thought struck. The national interest. That might be the way to do it. Drop the bomb on someone who not only had solid connections with national interest-protecting pillars of the establishment but could be trusted not to drop a bomb right back on him.

There were precious few of those McDermott could think of... but there was one, one who'd forever be in McDermott's debt for being allowed sight of a world-shattering national interest exclusive the paper's double-dealing top floor mafia considered such a threat to their money grubbing plans they'd ordered it strangled at birth.

chapter twenty-five

As McDermott barged his way through the bedlam of the London evening rush hour to rendezvous with his contact, Harry Wong was rewarding himself with a visit to a very select, very discreet massage parlour in the heart of Soho's Chinatown.

He deserved this, he told himself. After what seemed like a lifetime of orchestration, the fulfilment of a long-held ambition was finally within reach.

Having been instrumental in helping Ke-Ching gain the MCC boardroom seat it was so insistent it wanted, the way was now clear for Wong to capitalise on his success and step up his campaign to bring the ICC Cricket World Cup to China.

First planted during his years at Oxford, the seeds of the idea had lain largely dormant until the day Hu had approached him with the Ke-Ching front man job offer some three decades later.

In the microsecond it had taken Wong to realise that getting Lord's onto the Ke-Ching national treasures support list could help him fulfil his World Cup dream, the seeds had germinated, flowered and begun giving off the sweet scent of mega-profit.

By helping the MCC wave farewell to its financial worries how could its committee not accede to his request to consider proposing China as a future World Cup venue to the International Cricket Council?

Now he was on the MCC board that agreement was looking a formality but that wasn't the half of it. With the dream's fulfilment also dependent on winning the Chinese government's backing for the idea, now he knew how Ke-Ching had obtained its MCC seat, that too was looking a done deal.

Ever since the committee had finally caved in to his Hu-ordered offer to help the MCC out of its financial hole in return for a seat on the board, Wong had wondered how Hu Nei had come to learn of the funding shortfall. Such information would surely have been a closely-guarded MCC secret.

Now he knew the truth Wong scolded himself for not having worked it out for himself. For having to be told by a city banking contact that Ke-Ching and its handlers had known about the hole long before the MCC did.

* * *

Hardly had Wong been asked by Hu to approach the committee with Ke-Ching's sponsorship/bail-out offer than the banker was on the line beseeching him for help.

Assuming Wong's new role with Ke-Ching made him one of China's trusted, in-the-loop few, the banker's sole, very urgent request to Wong was for him to use his influence to get China to ask any favour of him but that.

If it ever got out that he'd been the one who'd conveniently 'lost' the MCC's money until told he could 'find' it again, pleaded the banker, hanging, drawing and quartering would be a lenient penalty compared with the social disembowelling that would accompany his being unmasked as the man who'd sold Lord's down the Yellow River.

Whilst not being unaware of the debt his bank owed China for coming to its rescue in 2008, the banker told the silently spellbound Wong, this was a price too far.

'You're my last hope Wong,' the banker had almost wept into the phone. If the man who'd arranged for Chinese funds to be channelled furtively to the banker's crash-hit bank couldn't help he'd be left with no option but to take the brandy and a loaded revolver into the library and do the honourable thing.

Wong's only contribution to the conversation had consisted of a few monosyllabic grunts and a completely disingenuous assurance that he'd see what he could do. Mostly he was having to bite his lip over China's sheer, unbridled audacity.

Insinuating Ke-Ching onto the MCC board by arranging things so the club got no hint it was being bailed out with its own funds was so deliciously deceitful that Wong had trouble not letting on that he wished he'd thought of it himself.

With great force of will, he didn't. Now his suspicion that Ke-Ching was nothing more than a front for some sort of Chinese government intrigue had been all but confirmed, it was important he kept his banking contact sweet. He could be a valuable asset in unravelling China's reasons for taking such an urgent and unprecedented interest in Lord's, knowledge that would undoubtedly be of great assistance when it came to swaying China into backing his World Cup bid.

* * *

Wong's plan for getting to that stage was to trade on the back of the Double Tops competition's success. If Ke-Ching – i.e. China – could be persuaded to capitalise on it and sponsor a China-hosted World Double Tops tournament in 2020 the way would then be clear for proposing that China should also one day host the far more prestigious fifty-overs World Cup.

The date he had in mind had been selected with a very specific purpose in mind. With 2031 being the year that, under the regular World Cup rotation order, India's hosting turn was due, the prospect of China stealing the tournament from under its historic adversary's nose would, Wong thought, have China's authorities drooling into their noodles.

But just in case that alone wasn't enough to win their support, Wong had been seeking an auxiliary instrument of persuasion. How China had gained that MCC committee seat and what had prompted it to take such a drastic step was just the sort of thing he'd been looking for. Although hoping he'd never have to use it – people with less damaging goods on China had found themselves working in the coal mines – if the hosting date alone didn't do it, Wong was fairly certain this snippet of information would be more than enough to win China's backing.

For the moment though, that could wait. First he had to fire the cricket authorities' imagination and Wong knew exactly where to start. Although it was the International Cricket Council which selected the World Cup venue, since no ICC decision was ever taken without MCC input, that undoubtedly was where his energies needed first to be directed. If the committee on which he now served could be 'persuaded' as to the likely beneficial effect their backing for China's World Cup bid would have on the 'wellbeing' of all involved in running English cricket…

It was something he planned to allude to at the following week's committee meeting but maybe he should test the waters first. A couple of 'consultation' calls to a select group of committee members should do it, calls he planned to make just as soon as he'd dealt with another pressing matter. There were certain people of his acquaintance who'd be anxious for news of how his strategy for relieving Cornwall of its long neglected and heavily under-exploited mineral deposits was going and now seemed a good time to issue a progress report.

* * *

Pretty well as it happens, thought Wong as the masseuse's hands put new fire into erogenous zones Wong thought had long gone extinct. In the light of Daffy Dimmock's response to Wong's more-than-generous bonus pay-out to his newly-acquired Cornish flower producers, he reckoned he could now put the minds of his business associates at rest.

Wong's reward to the growers following record Valentine's Day/Chinese New Year flower sales had had Daffy calling to say that if there was anything else he could help Wong with he was at the Hong Konger's disposal.

Coming from the man who also headed a cooperative set up to preserve the disused St Ruth tin mines for posterity, Wong felt his mining conglomerate colleagues would like to know that all was now in place for taking the scheme to its next level.

On the other hand, Wong thought on reflection, perhaps it would be better to discuss it with the conglomerate's CEO first.

Yes, that would be best. Over dinner perhaps?

chapter twenty-six

'Lunch. Simpson's. NOW!'

Lord Vernon Bleauforth seemed a tad overwrought, thought Turnball. Probably the prospect of having to share the Lords benches with veiled women following the European Court of Human Rights' overturning of the government's ban on the wearing of headscarves in the Palace of Westminster. Ah well, Turnball muttered to himself, at least that daft ruling didn't apply to Simpson's. Not yet anyway.

Bleauforth was already there, engrossed in a sheaf of papers spread out across their regular table and harrumphing into a sizeable tumbler of Glenmorangie single malt.

'Buggerbuggerbugger!' Turnball could hear Bleauforth frothing as he approached the table. 'Must be *something* that precludes it!'

'What?' asked Turnball. 'Not giving a quality whisky one's full and undivided attention?'

'THIS!' exploded Bleauforth. 'Or more precisely, what THIS doesn't say rather than what it does. There seems nothing here to prevent the ICC changing the World Cup venue rotation order!'

Turnball knew better than to interrupt Bleauforth in full rant, contenting himself solely with getting a glimpse of what 'THIS' was – the International Cricket Council's book of rules and regulations.

'If war broke out in the selected host country or the national cricket association of said country was caught with its fingers in the till,' fumed Bleauforth, 'I could understand it. But not because the ICC had received a better offer. Especially when that offer comes from a country with absolutely no cricketing history whatsoever! I mean, who in their right mind would want to watch a World Cup in bloody China?'

'China?'

'God's holy jockstrap, Turnball! Haven't you heard? The bloody chinks are trying to steal the 2031 World Cup from India! Word reached me this morning that bloody Wong has been casting around for reactions to the idea. The sheer, unbridled bloody cheek of it! Comes waltzing into the MCC, arms full of foreign dosh and thinks that's going to sway the committee into backing China's World Cup bid!'

'Won't it?'

'Over my dead… wait a minute. YOU wouldn't be thinking of backing it would you? You can't! You know as well as I do that this is flagrant blackmail. Or in this case, yellow mail.'

'Depends.'

'On WHAT, pray?'

'Well,' returned Turnball with a knowing smile, 'on what the committee thinks we should do with THIS.'

Reaching into his jacket pocket as he spoke, Turnball had fished out McDermott's summary of the *Daily Grind*'s publication-banned China exposé and placed it carefully on top of the ICC book of rules and regulations.

* * *

Once he'd extracted himself from the M25's Friday night madness, Turnball finally arrived at the MCC star chamber meeting he'd asked to be convened at Sir Oliver Gainsborough's country club at exactly the moment Harry Wong was ordering for his dinner guest, the scruples-deficient Afrikaner mining engineer 'husband' of Baroness Daphne DeWitt.

'Gentlemen,' Gainsborough began as a breathless Turnball rushed into the room, 'thank you all for coming. As you'll probably have guessed by now, were it not for the fact that an issue of some urgency and delicacy has arisen, this informal session would have been left until a more sociable hour.

'However, our esteemed colleagues Turnball and Bleauforth have jointly persuaded me that this is a matter that simply cannot wait, hence calling you all here tonight.

'As is by now common knowledge within this circle,' the MCC chairman told the twenty-two members of the Wong and DeWitt-less star chamber, 'moves are afoot to relocate the 2031 ICC World Cup from India to a place rather further east. While this proposal is on the agenda for discussion at our forthcoming regular committee meeting, Messrs Turnball and Bleauforth have alerted me to certain information relevant to the proposal to which, they feel, the attention of this group should be drawn prior to going into formal session.'

Had the star chamber meeting call come from Bleauforth alone its members would likely have found more pressing matters requiring their attention. Not so when they heard that Turnball's name was also on the invitation. His reputation for having more eyes and ears than the Stasi made missing a Turnball seminar as unthinkable as finding something better to do on the first day of a Lord's test match.

Not one of the assembly was to leave disappointed, each returning to his regular activities smiling the same sly smile that Turnball had been trying to suppress on rising to address them.

* * *

'Thank you, Mr Chairman,' he began. 'As you say, China's bid to host the 2031 World Cup is up for formal discussion at the next full committee meeting so any detailed discussion of the bid can wait until then.

'What can't is this group's deliberation over information that has come to light which is of some relevance to the bid... information which, as our chairman quite rightly points out, is of a somewhat delicate nature, concerning as it does the recently-publicised MCC/Chinese government connection.

'As I'm sure you won't need reminding, this apparent connection was the subject of a *Daily Grind* article alleging that our recently-acquired sponsor Ke-Ching was being used as the intermediary in a Chinese government plot to infiltrate the British Parliament via this very body.

'That story, as you will recall, was flatly denied by the Chinese government and resulted in the publication of an article in the official *China Daily* newspaper not only accusing the *Grind* of maliciously wishing China ill but lauding the Chinese private sector for stepping in to provide financial support to national cultural icons like Lord's.'

The twenty-one other heads in the room bobbed in accordance with Turnball's summary of recent events. To the committee, the allegation had been so preposterous that, to a man, they'd not only accepted the *China Daily*'s rebuttal as fact but had collectively vowed to never again take seriously anything the *Grind* had to say on the subject of the MCC, Lord's or cricket in general.

Because the paper hadn't even had the decency to either retract or justify its allegations once China, via the *China Daily*, had effectively challenged it to do so, it was abundantly clear to all that the *Grind* was guilty of indulging in alarmist sensationalism purely for the sake of sales.

The paper, in the committee's estimation, had sunk to the level of a *Fox News* broadcast on this one and there were even rumblings of suing for defamation.

'Having had a close association with the *Daily Grind* in the past,' Turnball continued, 'I felt it my duty to make certain enquiries regarding said story in order to gain an understanding of what could have prompted an otherwise responsible paper to run an article consisting, it seemed, more of smoke than fire.

'Gentlemen, I now have to inform you that, on the strength of those enquiries, it would seem that this body's general view that no fire exists may, in fact, be somewhat misplaced. All the evidence would seem to point to the inescapable fact that the only smoke emanating from this burning issue is that being carried on the breath of the dragon that would seek to use it to blind onlookers.'

The collective grinding of cerebral gears as the assembly attempted to de-code Turnball's convoluted delivery could be heard in the bar. Before they clicked into place and the anticipated group howl of protest ensued, Turnball moved swiftly on, taking advantage of the calm before the storm to launch into a full-out explanation for arriving at this apparently seditious conclusion.

'Yes, gentlemen, you heard me correctly. Information has reached me which not only confirms the *Grind*'s allegations but takes the story to a new, even more disturbing, level.

'In my hand,' said Turnball, his voice starting to rise as he waved aloft the byline-deleted summary of Amber Middlethorpe's story furtively delivered to him by the *Grind*'s incensed sports editor during a 'chance' meeting on a Piccadilly line tube at rush hour, 'are the results of an investigation which leave me no option but to conclude that the MCC is indeed being used by the Chinese government as the vehicle for infiltrating not only Westminster but every other seat of western power... up to and including that of the United States of America!

'These notes, gentlemen, prove conclusively that this body has been duped by our sponsor into believing that its motive for underwriting the future of Lord's goes no further than using cricket as the medium for promoting its internet-related product.

'Were it truly so. The product we have in fact been endorsing, gentlemen, is none other than the political doctrine of the People's Republic of China! In short, the MCC has not only been tricked into becoming a whore for the Chinese Communist Party but of paying for China's pleasure out of the MCC's own funds!!!'

Drained by this wholly uncharacteristic display of emotion, Turnball found himself in need of a restorative libation. As he raised his glass to his lips, twenty gaping train tunnel mouths greeted him through its base, the entire membership of the MCC star chamber less Bleauforth who'd already heard it.

'That's right, gentlemen,' he resumed quickly to nip the anticipated ensuing pandemonium in the bud, 'this august body has been compromised... implicated in an odious Oriental plot to unseat western capitalism and replace it with a political system that stems directly from the pen of one Mao Zedong, a man who regarded the democratic process as the work of Beelzebub.

'Were it not for investigations conducted by certain parties of my acquaintance, said plot would have gone unidentified until it was too late.

'Fortunately, China's insidious little conspiracy has now been exposed for what it really is, leaving those who find themselves both implicated in it and affected by it time to take remedial action.

'Gentlemen, although we teeter on the brink of succumbing to the onrushing tide of Chinese totalitarianism, all is not yet lost. There is, I would contend, a way to draw stumps on this pernicious plot through the instigation of an MCC rearguard action, details of which I intend to outline once, with your permission, I've first provided a summary of the evidence now in my possession confirming the existence of said plot…'

For the next ten minutes, the world for the members of the star chamber stopped spinning as Turnball systematically unfurled and laid before his colleagues China's world domination plan minus the source of the information. Letting it be known that the information had come not, as he was sure his colleagues were suspecting, from any national security agency with which he had a connection but from the sportsdesk of the very newspaper the star chamber had effectively declared *persona non grata*, might not, Turnball thought, serve to enhance the story's overall credibility rating.

As Turnball scanned the room for reactions to his presentation, the stunned silence that greeted it told him his colleagues were collectively thinking the same thing: 'Having effectively told us that the very future of the western world hangs on how our modest little grouping responds to the information you've imparted, you'd better have a bloody good plan for scuppering China's vile little wheeze!'

Turnball rather thought he had. A spitting cobra of a plan he privately considered so devilish in its ingenuity it'd leave the Chinese speechless and his colleagues slapping their thighs in relief and admiration.

'So, gentlemen,' he resumed with a small smile, 'from the evidence I've presented, I trust it has now become clear to all present that through its association with the Chinese government's mountebank Ke-Ching, the MCC has unwittingly wandered into something of a political minefield... one through which we must pick our way carefully for the sake of western civilisation itself. Put one foot wrong and we stand to lose everything we in the West have come to hold dear.

'On the other hand, there is a way of turning the invidious position in which we now find ourselves to our considerable advantage.

'Working on the assumption that the information received is accurate – and I would say at this stage that I have no reason to doubt its credentials – I've taken the liberty of drawing up a proposed plan of action which I believe will achieve all necessary ends, i.e. pulling the rug out from under China's contemptible feet whilst, at one and the same time, ensuring the MCC's funds are repatriated to it... with interest.

'For the sake of easy reference, I've given said plan of action a working title, viz Operation Pest Control – a title I trust members will find appropriate given that China's plan for infiltrating the western citadel is scheduled to climax in 2020, the Chinese Year of the Rat.

'In short, OPC as I'll refer to it for short, revolves around us doing... precisely nothing. Or rather, nothing more than privately making our friends across the Atlantic and certain selected ministers this side of it aware of the basics of what it is we've discovered. Widespread broadcasting of said information throughout Westminster is not, in my opinion, a matter of any great urgency given that Parliament is already protected from finding itself infiltrated by agents of the Chinese government via the MCC.

'To think, as the cadres in Beijing appear to do, that Lord's is not only an integral part of, but has influence in, Parliament's Upper House is at best laughable... as I'm sure my noble friend Lord Bleauforth will agree...'

Bleauforth nodded vigorously. The very thought!

'Nevertheless,' continued Turnball, 'it's a belief which might be utilised to the benefit of the MCC if played with a certain amount of guile. Allow me to explain.

'What we have here is a situation in which we have the decided upper hand, a situation in which the principle of asymmetric access to information pertains and might be employed under OPC to work very much in the MCC's favour.

'With the rat in the Lord's kitchen not knowing we know what we now know and with said rat firmly convinced we don't know what it knows, we find ourselves in the unique position of being able to select a diet of our own choosing to keep its hunger sated. In short, it can be persuaded to swallow virtually any little titbit we care to feed it, however non-nutritional.

'Provided that the "we" in this context is not this group but certain government figures specially selected by this group, once those figures have been alerted to the rat's rather unsporting ambitions, there is, in effect, nothing more this group needs to do. Well, nothing except keep taking back the money the rat owes us in return for introducing it to the "right" people…'

* * *

While Turnball was outlining his masterplan, Sir Oliver Gainsborough's face was going through a paint chart of colours, settling on a not altogether healthy shade of puce.

'And just how long do you think that money will keep flowing once the rat realises it's been rumbled?' interjected the decidedly under-impressed, finger-tapping chairman.

'When Beijing discovers it's being fed duff information, as it's inevitably bound to do, our "sponsor" will be gone as quickly as it arrived… taking our money with it.'

'An excellent point, Mr Chairman, and one to which we again have our good friend the asymmetric access to information principle to thank for providing a solution.

'As of this moment, none apart from Harry Wong, his paymasters in Beijing and this body are aware of China's interest in supplanting its old enemy India as the host nation for the 2031 World Cup, India least of all.

'While this situation remains current, should it come to this group's attention that China has, in your words Mr Chairman, rumbled us, I propose that Wong be advised that it might not be in China's best interests to consider revising "Ke-Ching's" level of MCC "sponsorship" while the MCC is in the process of deliberating on its World Cup recommendation to the ICC. That, if I'm not very much mistaken, should focus Wong's mind nicely.'

'Hmmm,' Turnball could hear the assembled gathering thinking. 'Not bad, but that can't be all of it surely.' Knowing the man as they did, that must have been no more than the Turnball tempter. In his pomp, Turnball had had the ability to make the ball sing and dance. The pedestrian long hop he'd just bowled had 'boundary' written all over it. If China didn't find some way of countering that sort of coercion tactic, they'd be most surprised. And if Turnball didn't have an unplayable follow-up jaffer ball up his sleeve, they'd be mortified.

To their relief he did.

'Gentlemen,' Turnball began softly by way of announcing its imminent delivery, 'should our sponsor remain resilient in the face of such advice, I propose that the India card then be played to remind all concerned that China is not the only player in the game.

'Were it to reach China's ears that the MCC is being courted by India to supplant Ke-Ching, i.e. China, as the MCC's prime sponsor, one might expect those ears to prick up somewhat. The loss of face associated with seeing China displaced somewhat publicly by its historic adversary could well result in a swift revision of Beijing's decision to pull the plug on the MCC.'

Could? To the assembled gathering, the only certainty such a word signalled was the certainty of being run out. If that was Turnball's wicket ball, his place in the team was most definitely in doubt. How, their faces asked, could Turnball be so sure of attracting India's support?

Turnball smiled inwardly. He'd done them with the old three-card trick. The clincher was in the third ball he was about to deliver, not in the second as they'd expected.

'Gentlemen, from your less than ebullient reaction I can see that you remain to be convinced as to the robustness of the plan thus far presented. Perhaps my final point might serve to tip the balance.

'In the event of Beijing remaining intransigent on the matter, that would be the moment for the playing of our India ace. Were it to be made apparent to our friends on the Orient that the MCC would be more than confident of receiving Delhi's substantial gratitude in return for being made aware by this committee, *prior to the ICC World Cup host nation decision*, that India faces a World Cup competitor bid from the East…'

Turnball had no need of finishing the point. His final words were already being drowned out by a crescendo of appreciative star chamber fingers drumming on the conference table to signal they'd at last got it.

With Indian sabres already being rattled over China's attempt to tap into vast oil and gas deposits recently discovered on the Indian side of the countries' joint border, for India to now learn that China was intending to add insult to injury through trying to steal the holy-of-holies – the Cricket World Cup – from under India's nose would be beyond India's bearing.

With cricket having achieved virtual, if not actual, religious status in India, Delhi's gratitude for being tipped-off in time to prepare a Chinese bid-sinking counterstrike, coupled with the MCC's backing for India's own World Cup bid, would be unbounded.

***

As Turnball drank in his colleagues' show of appreciation for a delivery to which the opposition's batsmen could surely have no response, he noted that only one of the twenty-one other sets of fingers around the table remained motionless. Sir Oliver Gainsborough sat staring impassively into the space separating his two ruddy, unmoving, hands.

Waiting until the MCC committee's version of a show of unbridled appreciation began to wane, Gainsborough coughed slightly and rose slowly to address the assembly.

'Gentlemen,' he said quietly. 'For sheer conniving Machiavellian duplicity, I've heard little to equal Sir Victor's proposed device for unseating those who would seek to destabilise the very bedrock of western civilisation.

'But before we lose our hearts – and heads – to his "plan", perhaps it might be worth pausing to reflect on the likely outcome of this particular horse shedding a particular shoe at a particularly critical moment.

'My primary concern, gentlemen, is that the invention that is the product of Sir Victor's bountiful and, it has to be said, fertile mind competes strongly with any Heath Robinson mousetrap for moving part requirement.

'With every part dependent on every other part to achieve the desired result, failure of any one part will inevitably lead to failure of the whole. And failure of the whole will inevitably lead to the rodent in question remaining at liberty to smear this august body's face with a considerable amount of rotten egg – something I'm particularly keen to avoid given the current circumstances.

'So it is for that reason that I intend to propose an alternative to Operation Pest Control.

'Simply put, I intend to propose that when our full committee meets in formal session, we do no more than give Wong the opportunity of answering our – sorry, Sir Victor's – allegations and act in accordance with his response.

'In like manner, I will also be proposing that our friends in India be alerted forthwith to China's World Cup hosting ambitions in order to allow them to deal with the issue in a gentlemanly fashion.

'That, gentlemen, is my personal position and having laid my own cards on the table I now invite others to do likewise.'

* * *

After a short pause to digest their chairman's deliberations, the first hand to rise was that of Turnball's closest confederate and wholly unpredictable batting partner, Lord Vernon Bleauforth.

'Thank you, Mr Chairman,' he said thoughtfully, 'and thank you Sir Victor for what I agree with the chairman is one of the most artfully fiendish stratagems I've ever had the privilege of hearing during my time serving on this committee.

'So artful, in fact, that it even resulted in me buying its originator lunch when he appraised me of its contents earlier today. To me, should the Turnball plan succeed, it will have achieved all we would want it to achieve and then some.

'Apart from having the potential of making sure our funds are repatriated to us, the plan could even result in the MCC relieving China of some of its own, thereby sending a clear message to others considering playing games with either this body or this great country that they do so at their considerable peril.

'While the accepted wisdom is that Britain is a spent force on the world stage, this plan should not only help set the record straight but restore to us something I thought had been lost forever. After years of allowing the pettifogging namby-pamby bed-wetting spoilsports to get their whiney wet blanket way in the field of international relations, the plan will, at last, see the sport put back in politics.

'With such considerations in mind, gentlemen, it will come as little surprise to you to learn that it was my intention to back Turnball's plan to the hilt tonight.'

A murmur of disquiet swept the room. If that's all Bleauforth had raised his hand to say, he could have said it in considerably fewer words.

Bleauforth was not to be distracted. For once in his life he'd rehearsed what he wanted to say and wasn't about to see all that hard preparation work go to waste.

'I say "was",' he said, pausing for a moment to let his announcement sink in.

'Having heard what the chairman has had to say, I now have to confess to being torn on the matter. As the chairman quite rightly says, what we have here is an issue requiring greater use of the head than the heart.

'As foreign as such advice is to your humble servant, I have, while the chairman has been speaking, been doing my best to follow it, weighing up the pros and cons of both sides.

'On the one hand, it would seem to me that we could go with the Turnball plan and hope it doesn't founder for the sake of a horseshoe lost. Or we could adopt the chairman's proposal and hope our sponsor doesn't walk once they've been appraised of the information now in our possession.

'I don't mind saying that having to make a choice between the two has exercised my own cerebral powers to the full given that both options have their pitfalls.

'But reason has finally prevailed and it's now abundantly clear to me as to which of them will best serve our requirements.

'Mr Chairman, your plea to act with prudence on this matter has not fallen on deaf ears.

'Even so, I'm still going with the Turnball plan... for two basic reasons. One, it seems to me that this is the only option that stands a snowball in hell's chance of preventing the Chinese from taking up their bed and buggering off with our money. Two, to my mind by going the route our chairman is proposing we'd actually be committing a cardinal sin – the sin of violating a code that's precious to us all, the code that rules the game of cricket. Allow me to explain.

'As we all know, gentlemen, cricket isn't just a game played between two opposing parties. It's a game of honour. A game with ethics and etiquette attached, much of which we carry over into our day-to-day lives away from the cricket field.

'Amongst that code of ethics is one which, in my view, defines all the others – the ethic of "playing the game". Break that fundamental law of the spirit of the game of cricket and in my opinion you break the whole code. By doing what the chairman is proposing, I would contend that this body could be accused of doing precisely that.

'The way I see it, going the chairman's route would deprive the parties involved of a chance to cross swords and therefore of a chance to learn from the encounter, one which in this case involves a master of the art of double-dealing deceit.

'That being the case, Mr Chairman, to prevent any such

deprivation I feel this body has an obligation to fulfil. We have a duty to ensure no barriers are erected to the staging of a masterclass in strategic swordplay and that the only way of ensuring that is to go the Turnball route.

'By going any other,' said Bleauforth, trying hard to suppress a small rising smile that would ruin his delivery of the punchline, 'our Chinese friends will be deprived of said masterclass, we'll be deprived of teaching the bastards what a run on the yuan really means and that, I would humbly contend Mr Chairman, just wouldn't be cricket old boy… would it?'

OTHER WORKS BY *MARK NEWHAM*

LIMP PIGS

China's offer for him to head up the Beijing Olympics official news service confirmed what the author had long been thinking.

China's claim to have changed was as credible as the news put out by his former employer, the official Chinese news agency Xinhua.

In the three years he'd been away, change in China seemed to have become the accepted wisdom. The author begged to differ and now he had the evidence.

The offer of such a position to someone with all the sports reporting experience of Mao Zedong proved that, fundamentally, China remained as unmoving as the Great Wall and as rational as the world's decision to make Tony Blair a Middle East peace envoy.

His Olympics experience supported the contention. Continued manipulation of the news proved China was the nation-state equivalent of the zebra – a black horse with white stripes able to change into nothing but the exact opposite.

Fleeing from the land that commonsense forgot as Beijing doused the Olympic flame in 2008, Mark Newham vowed to remind the world of the fact. The result is **Limp Pigs**, an irreverent myth-busting memoir-with-attitude designed to clear the smoke and smash China's hall of mind-bending mirrors.

Published in 2011 in both paperback and e-book formats, **Limp Pigs** *ranked NUMBER ONE in Amazon's censorship category for several weeks.* **The BBC called it 'Unique… Inspiring…'**

Limp Pigs 2013 *– an update of the original – is available as an e-book. A sample chapter can be viewed at* **www.moriartimedia.com**

www.ingramcontent.com/pod-product-compliance
Lightning Source LLC
Chambersburg PA
CBHW032030290426
44110CB00012B/743